AFROCENTRIC
VISIONS

AFROCENTRIC VISIONS

Studies in Culture and Communication

Edited by

Janice D. Hamlet

SAGE Publications
International Educational and Professional Publisher
Thousand Oaks   London   New Delhi

For information:

 SAGE Publications, Inc.
2455 Teller Road
Thousand Oaks, California 91320
E-mail: order@sagepub.com

SAGE Publications Ltd.
6 Bonhill Street
London EC2A 4PU
United Kingdom

SAGE Publications India Pvt. Ltd.
M-32 Market
Greater Kailash I
New Delhi 110 048 India

Printed in the United States of America

Library of Congress Cataloging-in-Publication Data

Main entry under title:

Afrocentric visions: Studies in culture and communication /
Janice D. Hamlet, editor.
     p.   cm.
   Includes bibliographical references and index.
   ISBN 0-7619-0810-2 (cloth: acid-free paper)
   ISBN 0-7619-0811-0 (pbk.: acid-free paper)
   1. Afro-Americans—Ethnic identity.   2. Afro-Americans—
United States.   3. Afrocentrism—United States.
 . 4. Afro-American arts.   5. Afro-Americans in mass media.
I. Hamlet, Janice D.
   E185.625.A388   198
   305.896'073—ddc21   98-25414

98 99 00 01 02 03 10 9 8 7 6 5 4 3 2 1

Acquiring Editor:	Peter Labella
Editorial Assistant:	Renée Piernot
Production Editor:	Diana E. Axelsen
Editorial Assistant:	Denise Santoyo
Copy Editor:	Joyce Kuhn
Typesetter/Designer:	Janelle LeMaster
Cover Designer:	Candice Harman

Contents

Foreword

J anice D. Hamlet's book, *Afrocentric Visions: Studies in Culture and Communication,* represents a significant advance in the history of Afrocentric theory and criticism. During the past 10 years there has been a growing interest in this evolving field of critical theory and practice in communication, culture, and the arts. Understanding this movement and capturing the elements of its expression have become factors in the new opening to human interaction called *diversity* by some and *multiculturalism* by others. Thus, this book represents another instrument in the endeavor to explain how human beings have responded to one aspect of this new opening, the Afrocentric idea.

Afrocentricity is the theoretical notion that insists on viewing African phenomena from the standpoint of Africans as subjects rather than objects. It is therefore a rather simple idea. The insistence on seeing African phenomena from the perspective of African people is neither novel nor extraordinary. What makes this view of reality so awesome for many people is the fact that it is stated in a way that suggests Africans have been viewed in the past as tangential to Europe, as peripheral to Eurocentric views, and as spectators to others. To theorize from the vantage point of Africans as centered is to provide a new vista on social, cultural, and economic facts. Thus, it is the orientation to data, not the data themselves, that matters.

Four areas of inquiry are developed in Afrocentric thinking: cosmological, axiological, epistemological, and aesthetic. The cosmological inquiry deals with classes, gender, sets, and general fields of experience and behavior. Axiological inquiry answers the questions of values. Epistemological inquiry concerns issues of proof and methods of knowing. The aesthetic area of inquiry asks the questions that deal with the good and the beautiful. Of course, authors who write papers dealing with Afrocentricity do not have to self-consciously write with these areas of inquiry in mind. Actually, what they write often does fall into one of these areas, even though they do not state that they are dealing with the particular issue.

Hamlet's organization of this book into four parts is brilliant in its progression from perspective on into the future. This is a logical progression that recognizes the importance of perspective, place, stasis, and one's own location in beginning a discussion of the discourse surrounding Afrocentricity. The two middle sections isolate specific areas for critical discussions: namely, communication and aesthetics. These are central constituents of human interaction. How we communicate and how we determine the good and the beautiful are key to human relationships.

The future of Afrocentric visions will depend upon the kind of scholars assembled in this volume by Professor Hamlet. She has chosen to highlight some of the emerging scholars in several fields, making her book cross-disciplinary. Therefore, those in literary criticism, women's studies, communication, and African American studies may find these chapters useful in their treatment of specific elements of culture. The scholars who have answered the questions of relationships, imagination, and religion are preceded by those who have paid attention to the issues of theory. Because practice follows theory in the natural world, these writers have demonstrated precisely the relationship between the Afrocentric perspective and various forms of critical commentary.

The reader should find the chapters in this volume readily accessible and geared to the college student as well as to the mass audience. Following the idea of a collective understanding, the reader, after an individual reading of the chapters, joins by virtue of his or her knowledge and experience with the book a growing and evolving audience for the Afrocentric theory.

Quite frankly, the evolution of the field has already seen several changes, some of them hinted at in the volume itself. For example, some writers prefer to use the term *Africology* to refer to the Afrocentric study of African phenomena, which is different from the old terms *Black Studies* and *African American Studies*. Beyond this, however, is the fact that the field has generated new research questions and, of course, now, new answers.

Afrocentric Visions: Studies in Culture and Communication adds a dimension to the study of culture and communication that does not appear in the general run of books on these subjects, most of which are written from a narrow Eurocentric perspective. This volume answers questions from an entirely different frame of reference. In so doing, it does not deny the value of other perspectives but argues that for African phenomena, the best system of analysis is Afrocentric. Of course, there are many possibilities within the Afrocentric paradigm, so being Afrocentric in one's analysis does not mean conforming to one "doctrine" of Afrocentricity—there are many ways to discuss the centeredness of a text, document, or person.

Finally, the reader of this volume should take into consideration the fact that this is not the final book on the subject. Indeed, Hamlet's final section asks the question "Where do we go from here?" The reply to this question requires numerous answers and an ongoing discourse of analysis and synthesis and of commentary and criticism. Only in this way can Afrocentric visions in culture and communication become meaningful to us.

—MOLEFI KETE ASANTE
Temple University

Preface

Afrocentricity, the efforts of some African American scholars to reclaim an African past and illuminate its presence in the culture and behavior of African American people, is one of the most intellectually innovative conceptual frameworks to emerge in the past decade.

The concept means literally placing African values and ideals at the center of any discussion and analysis that involves African culture, discourse, and behavior. Therefore, to understand African American experiences one needs to understand the rich culture and history of African Americans.

According to its major proponent, Molefi Kete Asante, the Afrocentric perspective allows Africans to claim their rightful place as subjects of historical experiences rather than objects on the fringes of European history and experiences. This implies that, rather than imposing Western constructs onto African Americans' behavior and phenomena, theorists and students grounded in Afrocentricity use the filter of African culture to understand African American behavior and phenomena. Rejected is the idea that these phenomena should be viewed and evaluated through European lenses and standards, which often result in inaccurate, misleading, and biased interpretations. African American phenomena deserve to be examined using methodologies and standards that are consistent with African culture's norms.

It is significant to note that it is a fallacy to assume that all African Americans are Afrocentric. The word *Afrocentric* is not a race-defining label. There are Eurocentric African Americans just as there are Afrocentric Europeans. The Afrocentric perspective refers to a worldview and an approach to data. Therefore, the purpose of an Afrocentric framework is not only to understand African American phenomena from a cultural framework but also to revise theories, methodologies, and ways of teaching and assessment that take this perspective into account.

Although numerous scholars have challenged Eurocentric thought, Asante offers one of the most intellectually sound and stimulating perspectives justifying a reexamination of how we should begin to evaluate African Americans and other people of color.

In an essay titled "Socio-Historical Perspectives of Black Oratory" (1970), Asante describes unique features of African American communication, followed by a second essay titled "Marking of an African Concept of Rhetoric" (1971). In these two essays one can begin to see his seminal move toward identifying an African-centered framework for the analysis and discussion of African American culture and behavior.

In later works, beginning with his book *Afrocentricity* (1980), Asante labeled this African-centered framework and elaborated on the arguments presented in his earlier works. Three later books most clearly defined this conceptual framework. In *The Afrocentric Idea* (1987), Asante introduces a way of thinking that replaces Eurocentrism as the universal perspective. Instead, he appeals for historical and conceptual legitimation when examining human phenomena that emerge from outside the historical and cultural experiences of Europe. As such, the study and analysis of African American culture, Asian American culture, Latino culture, Native American culture, and the cultures of other people of color aligns alongside European culture. Social equality is legitimized; ethnocentrism is eliminated. The diversity of the human experience is celebrated.

Kemet, Afrocentricity and Knowledge (1990) details Asante's principle issues of Afrocentric inquiry and the idea of centrism. He defines centrism as "the groundedness of observation and behavior in one's own historical experiences which shape the concepts, paradigms, theories, and methods of Afrocentric inquiry" (p. 12).

Asante's later contribution, *Malcolm X as Cultural Hero and Other Afrocentric Essays* (1993), explores major themes confronting African Americans, such as the lack of historical consciousness, gender, and African hunger. The essays are linked to one dominant argument: African Americans and American culture owe much to Africa. Africans owe deference to no one. Asante (1993) notes,

> On both sides of the continent, in different eras and under different conditions, African contributions and heritages have been victimized by others. We can no longer accommodate the wishes of others against ourselves. This means that language, which is a preeminent carrier of visions and myths, must reflect a new African person emerging from the twentieth century. Schools and colleges must consciously work to create the language that will coincide with the new conditions for humanhood. African leaders must not be afraid to stand upon the foundations of the past, building all the time toward the new situation, and remembering as they build that they are not alone in the world.
>
> When an African leader stands unapologetically before any audience and gives thanks to the ancestral deities for his or her fortunes we will have achieved at least one victory for the Afrocentric vision. When there are numerous international highways on the continent, connecting distant cities in several nations, another victory will have been achieved. When the economic links between nations of Africa are not simply based upon the patterns inherited from colonialism but on the concrete needs of the African people we will have achieved some success. Ultimately, when the rapprochement between those Africans who were taken from the continent and those who remain on the continent are regularly consecrated in memorials and ritual gatherings, the aims of the African world toward self-choosing realities will be truly in place.
>
> These are Afrocentric visions which are rooted in the ground of our own center and which allow us to view ourselves not as beggars but as productive and assertive human beings making our contributions to the human community. (p. 50)

The chapters in this volume represent Afrocentric visions, offering contributions from both senior scholars grounded in an African-centered consciousness and junior scholars who are seeking to understand and utilize this perspective. Together these scholars have illuminated the Afrocentric perspective through analyses of various aspects of African American culture yielding insights from a variety of backgrounds, experiences, and disciplines.

The text is divided into four parts. Part I focuses on African American culture and the Afrocentric perspective and methodology. Parts II and III provide applications of the Afrocentric perspective found in various disciplines and in diverse human interactions. Part IV's chapters challenge readers' thinking about the Afrocentric perspective and locating their own place in American society and the world.

It is my hope that readers of this book will then better understand African American culture and experiences, the Afrocentric perspective, and perhaps themselves.

Acknowledgments

I am grateful to the people at Sage for their interest in this project. Special thanks and appreciation are extended to Molefi Kete Asante, Professor of African American Studies at Temple University and founder of the Afrocentric School of Thought, who welcomed this project with enthusiasm and encouragement and provided me with valuable suggestions and contributions. May the ancestors continue to motivate and speak through him. I give honor and respect to my parents. I also give thanks for being blessed with two wonderful sisters who has marveled at every accomplishment and shared every tribulation as if each and every one were their own. Most important, I give thanks to my creator who protects and guides me, to the guardian angels who watch over me, and to the ancestral spirits who empower me.

References

Asante, M. (1970, October). Socio-historical perspectives of Black oratory. *Quarterly Journal of Speech.*

Asante, M. (1971, March). Marking of an African concept of rhetoric. *Speech Teacher.*

Asante, M. (1980). *Afrocentricity: Theory of social change.* Buffalo, NY: Amulefi.

Asante, M. (1987). *The Afrocentric idea.* Philadelphia: Temple University Press.

Asante, M. (1990). *Kemet, Afrocentricity and knowledge.* Trenton, NJ: Africa World Press.

Asante, M. (1993). *Malcolm X as cultural hero and other Afrocentric essays.* Trenton, NJ: Africa World Press.

THE AFROCENTRIC PERSPECTIVE: IDEOLOGY AND METHOD

W hat is the significance of culture and of viewing it from a cultural frame-work? The three chapters in Part I focus on African American culture and discussions on the Afrocentric perspective.

Linda James Myers offers in Chapter 1 a discussion on culture. She identifies the deep structure of the African cultural heritage in terms of a conceptual system, one in which autobiography plays a significant role.

Chapter 2 by Norman Harris focuses on how Afrocentric philosophy ought to structure any discussion of African people. Afrocentricity, he argues, interacts to be fundamental with African American life.

In Chapter 3, Terry Kershaw elaborates on the Afrocentric method and its significance to the discipline of African American studies.

The Deep Structure of Culture

1

Relevance of Traditional African Culture in Contemporary Life

Linda James Myers

Culture defined as the total way of life of a people is somewhat indestructible. As long as there are people they will have a way of life. Culture determines quality of life in large measure. The importance of cultural identity to people of African descent has been emphasized repeatedly (Asante, 1983; Cruse, 1967; Karenga, 1983).

Part of what is being responded to is what Nobles (1976) describes as the "conceptual incarceration" of black people in a hegemonous European-American-oriented culture.

> The natural consciousness of black people is forced to relate to a reality defined by white consciousness. That is, contemporary black people in the United States live in a psycho-social reality consistent [with] and supportive of white mental functioning. Such a situation is tantamount to black people living in [what for black people must be] white insanity.

It has been said that we must become "cultural scientists," learn the true nature of our African cultural heritage so that we might maximize its benefits in contemporary times (Asante, 1983). If we assume a single gene pool, accept the most current archaeological and anthropological evidence, and follow what has been shown to be true of dominant genes for color versus recessive, all people can be said to be of African descent depending on how far back they wish to go in tracing their ancestry. We owe it to ourselves to understand the nature of the conceptual system that yielded the first culture from which all other conceptual systems and culture evolved (Ben-Jochannon, 1971; Diop, 1974; Van Sertima, 1983). If our premises are indeed true, having clearly identified the nature of this ancient system of thought, we should be able to distinguish the transmittal of its elements to all late cultures. This chapter will identify the deep structure of the African cultural heritage in terms of conceptual systems, discuss methods for reclaiming it, and the consequences of nonreclamation. In this instance, our discourse will be restricted to comparing and contrasting the ancient African and modern Euro-American cultural worldviews as the polar referents of the cultural continuum.

The Deep Structure of Culture

Culture has been defined as the total way of life of a people. A people's way of life may be examined at the level of sensory observation or surface structures, which are subject to relatively rapid change, constrained by time and space, and nongenerative in nature. Or another level of analysis may be the deep structure, which is archetypal, not bound to the specific group, and generative in nature. At the deep level of structural analysis evidence of a certain set of rules or system is sought that affords diagnosis of the features of empirical phenomena (Hammel, 1972).

Nobles (1980) identifies the deep structure of culture as the philosophical assumptions (e.g., ontology, epistemology, axiology, cosmology) underpinning and reflected in the culture's worldview, ethos, and ideology. The outward physical manifestations of culture and its artifacts (i.e., specific languages, specific knowledge of *tribal* origins, customs, and rituals, African socioeconomic organization, and so on) are amenable to change and/or destruction. However, the worldview yielded by a particular set of philosophical assumptions can be preserved in the conceptual system those assumptions structure. In terms of African/African-American culture, what persevered and developed were the essential qualities of the African worldview, a view concerned with metaphysical rather than purely physical

cultural ethos
worldview

interrelationships, such as that between music and poetry, religious functions and practice, man and nature (Walton, 1972).

Others have detailed the existence of a traditional African worldview, and certain cultural ethos seem continually to predominate (Asante, 1980; Balander and Maquet, 1974; Busia, 1963; Diop, 1978; Forde, 1954; Gerhart, 1978, Levine, 1977; Mbiti, 1970; Nobels, 1972; Parrinder, 1954; Sowande, 1974; Thompson, 1974; Williams, 1976; Zahan, 1979). Dixon (1976) and Nichols (1976) have been particularly clear in delineating and articulating the philosophical assumptions of the worldview. Ontologically, the nature of reality is believed to be at once spiritual and material (spiritual/material, extrasensory as can be known through the five senses). Self-knowledge becomes the basis of all knowledge in Afrocentric epistemology and one *knows* through symbolic imagery and rhythm. In terms of axiology, highest value is placed on interpersonal relationships among people. Diunital (union of opposites) logic dominates this worldview and the process is ntuology (all sets are interrelated through human and spiritual networks).

The Afrocentric Conceptual System

Adherence to a cohesive set of philosophical assumptions, such as the one just described, creates a conceptual system, a pattern of beliefs and values that define a way of life and the world in which people act, judge, decide, and solve problems (Albert, 1970). It is this conceptual system that structures the worldview at the level of cultural deep structure to be reflected in surface structure across time/space. For example, in analysis of the sacred and secular dynamics of the African American communication system, Daniel and Smitherman (1976) identify the traditional African worldview as significant for understanding patterns of black communication in the United States, and the call response pattern as exemplary of a "deep structure" cultural difference.

We can therefore speak reliably in terms of a European conceptual (definitional) system as well as an African *conceptual* system, each being distinctly different from the other in terms of basic survival thrust and fundamental character (Baldwin, 1980). Describing people of African descent, Asante (1980) acknowledges that they are a people who appreciate the continuum of spirit and matter, not distinguishing between them. Frye (1978) discusses, as the first construct of traditional African philosophical thought, the notion that there is an all-pervasive "energy" that is the source, sustainer, and essence of all phenomena. In contrast, the Western world-view is fragmented with its separation of spirit and matter (Capra, 1975). Rather than emphasize the dynamic unity of all things, such a system focuses on the segmentation of the phenomenal world (e.g., separating mind and body, persons against nature, self and other, and so on). Only within the last quarter century do we find an awareness of this spiritual/material paradigm gaining ground in Western science (Capra, 1975, 1982; Gelwick, 1977; Jantsch, 1979; Pelletier, 1978). However, knowledge of the implications of the paradigm shift for daily functioning still seems to elude Western culture.

The concept of self will be used to illustrate how the Afrocentric system functions. In order to make these ideas more fully comprehensible within a Eurocentric frame of reference, let us first entertain the nature of spirit, and matter, the manifestations of spirit. *Spirit* is defined as that pervasive essence that is known in an extrasensory fashion (i.e., the fastest moving energy, consciousness, God). Think in terms of breaking down matter (the most outward manifestation of spirit). Chemistry has aided in this endeavor; with its periodic table we can identify all of the chemical elements known and their atomic (proton, neutron, electron) configurations. Subatomic physics then allows us to penetrate the nucleus of the atom and discover a particle world in which all particles of a given kind are completely identical. The constituents of particles are more elusive observationally. Strongly interacting particles (hadrons) are believed to be composed of elementary entities called quarks. Our technology does not allow us to "see" quarks or measure them. In modern physics, the question of consciousness has arisen in connection with the observation of these subatomic phenomena. Quantum theory has made it clear that these phenomena can be understood only as links in a chain of processes, the end of which lies in the consciousness of the human observer (Wigner, 1970). Subsequently, we have simultaneous levels of existence ranging from the most inward, pervasive, fastest-moving energy, consciousness, to its most outward crystallized form, matter.

In ordinary life in American culture we are not always aware of the unity of all things, but divide the world into separate objects and events. Western culture assumes this division useful and necessary to cope with the everyday environment; however, it is not a fundamental feature of reality. It is an abstraction devised by our discriminating and categorizing intellectual orientation (Capra, 1975). In contrast, the African mind functions holistically, emphasizing the interrelatedness and interdependence of all things.

Africans of traditional culture apprehended a sense of self extended in time to include all of the ancestors, the yet unborn, all of nature, and the entire community (Nobles, 1976; Zahan, 1979). Thus they identified themselves at the level of permeating essence rather than specific outward manifestation (i.e., as consciousness or spirit, rather than individualized material form). According to Zahan (1979), from this point of view the individual does not constitute a closed system in opposition to the outside world in order to better secure her or his own substance and limitations. On the contrary, the individual enters into the surrounding environment, which in turn perpetuates her or him.

Identifying self in this way reflects the idea of holonomy, the whole being contained in each of its parts, which is so characteristic of nature (Bohm, 1980; Capra, 1982; Chew, Gell-Mann, & Rosenfield, 1964). The African is at once seeing herself or himself as one with Infinite Consciousness and yet individually, a unique part of that consciousness manifesting. Zahan (1979) speaks of the very widespread, if not universal, belief among Africans in the ability of the individual to "double" herself or himself at certain moments in her or his life. Within this frame of reference, the extended self, Infinite Consciousness, possesses a point of fission that assures man or woman an infinite range of possibilities.

The African extended self is God manifesting, the human being is one with God having structured consciousness through conceptual systems to be divine or supremely good. It is important to note, however, that within this worldview one is not automatically given the status of human being, nor does "dying" automatically make one an ancestor. Both statuses are accorded on the basis of one either evidencing the potential to manifest good consciousness (correct awareness according to the structure of the conceptual system) or in the case of the ancestor, having realized good consciousness in individual/group experience (self-actualized).

The African conceptual system with its spiritual/material ontology and subsequent notion of extended self assumes a self-organizing universe (Jantsch, 1980). The process of ntuology, all sets are interrelated through human and spiritual networks, assures that highest value must be placed on interpersonal relationships between individuals. Zahan (1979) notes that things and beings are not an obstacle to the knowledge of God, rather they constitute signifiers and indices that reveal divine being (i.e., one knows through symbolic imagery and rhythm in the expression of self-

Things + beings may be indices of divine being

holistic (dview)
war

knowledge). Establishing the validity and reliability of the conceptual system is not the objective of this chapter per se (see Myers, 1984), but the current paradigm shift of Western science, and Eastern philosophies (Buddhism, Hinduism, and Taoism), endorse the acceptance of such an holistic worldview. It is from the deep structure of traditional African culture that we can learn how to apply the height of this knowledge to everyday experience.

Reclaiming the Afrocentric Worldview

Our purpose in supporting the resurgence of the deep structures of African culture is not for the replication of ancient surface structure culture in modern times. Even if possible, that would be unnecessary, and likely, unbeneficial. For example, ancient Egyptians taught a deification process whereby man or woman could achieve everlasting peace and happiness, called the Egyptian Mystery System (James, 1954). We do not, however, need to go through the form and ritual of the Mystery System itself to benefit from its teachings. Indeed the conceptual system that we would be seeking to achieve would preclude that, because its basic premise is to allow the outward form to change freely while focusing on its source, inward spirit that is unchanging. Once that is accomplished we will have ensured that outward materiality will "take shape" consistent with underlying spirit in a manner far superior to anything a segmented conceptual system could fathom.

Given an Afrocentric conceptual system, life is meant to be carefree (free of worry, anxiety, fear, guilt, frustration, anger, hostility, and so on). The way the system is structured we are one with the source of all things good, and, as such, infinite beings. To the extent, however, we entertain the dominant Eurocentric conceptual system, at best, aspects of that truth will be fragmented in our experience. The choice of conceptual systems is ours; and at all times we can know that the law of mind is working so that whatever we are believing is, is for us at the moment of belief. Power is the ability to define reality.

Asante (1980) speaks of five levels of awareness in our souls. The fifth level, Afrocentricity, occurs "when the person becomes totally changed to a conscious level of involvement in the struggle for his or her own mind liberation." This level of awareness is of course requisite for adoption and maintenance of the Afrocentric conceptual system. The consciousness of the person is totally changed and empowered when he or she establishes the conceptual system of the African culture deep structure. I will now briefly discuss three approaches that will facilitate the reclamation process.

Methods of Reclamation

Young and Hardiman (1983) argue that the Afrocentric perspective can be taught in an academic setting and have devised a curricular approach consisting of five phases for the teaching of literature. I believe their approach is applicable to all disciplines. The first phase they identify is reclamation. This phase entails the documentation of evidence verifying the true African historical record. Phase two is emotional and intellectual identification in which students conduct their own investigations, raising questions and answering them in terms of research of personal relevance. Phase three is demystification in which emphasis is placed on defining and clarifying structural elements, form, content, and other devices of the discipline. In phase four, understanding, students focus on integrating, synthesizing, internalizing, and reflecting what they have learned through analysis of western orthodox work. The last phase, mastery, requires that students demonstrate their understanding by applying the information in a product of their own creation for future generations of humankind and thereby taking their place in the African legacy continuum.

Having analyzed the psychology of black expressiveness, Pasteur and Toldson (1982) provide the following suggestions for realizing and maintaining the Afrocentric identity of being one with nature, a prerequisite to healthy living: cultivate relationships with elements in the natural world; access knowledge of holistic medicine; resist formalizing and standardizing existence; guard against repetitive routines of the same old thing the same way; do some things when you feel like doing them and negotiate for freedom from time compulsion; be as frank, honest, and to the point as possible; move as naturally, relaxed, and rhythmically as possible; love life and self, wishing to see self multiply. In terms of general orientation, they advise asking the question, "It is natural?"

I have devised a psychotherapeutic approach called Belief Systems Analysis for those who seek optimal well-being and wish to make a serious commitment to working at changing conceptual systems. Rooted in the Afrocentric conceptual system itself, it cannot be called a preferential rational-emotive or cognitive behavioral therapy with complete accuracy, although the elements are there. The client's particular worldview or belief system is juxtaposed against the Afrocentric system we have identified. One system is identified and selected as preferable based upon the consequences it holds for the believer. Depending on the choices made, reality restructuring then takes place in terms of perceptions, cognitions, emotional responses, and behavior.

Because basic universal truths have been identified in the Afrocentric conceptual system, we can find aspects of these same truths in a wide variety of places. Consequently, do not be surprised to find them in Christianity, Islam, Buddhism, Hinduism, Taoism, Human Potential Movements in the West, and so on. Each path taken seems to lead us back to Africa when exhaustive research is done.

Consequences of Nonreclamation

The consequences of not recapturing the deep structure of our cultural heritage are clear, when one considers the options. Adhering to the Eurocentric conceptual system, with its material ontology as primary, inherently means destruction, because by definition materiality is finite and limited. A consciousness rooted in such a worldview will terminate itself (i.e., believe with full expectation it is going to die). We can see the long- and short-term consequences of Eurocentric functioning. Three long-term effects are an ecology thrown out of balance (acid rain, soil erosion, climate shifts, the greenhouse effect), a world on the brink of nuclear destruction, and a bankrupt economy based on totally imbalanced utilization of resources. We likely experience the short-term consequences very personally; they are stress, anxiety, insecurity, jealousy, fear, hatred, anger, hostility, families torn apart, seeking peace and finding none.

Noted black psychologist Naim Akbar(1981) describes four categories of mental disorder among African-Americans based upon the consequences of being disenfranchised from our cultural deep structure and manifest in a false sense of self. The first category he identifies as an alien-self disorder. This group of individuals see themselves as material and evaluate their worth by the prevalence of material accoutrements. Assimilating into Euro-American society and denying those factors that have affected us historically and continue to shape us in contemporary society have succeeded in alienating these people from their very selves. Affectation best describes the demeanor of persons with this disorder and sexual problems and perversions are common.

The next category of disorder is the antiself, which adds to the alien-self overt and covert hostility toward the group of one's origin and by implication toward oneself. According to Akbar, individuals with this disorder are motivated by a personal self-interest, using the approval of the dominant white group as the main influence on their behavior. They are likely models of mental health, according to the standards of "democratic sanity" in this society. The apex of their self-rejection may sometimes be seen in the choice of a marriage partner from the dominant inferiorizing group. Fleeting glimpses of their isolation intensify, in members of this group, their effort toward acceptability by the white dominant group and they become even more aggressive toward their group of origin. People with antiself disorders are particularly susceptible to manipulation by the dominant group to aid in the suppression and control of progress in the African-American community.

The last category I will discuss here is the self-destructive disorder; people in this group are the most direct victims of oppression. Akbar states that these disorders represent self-defeating attempts to survive in a society that systematically frustrates normal efforts for natural human growth. Members of this category have usually found the doors to legitimate survival locked and out of the urgency for survival selected personally and socially destructive means to alleviate immediate wants. Included in this category would be pimps, prostitutes, substance abusers, and psychotics.

Conclusion

The issues raised in this chapter regarding the adoption of a conceptual system rooted in the African cultural deep structure are empirically verifiable and warrant further investigation. Autobiography comes as a most highly recommended methodology, simply because it is so purely consistent with the Afrocentric epistemology of self-knowledge as the basis of all knowledge. An open and honest encounter with yourself might be a first step in critical examination, particularly when dealing with the deepest levels of analysis. What are you assuming to be true? And having assumed it, how is it shaping your experience right now? How has it influenced your past? What better informed choices might you want to make in the future?

The adoption of an Afrocentric conceptual system prompts us to reevaluate every aspect of our being, we begin to see an old world in a new way. As we begin our exploration, we might want to pay particular attention to folklore. Messages that folk are communicating in ordinary day-to-day situations may certainly prove as valuable a source of knowledge as much published information. For example, the enthnocentric histories dominant white culture had produced (Preiswerk and Perrot, 1978) serve primarily to reinforce the status quo rather than enlighten, as is the case with much so-called scholarship. Rather than elaborate on these issues further, suffice it to say that we can afford to be creative, no area of interest should be left untouched. The consequences for not liberating our minds will be ours to pay.

If you can control a person's thinking, you do not have to worry about the person's action. When you determine what a person shall think, you do not have to concern yourself about what the person will do. If you make a person feel that he or she is inferior, you do not have to compel him or her to accept an inferior status, for the person will seek it for himself or herself (Woodson, 1933).

References

Akbar, N. (1981) "Mental disorder among African-Americans." Black Books Bull. 7, 2.

Albert, J. (1970) "Conceptual systems in Africa," pp. 99-107 in J. Padem and E. Soja (eds.) The African Experience, Vol. 1. Evanston, IL: Northwestern Univ. Press.

Asante, M. (1980) Afrocentricity: Theory of Social Change. Buffalo, NY: Amulefi.

Asante, M. (1983) "African linguistics and communication continuities." Presented at the Fifteenth Annual Conference of the African Heritage Studies Association, New York, April.

Balander, G. and J. Maquet (1974) Dictionary of Black African Civilization. New York: Leon Amiel.

Baldwin, J. (1980) "The psychology of oppression," in M. Asante and R. Vandi (eds.) Contemporary Black Thought. Newbury Park, CA: Sage.

Ben Jochannan, Y. (1971) Africa: Mother of Western Civilization. New York: Alkebu-lan.

Bohm, D. (1980) Wholeness and the Implicate Order. London: Routledge & Kegan Paul.

Busia, K. A. (1963) "The African world view," in J. Dracher (ed.) African Heritage. New York: Crowell-Collier.

Capra, F. (1975) The Tao of Physics. New York: Bantam.

Capra, F. (1982) The Turning Point: Science, Society and the Rising Culture. New York: Simon & Schuster.

Chew, G. G., M. Gell-Mann, and A. H. Rosenfield (1964) "Strongly interacting particles." Scientific American 210: 74-83.

Cruse, H. (1967) The Crisis of the Negro Intellectual. New York: William Morrow and Company, Inc.

Daniel, J. L. and G. Smitherman (1976) "How I got over: communication dynamics in the black community." Q. J. of Speech 62, 1: 26-39.

Diop, C. A. (1974) The African Origin of Civilization: Myth or Reality. New York: Lawrence Hill.

Diop, C. A. (1978) Cultural Unity of Black Africa: Matriarchy and Patriarchy in Antiquity. Chicago: Third World.

Dixon, V. (1976) "World views and research methodology," in L. King et al. (eds.) African Philosophy: Assumptions and Paradigm for Research on Black Persons. Los Angeles: Fanon Center.

Forde, D. (ed.) (1954) African Worlds: Studies in the Cosmological Ideas and Social Values of African Peoples. New York: Oxford Univ. Press.

Frye, C. (1978) Towards a Philosophy of Black Studies. San Francisco: R. & E. Research Associates Inc.

Gelwick, R. (1977) The Way of Discovery. New York: Oxford Univ. Press.

Gerhart, G. M. (1978) Black Power in South Africa: The Evolution of an Ideology. Berkeley: Univ. of California Press.

Hammel, E. A. (1972) "The myth of structural analysis: Levi-Straus and the three bears." Addison-Wesley Module in Anthropology (Module xxv). Reading, MA: Addison-Wesley.

James, G. (1954) Stolen Legacy. New York: Philosophical Library.

Jantsch, E. (1980) The Self-Organizing Universe: Scientific and Human Implications of the Emerging Paradigm of Evolution. New York: Pergamon.

Karenga, M. (1983) "Nationalism: the problematics of collective vocation." Presented at the Seventh Annual Conference of the National Council of Black Studies, Berkeley, April.

Levine, L. W. (1977) Black Culture and Black Consciousness. New York: Oxford Univ. Press.

Mbiti, J. (1970) African Religions and Philosophy. Garden City, NY: Doubleday.

Myers, G. J. (1980) "Belief systems analysis: an African based cognitive therapy." Presented at the Thirteenth Annual National Convention of the Association of Black Psychologists, Cherry Hill, NJ, August.

Myers, L. J. (1984) "The psychology of knowledge: the importance of world view." New England Journal of Black Studies 4: 1-12.

Myers, L. J. (forthcoming) Understanding an Afrocentric World View: Introduction to an Optimal Psychology. Dubuque, IA: Kendall/Hunt.

Nichols, E. (1976) "The philosophical aspects of cultural differences." Presented at the meeting of the World Psychiatric Association, Ibadan, Nigeria, November.

Nobles, W. (1972) "African philosophy: foundations for black psychology," in R. Jones (ed.) Black Psychology. New York: Harper & Row.

Nobles, W. (1976) "Black people in white insanity: an issue for Black community mental health." Journal of Afro-American Issues 4: 21-27.

Nobles, W. (1980) "Extended self: re-thinking the so-called Negro self-concept," in R. Jones (ed.) Black Psychology (2nd ed.). New York: Harper & Row.

Parrinder, E. G. (1954) African Tradition Religion. London: Hutchinson.

Pasteur, A. B. and I. J. Toldson (1982) Roots of Soul: The Psychology of Black Expressiveness. Garden City, NY: Anchor/Doubleday.

Pelletier, K. R. (1978) Towards a Science of Consciousness. New York: Delacorte.

Preiswerk, P. and D. Perrot (1978) Ethnocentrism and History: Africa, Asia and Indian American in Western Textbooks. New York: NOK.

Sowande, T. (1972) "The quest of an African world view: the utilization of African discourse," in J. Daniel (ed.) Black Communication: Dimensions of Research and Instruction. Washington, DC: National Endowment for the Humanities.

Thompson, R. T. (1974) African and in Motion. Los Angeles: Univ. of California Press.

Van Sertima, I. (1983) Blacks in Science: Ancient and Modern. New Brunswick, NJ: Transaction.

Walton, O. M. (1972) Music: Black, White and Blue. New York: William Morrow.

Wigner, E. P. (1970) Symmetries and Reflections. Cambridge: MIT Press.

Williams, C. (1976) The Destruction of Black Civilization. Chicago: Third World.

Woodson, C. (1933) The Mis-education of the Negro. Washington, DC: Associated Publishers.

Young, A. F. and W. J. Hardiman (1983) "A curriculum approach to the teaching of literature from an Afro-centric perspective." Presented at the Seventh Annual Conference of the National Council of Black Studies, Berkeley, March.

Zahan, D. (1979) The Religion, Spirituality, and Thought of Traditional Africa. Chicago: Univ. of Chicago Press.

A Philosophical Basis for an Afrocentric Orientation

2

Norman Harris

Background

By now, it is common knowledge that an Afrocentric orientation is one which places the interests and needs of African people at the center of any discussion. The awesome and ongoing intellectual contributions of Maulana Karenga; the works of several African American psychologists—particularly Wade Nobles, Asa Hilliard, Naim Akbar and Linda James Myers; and most certainly the work of Molefi Asante—all provide examples of how Afrocentric orientations structure ethical, psychological, socio-economic and cultural analyses. This chapter proposes to indicate basic philosophical assumptions which seem to structure the application of all Afrocentric approaches. It does not critique the work of Afrocentric scholars—though such an essay would certainly be useful. Rather, the writer's assertions and observations about the philosophical underpinnings of Afrocentricity are a result of having for a number of years read, reflected and acted on the fundamental idea that the Afrocentric philosophy ought to structure any discussion of African people.

This chapter originally appeared as an article in *Western Journal of Black Studies* (Vol. 16, No. 3, 1992, pp. 154-159). Copyright © 1992 Washington State University Press. Reprinted with permission.

This chapter has three related sections. The first indicates how Afrocentricity interacts with what the writer asserts to be fundamental motivations within African American life. The second section is an overview of Afrocentric ontological and epistemological orientations, and those are developed in terms of conceptions of time and logic. The third section illustrates that the way one thinks about time determines the role history plays in social change.

I.

Situated within the nucleus of the Afrocentric orientation is an assumption that a central motivation in African American life is the desire to achieve freedom and literacy.[1] Freedom is the ability to conceptualize the world in ways continuous with one's history. Literacy is the application of historical knowledge as the confluence between personality and situation dictates.

Freedom is an idealized conception derived from historical knowledge. This definition is one which turns analytical activity away from the quantification of gross changes in the socio-political and economic position of African Americans at any point in time (an end to chattel slavery, the passage of civil rights legislation, an end to various forms of discrimination, etc.) and towards a look at the way Africans in America define themselves and the extent to which they are able to implement their definitions of themselves. This definition of freedom therefore encourages research which seeks to distinguish between an appearance of change and the reality of change.

Historically, African Americans have been encouraged to confuse a rearrangement of reality with fundamental changes in reality. This phenomenon is facilitated through the implementation of various modes of socialization which undercut or minimize African and African American humanity. These modes of socialization include everything from changes in law to the inclusion of African American images in the print and electronic media. To be sure, this process has never been entirely successful, and we are now living in an historical period characterized by increased attention to the role of Africa in shaping humanity.[2] In response to that attention, one might perceive an increased pathology in Eurocentric scholarship[3] as it seeks to displace and discount the African origins of humanity and the fundamental role of African peoples in shaping western civilization at its point of conception. The contention here is commonplace and it is that the fundamental antagonism of Whites toward Africans, be they on the continent or in the diaspora, has not altered over time. What has altered in this relationship is the form and appearance which White pathology might take at any given point in time. The definition of freedom used here provides a basis for the African American consciousness to merge with the best traditions in African and African American culture in order to more fully contribute to the forward flow of human history than the current ideas, definitions and subsequent attempts to attain freedom now allow.

Literacy is the practical dimension of freedom and is defined as noted above for two reasons: first, the definition acknowledges the subjective dimension of the human experience which makes one-to-one correlations between being exposed to or deprived of any given stimuli and having a specific response to that exposure or deprivation impossible to predict. To be sure, there is a range of predictable behavior among African Americans that non-African Americans rely on in creating and perfecting the methods they use to maintain the myriad systems of oppression. Alluded to here is the stubbornness of African humanity; its unwillingness to do as objective circumstances dictate—that is to succumb to any number of limiting phenomenon. Secondly, literacy is materialist in its acknowledgement of differences over and within time relative to the situations people confront. More directly, the way literacy plays out in a given situation is in part a function of what the opportunities and limitations of the material conditions under question dictate. The most sublime expression of literacy is, of course rhythm. Here in *Roots of Soul,*[4] Pasteur and Toldson describe the phenomenon:

> At the essence of man's basic nature, enveloping vital forces, rhythm is a critical factor in the organization of human behavior. It is required for the attainment and maintenance of momentary perfection in human performance, which is the platform for achieving happiness. To be in rhythm is popularly recognized as a form of human efficiency . . . At such moments, one does not move in an analytical, step-by-step progression, one is the spontaneous, rhythmic unfolding of the progression. One does not try to do, one happens to be an instrument of the doing. During such moments, nothing is difficult, there is no anxiety. (76-77)

Literacy seeks to attain the state described above, and its attainment is dependent on the application of historical understanding as the confluence between personality and situation dictates. This writer's assertion is that all African American ethical, psychological, socioeconomic, political and cultural activity is an attempt to attain freedom and literacy.

Afrocentricity places the needs of African people at the center of all discussions. The quest to achieve freedom and literacy operates from that center.

II.

While not anti-materialistic, an Afrocentric orientation is one which asserts that consciousness determines being. Consciousness in this sense means the way an individual (or a people) think about relationships with self, others, with nature, and with some superior idea or Being. Certainly, the idea that consciousness determines being or the definition this writer gives to consciousness is not new. A variety of expressions drawn from classical and vernacular African and African American culture speak to this phenomenon. For example, the ancient Egyptian assertion, "Man Know Theory Self," indicates that the way one sees (thinks about and conceptualizes) the world precedes and determines life chances more so than exposure to or deprivation from various material conditions. The popular refrain of the "Funkadelics": "Free your mind and your ass will follow," is an example from vernacular culture of the assumption that consciousness determines being. Put another way, changes in the material world are possible only after one is able to think freely about those changes. In like manner, one can understand Marcus Garvey's assertion that what man has done, man can do; or Maulana Karenga's assertion that the crisis in the African American community is a crisis of values; or Jesse Jackson's insistent refrain, "I am somebody." In each instance, the assertion is that new thought precedes new action.

The idea that consciousness determines being derives from an Afrocentric ontology and epistemology. The Afrocentric ontology is characterized by a communal notion of existence, and can be stated as follows: we are, therefore I exist. This communal orientation is in contrast to the Eurocentric orientation that is best characterized by René Descartes's assertion, "I think, therefore I am." The Afrocentric epistemology validates knowledge through a combination of historical understanding and intuition. What is known, what can be proven is demonstrated through the harmonization of the individual consciousness with the best traditions in the African past. Again, by way of contrast, the Eurocentric epistemology validates knowledge through a combination of objectivity and "scientific method" wherein it is assumed that similar results obtained through similar steps under similar conditions is an indication of reality. Carl Jung, not always known for forward thinking on matters of race,[5] says that "Scientific materialism has merely introduced a new hypostasis, and that is an intellectual sin. It has given another name to the supreme principle of reality and has assumed that this created a new thing and destroyed an old thing. Whether you call the principle of existence "God," matter, energy, or anything else you like, you have created nothing; you have simply changed a symbol" (xxxi).[6] Jung's observations humanize science by noting its arbitrariness, and, implicitly, its juvenile quality. More directly, unable to understand relationships among the various expressions of reality (an inability to attain the literacy that rhythm occasions), western science seeks to sub-divide reality into angry little parts that barely know how to converse with each other. One may understand current events as flowing from the disharmony of implemented Western science.

The significance of Afrocentric ontology and epistemology is profound. The way one constructs reality, one's place in it, and the way one validates knowledge determines one's life chances. For example, the individualistic ontology into which we have all been socialized makes it all but impossible for many African Americans to conceptualize the idea of racial responsibility, particularly as it relates to racial empowerment. At worse, racial responsibility ends at the tip of one's nose, and at worse, racial responsibility is merely a romantic concept, a passing stage in the individual's development before one reaches maturity.

The Eurocentric notion of individualism rests on the assumption that being determines consciousness, and it is this assumption which infuses materialism with a spirit it could never have. A new or better job, more income, a car, an outfit, etc. are all assumed to carry intrinsic meaning that will at the level of consciousness create a new person. As long as a Eurocentric ontology of individualism obtains in the African American community, one may expect casual and justified inhumanity. A Black brother might say, "After all, if it's good for me, it's good for me. So step off, chump." The gangster image of the individualistic African American just described is, if you will, the whiter side of an all-White philosophical phenomenon that is not derived from the Black World experience. The eloquent stasis of neo-conservatives[7] is but the other side. The writer has written elsewhere about their tendency to write as if history has no abiding force in the world;[8] more directly, they assume that history has little if any contemporary and ongoing significance, particularly the history of enslavement, the various racist assumptions that sought its justification, and the continued phenomenon of institutionalized racism. More will be said about the way one conceives time and the impact that it has on the role that history plays in social change in the next section. Suffice it here to say that those the writer labels as neo-conservatives conceptualize time in a linear fashion, have difficulty in seeing a contradiction between appearance and reality, and therefore assume that changes in appearance actually represent a change in reality.

To sum up, an Afrocentric ontology is one which is communal; therefore, individuals find their worth, and their most sublime expression of existence in relationship to a community, to nature, and in relationship to some supreme idea or being. The Afrocentric ontology seeks to use rhythm to harmonize with those forces which appear external to the individual, but are in point of fact, simply expressions of the individual's potential. Na'im Akbar makes this point in his essay "African American Consciousness and Kemet Spirituality, Symbolism and Duality,"[9] when he asserts that

> African people are concerned about the invisible more than they are about the visible. . . . They are concerned about those forces that operate on a higher plane. . . . That's the nature of the spiritual orientation of African people. African people are more concerned about the infinite than they are about the finite. (106)

The idea of the infinite is similar to what might be referred to as potential; both are without limit and cannot be known in the context developed here except in association with other positive forces in the African world. Thus we see again the holistic—indeed, the limitless—nature of humanity that is possible from an Afrocentric ontological stance.

The Eurocentric ontology is individualistic and in it, the individual finds his fullest expression of existence in isolation or in opposition to man, nature, or some supreme idea or being. In this model there is no transcendent order to which the individual can attach herself. Indeed, attachments are at best pragmatic, and at worse they are parasitic. Tragedy, outrage and imposition are the hallmarks of Eurocentric cultural achievement and these can be understood as flowing from a view of the world in which humanity knows no collective and nurturing tradition to which it can attach itself. Like a child in a tantrum, one must be amazed by the ferocity of its self-destruction, particularly when it is all so unnecessary. A comparison between the "creative" culture associated with an Afrocentric orientation and that associated with a Eurocentric orientation would yield exciting psychological data about the way the African and the non-African think about reality.

An Afrocentric epistemology validates reality (or what it claims to know) through a combination of historical knowledge and intuition. In this epistemology, history is key because when the individual appropriately submerges himself in the reservoir of African history, then that submersion allows the individual to discover him or her self in the context of that history and thereby judge the reality of any given phenomenon. Wade Nobles[10] writes: "Unlike the 'stand for' connotation of the symbolic utilized today, the symbolic of ancient African times, and the contemporary African as well, was a symbolism that went beyond the 'representational-sequential-analytic' mode to the 'transformation-synchronistic-analogic' mode" (100). The last mode about which Nobles writes derives from a holistic view of reality; it is an aspect of a communal ontology. From this perspective, knowing is both rational and supra-rational, for it incorporates both that which can be understood in terms of methods to measure the material world, and that which transcends the material. Implicit in what Nobles writes, and, indeed, in what one sees in the writings of a number of scholars who explore classical African civilizations[11] is that reality follows essence, and that if one really wishes to know, then one must go beyond what is possible by the measuring and cataloging of material reality.

In a remarkable, and perhaps overlooked essay, "Hunting Is Not Those Heads on the Wall,"[12] Leroi Jones makes the point that hunting, like art, is a process and what is left—a dead head hung on the wall or the artifact—is not the reality; it is simply the artifact, the "leavings" of a process. So it is with reality as one has been taught to think about it: it is not the mere appearance of physical phenomenon; rather, reality is the essence which connects the multiple expressions of appearances.

This discussion could continue along these lines in terms of defining a relationship between how one validates claims to knowing (epistemology) and one's notion of what reality is (a version of ontology). But the purpose here is to pose what the writer sees as a fundamental difference between an Afrocentric epistemology and a Eurocentric epistemology. The Afrocentric epistemology assumes transcendent order in the world, and the Eurocentric epistemology assumes that the only order in the world is that which it can "scientifically" demonstrate and that which it can impose. An

Afrocentric epistemology attempts to validate claims to knowledge through immersion while the Eurocentric epistemology seeks distance from what it attempts to know and understand.

The differences between Afrocentric and Eurocentric epistemologies have pronounced effects on the way this society is organized and on the life chances of Africans in America. The more Afrocentric the epistemology of the African American,[13] the more profound will be his contribution to humanity. The less Afrocentric the orientation, the more narrow will be the contribution. To be sure, for an African American to have a Eurocentric epistemology is consistent with the way many Blacks have been socialized. That African Americans have not marched entirely into the various slave holes constructed for them is remarkable testament to the transcendent nature of our humanity.[14]

To sum up here, the Afrocentric epistemology assumes transcendent order in the world. It seeks to verify its claims to knowing through a combination of historical understanding and intuition. Its methods are both empirical and supra-empirical.[15] An Afrocentric ontology and epistemology are necessary to advance the quest for freedom and literacy.

The following discussion relates how the Afrocentric ontology and epistemology structure the way one thinks about time, and as a consequence, the way one thinks about the relationship of history to social change.

III.

The way one thinks about time determines the role that history plays in social change. If time is conceptualized in a cyclical fashion, then history lays a fundamental, one might say, a definitional role in social change. If time is conceptualized in a linear fashion, then history has little if any role to play in social change.

Deriving from its ontology (view of the world), and epistemology (verifications of those views of the world), an Afrocentric orientation conceptualizes time in a cyclical fashion. It assumes that the appearance of phenomenon always changes, but that the underlying essence of phenomenon remains basically unchanged. Part of life's journey, part of the quest for freedom and literacy is to systematically discover meaning (connections) beneath the surface of appearance. One may say in this regard, that an Afrocentric conception of time is not impressed by progress, which, in the Euro-Western context, means the endless rearrangement of appearances for their own sake. No beauty here, no ethics, only the unending march of progress.

The Eurocentric orientation of time is linear, and it assumes, at least at the level of the way it organizes its various socializing agents, that there is a one-to-one correlation between appearance and reality. But, as Public Enemy says, "Can't Trust It,"[16] meaning of course that the mere appearance of change does not signify actual change—that is, a change in the power relationships between African American and non-African Americans.

A cyclical conception of time encourages immersion in history at a level and in a way that marries individuality or personality to precedent. As is the way of education in classical African Civilizations, the immersion is consistent with and necessary to self transformation, or, in another fashion, it is consistent with being born again.[17] This transformation must happen not only for the individual African in America, but for all African Americans.

To clarify: the social transformation is possible from an Afrocentric conception of time, and that notion of time is cyclical. The transformation itself simultaneously involves immersion and expansion in Black World history; only then can the individual discover herself or himself; only then can the race discover itself. As outlined here, self-discovery is freedom; the ability to conceptualize the world in ways continuous with one's history. This self-discovery, this freedom is again consistent with what the Ancients taught, "Man Know Thy Self." Finally, on this part of the discussion, there can be no social change without freedom.

Literacy is the implementation of freedom and, as noted, is possible only when one thinks of time in a cyclical fashion. Social transformation is what is being struggled for. This is not a chapter intended to list specific items or accomplishments that would signify social transformation. The Urban League and like organizations routinely publish these kinds of things. Rather, it would be more useful here to repeat and elaborate upon what has been said: literacy is the implementation of freedom, and the increasing ability of African Americans to implement freedom does signify social transformation.

IV.

This chapter has sought to indicate the philosophical infrastructure on which Afrocentric scholarship rests. This will, the author thinks, provide others with a way of operationalizing the definition of Afrocentricity.

Notes

1. I have been working with and expanding these terms since I came across them a decade ago while writing my dissertation. My acquaintance with the concepts of freedom and literacy comes from my reading of Robert Stepto's *From Behind the Veil,* and from a variety of things I have read by Northrop Frye. While African American literary analysis was the specific reason for my usage of these terms, further reading indicated that their philosophical basis rested in what Carl Jung calls the collective unconscious. Additional reading indicated that Jung's notion of a collective unconscious is consistent with Richard Wright's prosaic, yet profound observation of things unseen, and the more fundamental African orientation concerning death, ancestor veneration, and the role of the past (if indeed it is that) in structuring the present. In short, the idea that African American life is structured by predispositions that cannot be fully explained by reference to empirical data is the basis for what I am doing here. In effect, the desire to achieve freedom and literacy is a supra-rational desire that is consistent with the African philosophical assumption that consciousness determines being.

2. The systematic rescue of Nile Valley Civilizations by writers and scholars as diverse as Charles Fitch, Ivan Van Sertima, Asa Hilliard, Larry Williams, W. Joye Hardiman, Martin Bernal, Jacob Carruthers, and organizations like the Association for the Study of Classical African Civilizations are indicators of this fact.

3. See Daudi Azibo's article in the Spring 1992 issue of *Word,* "Eurocentric Psychology and the Issue of Race."

4. Ivory Toldson and Alfred D. Pasteur, *Roots of Soul* (Garden City, New York: Doubleday Anchor Books, 1982).

5. Naim Akbar notes in a speech that Jung asserts that the problem with America is that it is more or less infected by the African.

6. W. Y. Evans-Wentz, *The Tibetan Book of the Great Liberation,* commentary by Carl Jung. New York: Oxford University Press, 1977.

7. I would include in this group those African Americans who are more concerned with mashing what is unique in African and African American culture into existing paradigms than they are with indicating what is unique. See my essay, "Who's Zoomin Who: The New Black Formalist," for a criticism of Henry Louis Gates, Jr., Robert Stepto and Houston Baker; see also my forthcoming book, *Signposts,* for more discussions.

8. See my review of Shelby Steele's *The Content of Our Character in Word* and also my review of *Reflections on An Affirmative Action Baby* in the Spring 1992 issue of *Word.*

9. This essay can be found in *Reconstructing Kemetic Culture, Papers, Perspectives, Projects,* edited by Maulana Karenga. (Los Angeles: University of Sankore Press, 1990), pp. 99-114.

10. Wade W. Nobles, "Ancient African Thought and the Development of African (Black) Psychology," in *Kemet and the African Worldview,* edited by Maulana Karenga and Jacob H. Carruthers.

11. See the works of Schwaller de Lubcitz, Na'im Akbar, Asa Hilliard, et al. For each, reality is essence, that which is at the center of physical phenomenon and consequently that which does not change. One of the most remarkable elucidations of this is a speech that Louis

Farrakhan gave on the Black Man (I heard on a colleague's tape machine and cannot give a specific reference) in which he discussed who and what the Black man is in terms of what reality is.

12. See Leroi Jones, "Hunting Is Not Those Heads on the Wall," *Home Social Essays*; see also his essay, "Black Ethos," in *Raise Race Rays Raze*.

13. It should be noted here that no one is necessarily born with a full-blown Afrocentric orientation, complete with an articulated ontology and epistemology. It should also be noted that people more directly of African descent (by whatever combination of scientific and cultural measures that seem appropriate) are more likely to be predisposed to an Afrocentric direction than are those who are of European or Asian descent. Nonetheless, people who are of European descent—Count Volney, De Lubicz, Gerald Massey, Melville Herskovits, Martin Bernal, and others are examples—can have an Afrocentric orientation. And this rather unremarkable observation achieves its strength based on the tendency of mainline scholarship to deny or denigrate the intellectual influences that Africa has exerted over its offspring in Europe and Asia.

14. It would be interesting here to explore as an historical continuum the Kemetic idea found in all of Africa that the purpose of all education is the deification of humanity. Could the stubbornness of this aspect of Classical African Civilization account for the transcendent nature of our humanity? This would be an intriguing question to explore.

15. To demonstrate this claim requires an elaboration on Nobels' discussion of the symbolic quoted earlier—specifically, the difference between "representational-sequential-analytic" mode and the "transformation-synchronistic-analogic" mode. I would refer the reader to Nobles' article as a beginning discussion of the methods the ancients used to verify knowledge.

16. Their video of this song cuts between an enslaved African American whose female interest is raped by the White man, to a brother working in a factory whose female interest is harassed by a White man. The effect is to emphasize that the more things change the more they remain the same. "Can't Trust It!" What you cannot trust is the mere appearance of change. *Word.*

17. See Asa Hilliard's "Pedagogy in Ancient Kemet," in *Kemet and the African World-view,* op. cit.

Afrocentrism and the Afrocentric Method 3

Terry Kershaw

Introduction

In the academy, the study of Black people has tended to follow the study of White people. The descriptions and analysis of Black life experiences have been formulated on the models set forth by White life experiences. The problem with this practice is the obvious one: Black and White life experiences are not the same. Although they are intertwined, they are not mirror images. Consequently, to describe and interpret those different experiences as if they were the same is the height of intellectual arrogance. The basis of that arrogance is the myth of White supremacy and the power to impact on people's life chances.

One way the academy helps in the maintenance of White supremacy is through the generating of knowledge designed to enhance the status quo. Generating knowledge in all disciplines is designed to articulate particular ideological and philosophical world views. To say this does not suggest that other groups could not benefit from the knowledge being generated for these purposes (e.g., cancer research). However, the knowledge that tends to be generated in the social sciences and humanities is much more cultural

This chapter originally appeared as an article in *Western Journal of Black Studies* (Vol. 16, No. 3, 1992, pp. 160-168). Copyright © 1992 Washington State University Press. Reprinted with permission.

specific. Of course, the natural sciences are not immune to cultural arrogance (Gould, 1981).

Therefore, the study of people of African descent can be liberating or oppressive. Black Studies as an interdisciplinary and multidisciplinary approach to the study of inter and intra group relations must always center on the forces that impact on the life experiences and life chances of people of African descent. Not only must Afrocentric scholars describe those forces (both social and "non" social), they must also generate knowledge to help change negative into positive forces as they impact on life experiences. In other words, a major purpose of Afrocentric generated knowledge must be to humanize.

Discussion

The core of any "discipline" of study is directly related to its subject matter, methodology and paradigmatic assumptions which in turn help generate various types of knowledge. The basic paradigmatic assumptions that give shape to the field alternately called Black Studies, African American Studies, Africana Studies and Africology revolve around the concept of Afrocentricity. According to Asante (1990), Afrocentricism as a framework for Black Studies treats African people as subjects, rather than as objects, of study. For Asante and other serious Afrocentric scholars this assumption is a given; "The Afrocentrist will not question the idea of the centrality of African ideals . . . " (Asante, 1990: 6). Asante goes on to state, "Centrism, the groundedness of observation and behavior in one's own historical experiences, shapes the concepts, paradigms, theories, and methods of Africology" (Asante, 1990: 12).

In terms of paradigm and method, the idea of centrism is crucial. According to Asante (1990), we must always keep in mind that knowledge is generated by humans who are products of a particular historical and cultural context. Therefore, the knowledge generated by these researchers tends to be reflexive of a particular philosophy and ideology and serves the interest of supporters of that philosophy and ideology. Consequently, Afrocentricity asserts that the life experiences of all people of African descent must be the focal point of Afrocentric generated knowledge (Asante, 1988). It emphasizes an analysis rooted in the historical and contemporary realities of Black people without negating nor minimizing the experiences of other groups. Rather, Afrocentricity emphasizes the particular and distinct experiences of people of African descent that have helped shape Black reality and vice versa. The following assumptions of a Black Studies discipline are informed by Afrocentrism:

1. That Black experiences are worthy of intellectual pursuit (Kershaw, 1989);
2. That the historical and contemporary experiences of people of African descent can prove instructive about human relations (Kershaw, 1989);
3. That the cultural, historical and contemporary experiences of African descended people are unique (Kershaw, 1989);
4. That one of the most significant tasks of an Afrocentric scholar is to help develop tools that help generate knowledge designed to describe, analyze and empower people of African descent to change negative social forces into positive social forces as they impact on life chances.

The first assumption emphasizes the significance of Black experiences. The term "Black experiences" refers to the diversity of the total life experiences in the past, present and "future" of African descended people. It assumes that a knowledge of the behavior, attitudes, beliefs, values, etc., of Black people, whether oppressing, being oppressed, or just plain living and the action that follows will add to the development of tools for the humanization of the world. A case in point is the Civil Rights Movement in the United States during the decade of the 1960's.

The Civil Rights Movement forced European American people in the United States to confront the system of racial preference. The obvious contradiction of overt racism and professed democratic principles became an international embarrassment for the self-proclaimed leader of the free world. It was difficult to ignore a pattern of racial oppression in a country that assumed the mantle of "protector of the free world."

In the process of getting passed various civil rights laws, an enlightened era in human relations was advanced. This era came into being not just for people of African descent in America, but also for those of European, Indian, Hispanic, Asian descent and many others. For example, in 1964 President Johnson signed into law the Civil Rights Bill with public accommodation and fair employment sections. For purposes of this discussion the focus will be on the fair employment section. The purpose of Title VII stated that through the use of formal and informal procedures, discrimination in employment based on race, color, religion and national origin would be eliminated. This act laid the foundation for Affirmative Action (Walters, 1982).

Most people will not take issue with the statement that other groups besides African Americans have benefitted from Affirmative Action. Even those people who have labelled Affirmative Action as reverse discrimination would be hard pressed to argue substantially with the preceding statement. European descended Americans have benefitted through women while the other previously mentioned groups have benefitted through both men and women. As a matter of fact, it is not unusual for employers to play the Affirmative Action "game" by playing one affected group against another. The argument has been made many times that the greatest beneficiaries of Affirmative Action has been White women (Walters, 1982).

Another example of civil rights legislation that came about because of the agitation of African Americans yet benefits everyone is the Voting Rights Act of 1965. The Voting Rights Act was the result of, among other forces, the constant pressure applied by Martin Luther King and the Southern Christian Leadership Conference. Prior to the passing of this Act, states could decide on who could exercise the right to vote. The push from King's group was to get federal registrars to protect the voting rights of Black Americans. In effect it was to get the federal government involved in enforcing the constitutional right of Blacks and to put a stop to the blatant discrimination faced by potential Black voters. As King reasoned, in a "democratic" society one of the greatest resources people have available to them is the vote. It is through the vote that leaders can be held accountable for their actions.

With the passage of the Voting Rights Act the interests of all Americans who were disenfranchised were served. The voting rights of Native Americans, Hispanic Americans and Asian Americans were protected as a result of this act. These confrontations and ending results forced most Americans to deal with the contradiction between the American creed and racism. Americans had to make hard decisions about what America was going to be. This kind of action advanced human relations because it spurred on future action directed towards the humanization of inter and intra group relations. Also, and it goes without saying, the study of the behavior and life experiences of millions of people is in and of itself a worthy intellectual endeavor.

The second disciplinary assumption stresses the importance of describing and analyzing both historical and contemporary relations with people of African descent as the focus. History is important because it describes what used to be, and provides some of the necessary linkages to the present, as well as helping to identify potential future actions. To attempt an understanding of present race relations, a knowledge of past relations is essential.

For example, in order to understand present American race relations between Blacks and Whites one needs to understand how much a part of the culture and society the belief in White supremacy and Black inferiority played. If one looks at when the imposed status of slavery was first applied to Africans by the English colonist, one is faced with some stark reality. From 1660 until 1865, the African was in legal bondage. Although not all Africans were enslaved, even those who were not did not enjoy full freedom; hence the term "quasi-free."

The period from 1865 to 1877 was a time of significant changes affecting the status of the enslaved African. In 1865, the 13th amendment to the constitution, which abolished slavery, was passed by Congress. In 1868, the 14th amendment was passed, that gave the enslaved African citizenship rights, and in 1870, the 15th amendment was added to the constitution, "securing" the right to vote for the newly formed group of African Americans. Also, during this time the Civil Rights Bill of 1875 gave African Americans the right to equal treatment in inns, public conveyances, theaters and other places of public amusement. For all intents and purposes it seemed as if Black-White relations were moving towards the positive side of the continuum.

However, in 1877, with the Hayes-Tilden compromise, the status of African Americans took a turn for the worse. Federal troops, which had been dispatched to the South to protect the rights of Black Americans, were withdrawn, leaving the plight of African Americans in the hands of their former slave owners. Numerous practices were instituted and intensified with the sole purpose of reinforcing the myth of White supremacy. For example, practices such as the "grandfather" clause as a requirement for Blacks to be able to vote, the intensification of the quasi-slave system known as sharecropping, the Supreme Court declaring in 1883 that the Civil Rights Act of 1875 was unconstitutional. Finally, culminating in the 1896 *Plessy v. Ferguson* Supreme Court decision that stated separate but equal was constitutional.

It was not until 1954 that the *Plessy* decision was overturned by the Supreme Court in the *Brown v. Board of Education* case. In 1964 the Civil Rights Bill was passed and in 1965 the Voting Rights Act was passed. If one takes a look at the years of legalized White supremacy and compares it with the years of legalized Black equality, one is struck by the overwhelming years of legalized White supremacy to the underwhelming years of legal-ized Black equality. Legalized White supremacy was the theory and the practice of colonial America and postcolonial America for 293 years, while legalized Black equality has been the theory and "practice" for 38 years. The quotation marks around practice are used because of the difference between de facto and de jure segregation.

The distinction between de jure and de facto segregation becomes clearer when one understands how societies develop culture, traditions and institutions. De jure segregation refers to legal segregation while de facto refers to the practice whether the law supports it or not. Culture, traditions and institutions develop over time. They become firmly entrenched in the practice of the people—so much so that they are transmitted from one generation to the next as the key to survival. If for 293 years the beliefs, attitudes and behavior patterns reflecting White supremacy were the norm, then it is safe to assume that the culture of White supremacy has been institutionalized (see college curriculums, for example). The 38 years of legalized Black equality, of which only 26 have been during any present person's lifetime, have not nearly been enough to eradicate the effects of the previous 293 years, especially in the practice of White racial superiority. To verify this point one needs to only look at the recent violent racial conflicts in this society as well as the continuous attacks on any type of policy that implies a Black focus.

Therefore, if an individual were serious about understanding present race relations they must understand the history. They must understand that society does not change overnight and the longer beliefs, attitudes and practices have been around the more difficult it is to change them. Consequentially, if one does not explore and identify the historical base of race relations, how can one understand if the basis of status has changed, how it has changed and why it has changed?

The third paradigmatic pillar focuses on the uniqueness of Black people and their relationships with other groups. This assumption is rooted in an Afrocentric perspective. It emphasizes the differences within Blacks and between Blacks and other groups of people as well as the similarities.

If one looks at the descriptor "African American" it may help illuminate this point. The term African American suggests that the cultural heritage of Black Americans is both African and American resulting in a variation of African culture influenced significantly by living in America. However, one way an Afrocentric scholar might look at this relationship is by studying the effect of basic "American" values and/or its potential effect on African

American life chances. Take, for example, the American emphasis on individualism. Individualism is seen within American culture as the prime motivator for success and the prime cause of failure. You, the individual, are held responsible for your lot in life and that becomes the key to evaluating people's success or failure.

For African American people living in a racist society where they are the victims of racism, this value could be dysfunctional for both the group and the individual. It would be dysfunctional if Black individuals are not judged on their merit. Under the current culture and structure of American society race is a significant factor in determining opportunities, experiences, and life chances. If race has a significant effect on a Black person's life then strategies for change that emphasize individual over group goals become dysfunctional. If Black people buy into the individualist argument their commitment to helping the group as a group becomes problematic.

Also, the way groups (individuals) respond to social forces will tend to vary as the social forces that impact their lives vary. Most "Americans" have not been victims of racism; on the contrary, most "Americans" have benefitted either directly or indirectly from racism. Therefore, one cannot assume a similarity of all experiences. This discussion, however, does not suggest that the only subject of study for the Afrocentric scholar is racial differences. All groups in America have had to deal with rapid technological changes. How they have dealt with them may vary but they all have had to deal with their class differences, religious differences, and ideological differences. Each of these topics is worthy of Afrocentric research.

However, any knowledge generated with Black people as its focus does not automatically qualify as Black Studies. Rather, it must be knowledge generated Afrocentrically. The basis of any type of knowledge generated within the paradigm of Black Studies must be rooted in an interpretation of "social" conditions by people of African descent which will direct the researcher to areas of study. Therefore, Afrocentric scholars must constantly engage in dialogue with the non-academic Black community because the focus of any research undertaken by Afrocentric scholars must be an extension of the group's understandings in order to help in the self-empowerment of the group.

William Wilson's discussion of the declining significance of race is an example of research focusing on Black experiences that is not Afrocentric scholarship. According to Wilson (1978), the traditional racial patterns between Whites and Blacks, particularly in the labor market, have been fundamentally altered. They have been altered in such a manner that class has become more important than race in determining Black access to privilege and power. However, the Black underclass is in a helpless state of economic stagnation. They, the underclass, need to improve their class position and then they will be able to enjoy the benefits of living in America.

Wilson's study has Black people as its subject matter; however, this writer contends that it is not Afrocentric scholarship. It is not Afrocentric for the following reasons: the first reason has to do with the fact that Wilson is telling the story as he interprets events. Where is the story that Black people tell? The question that becomes significant here for the Afrocentric scholar is "Does the story Wilson tells differ, and if so how much does it differ from the story told by the masses of African Americans?" He did not generate data from the people who were his subject matter. This last statement also brings up an interesting point in that Wilson, by not including "the" Black story is guilty of treating Black people as objects of study. How they (Black people) interpret the world would place them at the center rather than at the periphery. They become the subjects of study, not the subjects to be studied.

Secondly, when Wilson talks about changes in American race relations he identifies the reciprocal relationship between the economic and political institutions as significant factors. There is no acknowledgment of the impact of the "movement" during the 1960's. No significant discussion about the impact of Black people's actions as a significant factor. Again, he did not place the ideas and actions of Black people at the center of his analysis or as the initiators of change that effects their life chances.

Thirdly, when Wilson talks about solutions to help solve the problems of the underclass he suggests universal social policies rather than race specific policies. In drawing this conclusion, the question, "Is this in the best interest of Black people according to Black people?" was never asked. The solution proposed by Wilson seems to be answering the question, "Will White people perceive this to be in their best interest (and thereby benefit)?" What happens to Black people if they don't perceive it to be in their best interest? The argument put forth here about Wilson's work is not to minimize the significance of his work. It is to argue that because research focuses on African American people that in and of itself does not make it Black Studies.

The fourth pillar helps to strengthen the relationship between the academic and the non-academic communities. The purpose of generating Afrocentric knowledge is to describe the life experiences; to analyze the effect of forces that impact on life chances; and, to help develop tools designed to change negative forces into positive forces as they impact on the life chances of people of African descent. This pillar connects the Afrocentric scholar with the community because the generating of Afrocentric knowledge begins in the communities of "African" people. This assumption emphasizes the importance of using knowledge to empower people of African descent with tools to be the shapers of their reality. In other words, this is a reciprocal relationship between the Afrocentric scholar and the community of subjects.

To summarize, Afrocentricity as a paradigm for Black Studies places the following parameters on its practitioners: the knowledge base must come from the life experiences of people of African descent; the specific purpose of the knowledge generated is to empower Black people to effect positive social change and to describe Black life experiences as determined by Black people's understandings, interests and experiences; finally, the researcher (scholar) must always maintain a dialogical relationship with the subjects.

If one accepts these assumptions as valid, the range of phenomenon becomes self-evident. The second and third assumptions help set the limits of the discipline and the fourth assumption helps to define the role of the researcher. The life experiences of Black people include sociological, political, economic, historical and creative experiences, to name a few. Therefore, the range of phenomenon for Black Studies tends to be tied to various "traditional" disciplinary categories: Sociology, History, English and Psychology. In other words, Black Studies provides an interdisciplinary look at the life experiences of people of African descent utilizing the tools developed in each of the "disciplines" to help generate and analyze data (life experiences). Just as important to the interdisciplinary study of Black people as the Afrocentric paradigm is the generating of knowledge.

Knowledge can fall into any one of three categories: technical, practical and emancipatory (Habermas, 1972). However, for it to be generated Afrocentrically and to be Black Studies a key question must be posited: "Is the knowledge being generated with the purpose of describing, analyzing and evaluating Black life experiences and articulated by Black people, with the specific purpose of identifying negative social conditions and helping to develop the tools to change the negative into positive forces as they impact on Black life chances?"

The purpose of technical knowledge is to enhance prediction in order to control an environment. In terms of the natural sciences, technical knowledge is developed for the purpose of manipulating the natural environment. In the case of the social sciences, technical knowledge is used to control the social environment. Technical knowledge practitioners attempt to develop knowledge that allows one to predict outcomes in order to control those outcomes, to explain phenomena by linking the important factors in a logical manner that can be empirically verified (in other words, to find the most efficient means to a particular end). Therefore, theories are rated to determine their degree of predictability. If prediction can be relatively certain, the application of the theory allows for control over the particular end.

Positivist methodology, which is used to generate technical knowledge, consists of the following seven steps: (1) to identify a scientific problem by studying the results of past empirical and theoretical work; (2) to develop empirically testable hypotheses which will improve the theory's explanatory and predictive power; (3) to select the proper setting; (4) to develop measures and data collection based on previous research, observations, interviews in the setting, the researcher's common sense or knowledge of social processes; (5) to gather data through experiments, existing documents and texts, surveys, interviews and observation; (6) to analyze data to test hypotheses; (7) to alter laws and theories in lieu of findings and state the next researchable stage of the problem (Kershaw, 1989).

The role of the researcher in generating technical knowledge is to detach himself from what it is he is observing, that is if it is to be value free. This perspective operates on the assumption that if one is detached from what it is one is observing then one's values will not affect how one interprets what is observed; either the theory is supported or it is not. Science should not be determined by one's political or cultural values, but rather by what is observed, by what is analyzed and what can be empirically verified. This is a worthy goal, but one knows how difficult this can be because all too often when the evidence differs from the theory the "blame" is placed on the group that the theory is being used on (Gould, 1981). The group behavior is described as deficient or deviant and needs to be changed, especially if that group is lower on the wealth, power, and prestige scale. This does not prevent Afrocentric scholars from generating technical knowledge. The development and testing of Afrocentric generated theories is a necessary pursuit of Afrocentric scholars. Especially during this present historical period the importance of generating technical knowledge that empowers cannot be overstated.

Wade Nobles' (1985) Africanity theory is an example of how technical knowledge can empower. Nobles' basic assumption, which comes from past "Afrocentric" empirical and theoretical work, is that there is a continuity between African and African American cultural forms. Therefore, he concluded that African American families are African by nature and American by nurture. A problem to study could be what effect does each of these cultural forces have on contemporary African American family structure and inter-familiar interaction. Which values are present, do any values dominate that significantly effect the structure and values of the family are questions that can be raised.

One of the hypotheses that Nobles generated was that in periods of "crisis" or at "ceremonial" times, the "African nature" of the family is most visible. He developed measures, Afrocentrically, to define or operationalize crises, ceremony and African nature (interconnectedness and oneness of being). He gathered data by centering on African American families through interviews and surveys. What he expected to find was that the African nature would be manifested in family interpersonal relations (multiple parents and inter-family consensual adoptions).

Upon analysis of the data he found that Black families in America have a system that is primarily inclusive, responsive and interconnected. This he attributes to African ontological and cosmological understandings of the universe, and not to enslavement. The utility of the model is that it allows one to see that while some of the features of Black families may be attributed to some of the concrete conditions of living in America, the underlying dimensions of the family system may have emerged from a cultural basis strongly rooted in an African base. This is empowering because it helps to generate a basis of knowledge rooted in the experiences of the people. It is also empowering because it challenges the beliefs that if Black families differ both structurally and interrelationally from White families, they (Black families) are deficient models of White families.

Contrary to the technical type, practical knowledge is designed to describe the subjects' understandings and to help ground theoretical models. Special care is given to ensure that the subjects of investigation are the actual creators of the data via their interpretations of social conditions. Such endeavors will accumulate the necessary data to generate Afrocentric rooted theories. Indeed, the development of theoretical perspectives which can be tested after the accumulation of a sufficient degree of data is another important purpose for the generating of practical knowledge.

An excellent example of Afrocentric generated practical knowledge is the work of John Gwaltney. In Gwaltney's study entitled *Drylongso* he attempted to construct a self-portrait of Black America (Gwaltney, 1980).

In particular, he utilized personal narratives to describe what he refers to as core Black culture. As he himself states, "My main intent is to be an acceptable vehicle for the transmission of their views" (Gwaltney, 1980: xxii). Their views that Gwaltney wanted to describe were not the put-on views, rather they were their everyday views. Gwaltney also argues that practical knowledge generated from and about Black people clearly point out the potential for theory building. According to Gwaltney, "An internally derived representative impression of core Black culture can serve as an anthropological link between private pain, indigenous, communal expression and the national marketplace of issues and ideas" (Gwaltney, 1980: xxvi).

A major difference revolves around the role of the researcher in generating the two aforementioned types of knowledge. When generating technical knowledge, the investigator is guided by a predetermined set of relationships (*a priori*). The parameters of the study are restricted by a specific hypothesis. On the other hand, the researchers creating practical knowledge allow the subjects to shape the knowledge of the study. Similarly, the types of methods and knowledge generated differ. When generating technical knowledge, survey research and statistical analysis tend to dominate, while in-depth interviews and participant observation used in the development of ethnographs represent the prevailing methods in the creation of practical knowledge.

For some scholars these are the only types of knowledge they are interested in generating. For example, Wade Nobles (1985) argues that methodological issues proceed in three steps:

> The first involves clearly describing the philosophy or cultural world view which guides and defines the phenomena [In other words, the generating of practical knowledge]. The second involves the developing and testing of theoretical models which [is] consistent with the philosophical world view [Another way of saying technical knowledge]. [Finally], demonstrating the particular way in which that world view manifests itself or is affected by contemporary factors [Again, generating technical knowledge].

However, this bifurcated interpretation of knowledge overlooks an important tenet of the Black Studies discipline, the nexus between the academy and the community. If the field of Black Studies is to be intrinsically connected to the non-academic Black community, additional knowledge is warranted. Emancipatory knowledge is the third, and essential, ingredient in realizing the empowering aims of a Black Studies discipline.

Emancipatory knowledge, as with the other types of knowledge discussed, is generated with specific purposes in mind. The first is to identify contradictions between a group's understandings of social forces that impact their life and the empirical "reality" of the impact of those forces. The second operates out of the assumption that when contradictions are uncovered the people who are victims of the contradiction(s) resolve it. They either resolve it by changing their understandings/changing the forces, or by doing nothing. The do-nothing approach would be identified as a negative resolution while the other two would be described as a positive resolution. Therefore, given this assumption, a second purpose of emancipatory knowledge is to help lay the foundation for the development of tools to resolve the contradiction(s) in a positive manner.

To generate emancipatory knowledge one needs to first generate practical knowledge. Then one needs to generate technical knowledge that helps one to identify and assess the empirical relationships described from the practical knowledge. One needs to begin by operationalizing then describing and analyzing the effect of those social forces on the life chances of people of African descent. Finally, there is the need to participate in action that improves the life chances of African descended people.

Afrocentric Emancipatory Methodology

The following steps are involved in generating emancipated knowledge:

1. To use qualitative methods (i.e., in-depth interviews, participant observation, case studies) to generate practical knowledge about the forces that impact on African American life chances. Describe them and how they affect "African" life chances according to the subjects and understandings.

2. To use the understandings generated from step one as a guide to describe and analyze "the" empirical reality of the relationships identified from the data gathered during step one. For example, in interviewing Black respondents they identify a relationship between educational level and acceptance by Whites. They basically believe that the more formal education a Black person receives the more they "leave" Black and try to be

"White," which leads to a greater acceptance by Whites. The ramifications of this belief are far reaching when cooperation is called for by the "less" and "more" educated African Americans in the cause of improving Black life chances.

The Afrocentric scholar, in trying to generate emancipatory knowledge, utilizes methods and analysis consistent with uncovering relationships between variables. In other words, generating technical knowledge that allows the researcher to test the stated relationship. A key step in the development of testable hypothesis is the operationalization of variables so they can be empirically tested. In the current example, the operationalization of formal education is well documented; however, the operationalization of trying to be White "and a greater acceptance" is not. These variables are operationalized from the practical knowledge generated.

Given the state of knowledge available to Black Studies scholars at this time, a greater emphasis should be placed on generating practical knowledge rather than technical knowledge. Practical knowledge helps to generate new concepts, variables and ultimately Afrocentric theories which are grounded in the attitudes, behavior and historical relationships of the people being studied. Such an endeavor is important in light of the paucity of Afrocentric theories that seek to explain the experiences of people of African descent. The prevailing tendency is to employ Eurocentric-based theories to explain the behavior of a non-Eurocentric-based people. The obvious shortcoming ensuing from this approach is that such theories seek to understand and predict behavior without consideration of the significantly different cultural perspectives, social conditions and historical realities. A risky endeavor, to say the least. In short, the utilization of the qualitative approach will yield enormous benefit currently; however, once Afrocentric theories have been developed, a quantitative analysis of these will be necessary. Always keeping in mind, however, that these theories are not stagnant because people are always changing their attitudes and behavior.

3. To identify any apparent contradictions as well as convergence of the group's understandings and the "objective" reality. This step depends on the data obtained in both step one and two. The Afrocentric researcher would then generate technical knowledge as it relates to relationships between race and life chances. Of course, other factors mentioned by the subjects as significant would be analyzed (i.e., class, age, gender).

The two "realities" are compared with the comparison being described and analyzed. The purpose is to identify social forces that impact on life chances, both positive and negative, and to describe how they impact. When a convergence occurs, validation results. When a contradiction emerges, the researcher moves to step four. (The researcher can also move to step 4 when validation occurs, or can go to step 5.)

4. To participate in a program of education and action with the subjects by presenting the findings to the group of study and by participating in the development of tools that empower the group to identify contradictions and take action to rectify the situation.

A point that cannot be stressed enough is that regardless of the type of knowledge being generated, the role of the Afrocentric scholar is to generate knowledge to humanize the world and to help destroy those forces that help in the dehumanization of the world in general and people of African descent in particular. The findings of the research must be made accessible to as many "African" people as possible (i.e., publication in journals, newspapers, popular magazines).

Finally, the role of the researcher must be as an active participant in a dialogical relationship with the subjects. This relationship is not purely dialogical since the development of tools may require more than dialogue. The subjects come to a conclusion that their understanding of the significance of race on their life chances was different than they had believed. Consequently, the discussion should move to how to change the negative force, racism, into a positive force as it affects life chances. The researcher participates in that discussion and, if necessary, action to change that relationship. Therefore, being an Afrocentric scholar obligates the researcher to be an activist and a scholar working in the interest of improving life chances for people of African descent and, in general, for all people in similar situations.

5. To move on to the next potential researchable phase in the generating of technical, practical, and emancipatory knowledge and to contribute to the body of Afrocentric knowledge through the utilization and critique of existing Afrocentric and non-Afrocentric based knowledge. We must always be mindful of the relationship between theory and practice. As we uncover new interpretations of social conditions we add or subtract from existing theories and develop new ones. Practice defines theory rather than

theory defining practice. In other words, Afrocentric scholars must let the practice be the means of evaluating theory, not vice versa. When theory informs practice the practice is forced to comply to the theory, especially when the practice is perceived as negative. In a racist society the generating of knowledge is dominated by the group holding most of the power (which can be distinguished among other characteristics by race) and whose purpose in generating knowledge is to enhance their life chances. In the enhancement of "their" life chances they are often times contrary to the best interest of groups identified by the more powerful group as "out" groups (i.e., minorities). Therefore, theories of Black people in Black Studies must be Afrocentrically grounded and must be constantly satisfied relative to the practice of African people.

Conclusion

This discussion on generating knowledge along with the basic assumptions discussed earlier help define Black Studies subject matter and methodology. This is an initial attempt at defining a paradigm that helps shape the discipline and by no means is this research suggesting it is the only paradigm, nor should it be the only attempt to develop one. As with all new disciplines, its development depends on the continual and the critical contributions of its scholars who are trained in a Black Studies ethic, in a Black Studies paradigm and as Afrocentric scholars. Black Studies is ready to take its rightful place in the academy as the leader in the development of research and scholarship centering on Black life experiences. It must also be clear that Black Studies is not only connected to the academy but must also be connected to the community. It is the community that helps to give shape to the research problems, to the kinds of solutions that we must try to uncover and in actuality give shape to the very existence of the discipline of Black Studies. Black Studies cannot hide away in the ivory tower; Black Studies must be an active participant in the development, description, and analysis of Black life experiences. And, where Black life experiences are impacted negatively by social forces, the Black Studies scholar should be about the business of identifying those social forces and developing the tools and understandings to change those social forces from a negative to a positive—which requires an interactive relationship with the subjects. Asante (1990) identifies three additional features within the role of the Afrocentric scholar. They are: (1) Provide logical explanations of African peoples' experiences from the origin of civilization to the present; (2) Develop a holistic approach to the role of Africa in world culture; (3) Explain the behavior of African people by interpretations and analysis derived from an Afrocentric perspective. Therefore, the world of the researcher is to be an active participant in the generating of Afrocentric knowledge, not a passive participant as is emphasized by the positivistic approach. Even in the development of theory the researcher cannot afford the luxury of standing back from the problem, but must become actively engaged in the development of knowledge.

Because of historical and contemporary race relations disciplines such as Sociology, Psychology, History and Music cannot provide Afrocentric leadership in the study of Black people. Now this is not to say that Black Studies scholars cannot be sociologists, cannot be psychologists, cannot be historians, cannot be economists, cannot be political scientists, etc. Each of those disciplines provides tools that can be used in the discipline Africology. However, in terms of looking at the life experiences of people of African descent, it must be shared by an Afrocentric paradigm. The people of African descent must be centered in that discipline or else it is not Black Studies. Because one studies Black people, does research on Black people, publishes on Black people, that does not make it Black Studies. What makes it Black Studies is that it is Afrocentric. What makes it Black Studies is that it connects to the kinds of issues that impact the life chances of people of African descent. What makes it Black Studies is going to try to bring about a better world, not only for people of African descent but also for people of European descent, Asian descent, of Indian descent, etc. The honor and responsibility of studying, analyzing, describing people of African descent belongs to interdisciplinary Black Studies.

Therefore, in terms of where Black Studies is and the type of knowledge that Black Studies scholars need to be generating it is the writer's opinion that most of the present emphasis needs to be placed on the generating of practical and emancipatory knowledge. The reason is because practical knowledge allows one to begin to ground theory and more importantly, generate emancipatory knowledge based on the life experiences of people of African descent. Black people need to emphasize the importance of emancipatory knowledge at this time because it can serve as a catalyst for social change. It is extremely important that people of African descent begin to question their understandings, begin to question the forces that impact their lives. And where possible, to identify the contradictions between their understandings and the social forces that impact their lives.

One of the basic means by which one begins to challenge, to reconstruct, to define their reality is to deal with the concept of false consciousness. Consequently, emancipatory knowledge which allows one to begin to raise questions that bring one directly into confrontation with false consciousness needs to be a priority. To say the above is not to deny the fine work being done by Afrocentric scholars who are presently developing and testing theories (Baldwin, 1990; Azibo, 1990). However, this chapter looks at the overall state of the discipline, the overall state of knowledge on Black life experiences, the relationship between the two and how Black Studies connects to the "community" as a facilitator of improved life chances.

To conclude, the emphasis here is on the maintenance and viability of an interdisciplinary "discipline" that raises epistemological questions about what is and why it is, about what is knowledge and how one generates that knowledge. Black Studies is revolutionary, Black Studies is reactionary; above all else, Black Studies is necessary if the society is going to move forward in its quest for human knowledge. Black Studies is necessary if Afrocentric scholars are going to be generated who have a commitment to being scholar-activist for people of African descent.

References

Asante, Molefi. 1988. *Afrocentricity*. Trenton, N.J.: Africa World Press.

———. 1990. *Kemet, Afrocentricity and Knowledge*. Trenton, N.J.: Africa World Press.

Azibo, Daudi. 1990. "Personality, Clinical, and Social Psychological Research on Blacks: Appropriate and Inappropriate Research Frameworks." *In* T. Anderson (ed.), *Black Studies: Theory, Method, and Cultural Perspectives*. Pullman, Wash.: Washington State University Press.

Baldwin, Joseph. 1990. "Notes on an Afrocentric Theory of Black Personality." *In* T. Anderson (ed.), *Black Studies: Theory, Method, and Cultural Perspectives*. Pullman, Wash.: Washington State University Press.

Gould, Stephen J. 1981. *The Mismeasure of Man*. New York, N.Y.: Norton.

Gwaltney, John. 1980. *Drylongso: A Self Portrait of Black America*. New York, N.Y.: Random House.

Habermas, Jurgen. 1972. *Knowledge and Human Interests*. Cambridge, England: Polity Press.

Kershaw, Terry. 1989. "The Emerging Paradigm in Black Studies." *The Western Journal of Black Studies*, 13(1): 45-51.

Walters, Ronald. 1982. "The Politics of Affirmative Action." *The Western Journal of Black Studies* 6(3): 175-181.

PART II

AFROCENTRIC APPROACHES TO UNDERSTANDING INTERPERSONAL, GROUP, AND PUBLIC COMMUNICATION DYNAMICS

The process of human communication is central to our existence. Communication defines our friends, enemies, lovers, students, teachers, leaders, and any of a myriad of different roles and experiences. The four chapters in Part II offer Afrocentric studies focusing on interpersonal, group, and public communication patterns among African Americans.

In Chapter 4, Yvonne Bell, Cathy Bouie, and Joseph Baldwin focus on African American male-female relationships. They present findings that support this major prediction: that Afrocentric cultural consciousness is positively related to perceptions that prioritize an Afrocentric value orientation in African American heterosexual relationships.

Jerome Schiele (Chapter 5) reconceptualizes organizational theory by employing an Afrocentric paradigm. He identifies and discusses some of the characteristics of an Afrocentric organization and the extent to which some of these characteristics are congruent or incongruent with Western theories of organization.

In examining communication in the public sphere, Chapter 6 by Janice Hamlet focuses on the African American oral tradition, identifying and discussing the characteristics of African American communication, or what is known in Afrocentric thought as "manifestations of nommo." She argues that in evaluating African American communicators critics should use the lens of African American culture to understand African American discourse rather than impose Western constructs. By understanding and accepting the constituents of African American communication patterns, we extend our understanding of human communication.

In Chapter 7, John Smith evaluates culture and Afrocentrism in terms of their significance to the African American community. Smith maintains that a new world order or way of looking at the world has developed as a result of the African American community embracing Afrocentrism.

Afrocentric Cultural Consciousness and African American Male-Female Relationships

4

Yvonne R. Bell
Cathy L. Bouie
Joseph A. Baldwin

T he subject of Black male-female relationships is not a new area of focus in psychology. However, the dominant thrust of the existing research has been pathology-centered. It suggests that Black heterosexual relationships are characterized by a plethora of conflicts and problems (Farley & Hermalin, 1971), such as instability, disintegration, and pathological weaknesses (Frazier, 1957; Glazier & Moynihan, 1965; Thomas & Sillen, 1972).

In this type of pathology-centered research, it is typically assumed that Black heterosexual relationships are based on the same values, beliefs, and life-styles as those governing Euro-American heterosexual relationships. Supportive of this viewpoint is the emphasis on Black-White comparisons

This chapter originally appeared as an article in *Journal of Black Studies* (Vol. 21, No. 2, December 1990, pp. 162-189). Copyright © 1990 Sage Publications, Inc.

and the cross-cultural insensitivity of the item content in the various measures of heterosexuality used in this research (Allen, 1978; Nobles, 1974; Staples, 1971). The various measures have focused on issues pertaining to communication barriers, an egalitarian relationship structure, gender-role differences, and educational-professional status, among other issues (Cazenave, 1983; Fairchild, 1985; McAdoo, 1983). These issues, it has been argued, are a primary focus of relationships in the Euro-American worldview or cultural orientation (Akbar, 1981; Baldwin, 1985; Dixon, 1976; Nobles, 1974). Hence, the dominant conceptual framework suggested by the research on Black heterosexual relationships is primarily based on the worldview or cultural orientation of the Euro-American community (Baldwin, 1985; Harper-Bolton, 1982; Nobles, 1974).

The Euro-American Worldview and Cultural Orientation

The basic principles defining the Euro-American worldview are "survival of the fittest" and "control over nature" (people, objects, material possessions). These principles emphasize the high priority, historically and today, that European people tend to place on individualism and gaining control over the environment or surroundings (people, ideas, objects-property). Mastery is achieved through competition, aggression, materialism, domination and power, oppression, independence, and the transformation and rearranging of objects in nature (Akbar, 1984; Baldwin, 1980, 1985; Carruthers, 1981; Dixon, 1976; White, 1984). Since Euro-Americans are socialized in a cultural system (values, beliefs, attitudes, and behaviors) that prioritizes an individualistic-dominating and controlling orientation to survival and self-affirmation, they naturally project this orientation as normative in their varied social interactions, including heterosexual relationships (Asante, 1981; Baldwin, 1985; Nobles, 1974; Nobles & Goddard, 1984).

Male-Female Relations in Euro-American Culture

Consistent with the Euro-American worldview, the values of power, competition, material affluence, and physical gratification (or pleasure) have been shown to govern heterosexual relationships in Euro-American society (Akbar, 1981; Asante, 1981; Braithwaite, 1982; Cade, 1970; Karenga, 1978; White, 1984). For example, some researchers (Asante, 1981; Baldwin, 1980, 1985; Nobles, 1978, 1980) have shown that relationships in Euro-American culture are based on the principles of control and domination, or a hierarchy of power. The male is defined as the power-figure in such relationships (Basow, 1980; Beale, 1970; Blood & Wolfe, 1960; Frazier, 1932; Lewis, 1955; Moynihan, 1965; Pettigrew, 1964; Sizemore, 1973). He is expected to be the dominant and controlling family member, the major decision-maker, and/or the primary supplier of the survival-related needs of the family (Basow, 1980; Moynihan, 1965; Podell, 1966; Rainwater, 1966). Thus, his role is defined as superior to the female. The female, on the other hand, is viewed as the subordinate member in Eurocentric heterosexual relationships. Her role is defined as distinct, separate, and subservient (or inferior) to the male (Beale, 1970; Bird, 1968; Cade, 1970; Harper-Bolton, 1982; Nobles, 1974; Sizemore, 1973).

An example of the strong emphasis in Euro-American society on female subordination and male superordination is reflected in the widely held male attitude toward household duties as "woman's work" (Harper-Bolton, 1982; Staples, 1971). Many Euro-American male partners resist assuming or assisting with domestic responsibilities, such as managing the household and rearing the children, even in instances where such support is needed and/or desired (Cade, 1970). Such an attitude on the part of Euro-American men no doubt exists because such responsibilities have been associated with femininity or womanliness, which, as previously noted, suggests weakness and subordination, or a deficit state of being in Euro-American culture (Harper-Bolton, 1982; Ladner, 1971). Another example is reflected in the observation that many women in contemporary America resent and reject their traditional roles as wives and mothers, because these roles have relatively low value in Euro-American culture (Cade, 1970; Karenga, 1978). Many Euro-American women, especially in recent times, tend to think being a parent and/or wife brings them little social respect and sense of dignity or personal gratification (Astin, 1975; Brothers, 1984; Cade, 1970; Hoffman, 1977; Tangri, 1972). These women, therefore, seek "liberation" from their subservient roles in heterosexual relationships, and they advocate "equal rights" with their male counterparts in all sectors of American society (Basow, 1980; Braithwaite, 1982; Hoffman, 1977). Thus, it has been argued that the rigid and hierarchical nature of definitions of heterosexuality and gender roles in

Euro-American culture (Nobles, 1978) probably contributes considerably to disharmony in heterosexual relationships governed by this cultural orientation (Cade, 1970; Harper-Bolton, 1982).

The materialistic emphasis of Euro-American culture has been shown to generate high priority for material affluence as a determining factor in the success of male-female relationships (Akbar, 1981; Hampton, 1979; Harper-Bolton, 1982). Studies have found, for example, that socio-economic status, as indexed by level of income and education, is a major criterion in the mate-selection process and is positively related to marital stability in American society (Bernard, 1966; Carter & Glick, 1976; Cruse, 1982; Cutright, 1971; Glick & Norton, 1971; Hampton, 1979; Scanzoni, 1975).

The emphasis in Euro-American culture on material reality or the accumulation of material wealth has been found to be highly correlated with an overemphasis on physical characteristics, physical appearance, and sexual gratification as primary dimensions of heterosexual relationships (Akbar, 1981; Cruse, 1982; Karenga, 1978). Some researchers, for example, have shown that in American society, physical characteristics and gratification have a higher priority in choosing a mate than many psychological qualities and character traits (Braithwaite, 1982; Cruse, 1982; Fairchild, 1985; Fisher, 1981). Overall, then, the evidence seems to strongly support the contention that heterosexual relationships in American society are heavily influenced by the Eurocentric cultural orientation emphasizing individualism, materialism, and physical gratification.

▬ The Impact of Racial/Cultural Oppression on Black Male-Female Relationships

In varying degrees, it has been shown that African-Americans manifest some Euro-American cultural values in their relationships with each other (Akbar, 1981; Asante, 1981; Baldwin, 1985; Cade, 1970; Hammond & Enoch, 1976; Karenga, 1975, 1978; Nobles, 1978). This is probably the case because African-Americans continue to negotiate their survival in a society where the major institutions are governed by the principles and values of the Euro-American worldview (Amini, 1972; Baldwin, 1979, 1980, 1985; McGee, 1973). Having existed in a Eurocentric social reality over several centuries, evidence suggests that African-Americans have become psychologically dependent, in varying degrees, on that reality (Akbar, 1981; Baldwin, 1980, 1985; Nobles, 1976). Consequently, they have accepted an orientation to social relationships which is more consistent in many respects with Eurocentric cultural definitions than with their own Afrocentric cultural definitions (Baldwin, 1980; Braithwaite, 1982; McGee, 1973). This state of psychological oppression (Baldwin, 1980, 1985) means that many African-American males and females have internalized Eurocentric definitions/values and practice them in their relationships (Braithwaite, 1982; Cade, 1970; Harper-Bolton, 1982).

Support for the contention that Black heterosexual relationships are victimized by racial and cultural oppression in America comes from research on the values held by Black males and females. The research evidence on Black heterosexual relationships clearly suggests that many African-Americans (Jewell, 1983; Podell, 1966; Scanzoni, 1975) are influenced in their relationships by values and beliefs that are more congruent with the Euro-American worldview. Eurocentric values of high financial status, physical gratification, gender role differences, and education-professional status tend to play major roles in many Black male-female relations (Jewell 1983; Podell, 1966; Scanzoni, 1975).

Further support that this psychological oppression exists is found in the negative images African-American males and females have of each other (King, 1973). In this regard, American society defines Black men and women as being inferior to Whites. The electronic media, especially television and film, the mass media, and the American educational system in general have been shown to perpetuate negative Black male and female images (Benjamin, 1983; Caution & Baldwin, 1980; Jewell, 1983). Negative Black female images such as matriarchal, domineering, emasculating, and aggressive (Benjamin, 1983; Cade, 1970; Staples, 1971; Wallace, 1979) and Black male images as "Uncle Tom," passive, "stud," and criminal, among many others (Burgest & Bowen, 1982; Jewell, 1983), have been popularized by the electronic media. These negative images no doubt affect how many Black men and Black women view and relate to each other. According to sociological studies, for example, some Black males tend to perceive Black women as emasculating and aggressive, and conversely, some Black females tend to perceive Black men as shiftless, passive, and irresponsible (Benjamin, 1983; Houston, 1981; Staples, 1971; Turner & Turner, 1974).

Furthermore, some Black males tend to believe that Black females are the antithesis of beauty, femininity, and womanhood (Burgest, 1981; Burgest & Bowen, 1982; Nelson, 1975; Turner, 1982). Similarly, some Black females tend to believe that White men treat White women much better than Black men treat Black women (Turner, 1982). This kind of evidence clearly suggests that many Black men and women have internalized the negative Eurocentric images of their heterosexual roles, and that these internalized negative images probably contribute to much of the conflict in Black male-female relationships (Akbar, 1981; Amini, 1972; Braithwaite, 1982; Cade, 1970; Jewell, 1983; McGee, 1973).

Given the dominance of the Eurocentric worldview in American society (Baldwin, 1980, 1985), Black male-female relationships which prioritize Eurocentric values seemingly would be less stable than Black heterosexual relationships with a stronger Afrocentric cultural foundation (Akbar, 1984; Asante, 1980, 1981; Baldwin, 1984). There are several reasons why this position seems tenable. One is related to the transient and satiable nature of needs for pleasurable sensations (Akbar, 1981). Physical attractiveness and sexual potency decline with age in both men and women, and sensual pleasure provides only a temporary and intermittent source of self-satisfaction. Hence, while these needs do have a place in relationships, they do not constitute the total experience involved in sustaining healthy, culturally effective, and successful relationships between men and women (Asante, 1980, 1981).

Another reason for the tenability of this analysis concerns the issue of physical attractiveness. This issue is especially critical for African-Americans, given their existence in a society that projects and reinforces Eurocentric standards of beauty (Jewell, 1983; Murstein & Christy, 1976; Turner, 1982). Blacks who assign disproportionate priority to physical attraction/attributes in their relationships are probably more vulnerable to using Eurocentric criteria instead of Afrocentric cultural standards, such as human qualities or personal character. That is, the adoption of Eurocentric standards of physical attractiveness may cause a shift to physical rather than human/character qualities in assessing personal worth (Akbar, 1981; Harper-Bolton, 1982). This contributes to Blacks' perception of each other in many instances as deficient and inferior (Burgest, 1981; Jewell, 1983).

A third reason for the tenability of this analysis relates to the materialistic emphasis in relationships. The value of material affluence (prestige) could pose a threat to the establishment of serious and intimate relationships between Blacks because of racial oppression. That is, it is probably more difficult for Blacks than Whites to obtain definitive or absolute security through a self-image based on quantity of material possessions (Karenga, 1978). Furthermore, material affluence does not ensure the presence of those human qualities like strong moral character, mutual respect and sharing, or sacrifice which are so vital to healthy relationships between Black men and women (Asante, 1981).

The power emphasis in relationships suggests another basis of support for this analysis. Relationships with a power focus are concerned with hierarchy, manipulation, and control (Braithwaite, 1982). Partners (either one or both) in relationships with this focus tend to objectify competition with and exploitation of each other in order to maintain their self-worth. Thus, power-centered Black heterosexual relationships could be considered as maladaptive from the framework of African-American culture, because they lack reciprocity or mutual sharing and support, which define the essence of relationships in African-American culture (Asante, 1980; Nobles, 1974). Blacks in heterosexual relationships with a strong Afrocentric cultural orientation would be more spiritually balanced and thus place greater emphasis on personal-human qualities rather than physical-material qualities. Thus, Afrocentric relationships would be more healthy and culturally successful for Blacks. They would also be more resistant to Eurocentric racial cultural oppression, because by virtue of their Afrocentric value base, they should be less vulnerable to manipulation and control by alien cultural institutions (Baldwin, 1984, 1985).

The African-American Worldview and Black Heterosexual Relationships

An alternative approach in conceptualizing Black heterosexual relationships is derived from the African-American worldview. A basic assumption of the Afrocentric conceptual framework, as compared to the Eurocentric/cultural deprivation framework, is that African-Americans have a distinct cultural orientation (Akbar, 1984; Asante, 1980; Baldwin, 1980, 1985; Dixon, 1976). Hence, it is assumed in this model that African-Americans, notwithstanding some Euro-American cultural influences, tend to operate within the framework of the African worldview, which is distinct from the Euro-American worldview (Baldwin, 1985; Harper-Bolton, 1982; Nobles, 1980, 1986). Therefore, African-American scholars contend that a valid understanding of African-American relationships must logically incorporate the values and principles of the African-American worldview (Akbar, 1984; Asante, 1980; Baldwin, 1980, 1981, 1984; Nobles, 1980; White, 1984; Williams, 1981).

The African-American worldview is rooted in the historical, cultural, and philosophical tradition of African people. This worldview interprets Black behaviors and psychological functioning from the perspective of a value system which prioritizes the affirmation of Black life. The African-American worldview is defined by two guiding principles: "oneness with nature" and "survival of the group" (Baldwin, 1980; Mbiti, 1970; Nobles, 1980). The principle of "oneness with nature" asserts that all elements in the universe (humans, animals, inanimate objects, and natural phenomena) are interconnected (Nobles, 1980). That is, humanity, nature, and the self are conceptualized as the same phenomenon (Baldwin, 1985; Dixon, 1976; Nobles, 1980).

The principle of "survival of the group" prioritizes the survival of the corporate whole (the community), which includes all Black people, rather than the individual or some segment of the community apart from the corporate whole (Baldwin, 1985; Dixon, 1976; Nobles, 1980). The essence of both principles is best summarized by the African adage: "I am because we are, and because we are, therefore, I am" (Mbiti, 1970).

Cultural values consistent with the basic principles of the African-American worldview are interdependence, cooperation, unity, mutual responsibility, and reconciliation (Dixon, 1976; Harper-Bolton, 1982; Nobles, 1974, 1980). The African worldview, thus, characterizes the natural/normal cultural orientation of Black people and no doubt influences their behavior and social relationships.

An Afrocentric Model of Black Heterosexual Relationships

A model of Black heterosexual relationships based on the African-American worldview has been proposed by Asante (1980, 1981). Asante's model defines healthy Black heterosexual relationships as those that are governed by an "Afrocentric imperative." By an Afrocentric (or collective cognitive) imperative, he means the spiritual and intellectual commitment of Black couples to the cultural affirmation of their people. Thus, Asante's model emphasizes that Afrocentric cultural values should constitute the foundation of Black relationships.

Black relationships with an Afrocentric cultural basis, in terms of Asante's model (1981), are based on four major value components: sacrifice, inspiration, vision, and victory. Sacrifice as a value component suggests that partners should prioritize spiritual-communal character qualities as equally (if not more) important as physical-material qualities in the foundation of their relationships. This component means that couples should use their sense of corporate responsibility and interdependence to benefit their relationship as well as their families and the community at large. Hence, couples should be committed to giving of themselves, wherever they are located in time and space, for the continued survival and well-being of their families and the Black community.

Inspiration as a component of Afrocentric relationships emphasizes that partners should relate to each other in a mutually affirmative and/or holistic, as opposed to fragmented, manner (Asante, 1980). In a holistic relationship, each partner provides for the other's physical, intellectual, emotional, and social stimulation. Neither partner exploits the relationship; instead, both encourage, inspire, and support each other in their productive and creative work and responsibilities. Thus, the inspiration component of the Afrocentric relationship identifies mutuality and reciprocity as core ingredients of healthy Black heterosexual relationships.

Asante also defines Afrocentric relationships as being visionary. This component emphasizes the couple's role in future planning as related to family-community building. This means that the couple should be committed to goals, accomplishments, and aspirations that are related to the survival and development of the Black family in the Black community. This component, therefore, suggests the belief in Black community involvement that is designed to revitalize and preserve African-American culture.

Finally, victory as a value component of Afrocentric relationships defines the couple's belief and faith that all goals related to African affirmation are achievable. This component, according to Asante (1980), means that couples celebrate themselves, their achievements, aspirations, and developments as African people, since these are viewed as culturally relevant. This concept of Afrocentric celebration incorporates self-development and/or race-cultural-related accomplishments (e.g., the attainment of joy, peace, and power on behalf of the family and the Black community). Hence, family-community participation in the celebration of such accomplishments is more highly valued than (or is certainly considered equal in value to) the material-physical aspects of celebration (e.g., gift-giving). In terms of Asante's model, then, Afrocentric relationships are based on African-American cultural value themes, such as holistic relationships, spiritual/character values, and Afrocentric cultural consciousness.

Based on Asante's (1980, 1981) model, there should be a positive relationship between Afrocentric cultural consciousness and healthy (self-affirming) Black heterosexual relationships. Obviously, the value themes in Asante's model are in opposition to those that undergird relationships based on Euro-American values. Hence, African-American heterosexual relationships based on the African-American worldview would be expected to manifest, to a considerable degree, more Afrocentric/self-affirming attitudinal (cognitive) and behavioral orientations. To date, no research to our knowledge has been conducted which attempts to examine this notion or any aspect of Asante's model.

▬ Proposed Research and Hypothesis

The purpose of this study is to examine the relationship between Afrocentric cultural consciousness and perceptions of male-female relationships among African-Americans. Based on the assumption that Afrocentric cultural consciousness is positively related to healthy Black heterosexual relationships, perceptions (values, attitudes, and beliefs) of Black heterosexual relationships should vary as a function of levels of Afrocentric cultural consciousness. Therefore, it is predicted that Afrocentric cultural consciousness will be significantly related to how Blacks perceive heterosexual relationships. More specifically, the hypothesis is that those subjects who exhibit high Afrocentric cultural consciousness will prioritize Afrocentric cultural values in heterosexual relationships, as opposed to Eurocentric cultural values. And conversely, it is hypothesized that those who reflect low Afrocentric cultural consciousness will prioritize more Eurocentric cultural values (e.g., power, prestige, income and/or financial status), or perhaps a diffusion of both Afrocentric and Eurocentric values in heterosexual relationships.

Methodology

▬ Subjects

The subjects in this study were 88 Black males and 89 Black females from Gadsden and Leon counties in north Florida. A deliberate effort was made to obtain a cross-sectional sample by selecting subjects at different ages, educational, and occupational levels. Relative to each of these categories, the subjects were selected from four population categories: college students, unskilled workers, professionals, and the elderly. The college students were enrolled in various sections of the introductory psychology course at Florida A&M University. The unskilled workers and professionals were selected from a roster of names and work phone numbers provided by a state employment agency in Florida. Black churches in Gadsden and Leon counties selected the elderly subjects and provided names and phone numbers, with the person's permission. In each category at least 40 subjects were selected on the basis of whether they were presently or had been involved in a heterosexual relationship and whether they were willing to participate.

▭ Instruments

African Self-Consciousness (ASC) Scale. The ASC was developed by Baldwin and Bell (1985) and is designed to assess the Black personality construct of African self-consciousness (Baldwin, 1981, 1984). It consists of four competency dimensions that are reflected in the questionnaire's 42 items. The competency dimensions are: awareness and recognition of one's African identity and heritage; recognition of Black survival priorities and the necessity for institutions (practices, customs, values) which affirm Black life; participation in the survival, liberation, and development of Black people and defense of their dignity, worth, and integrity; recognition of how racial oppression hinders the development and survival of Black life and resistance to anti-Black forces. Also included in the ASC Scale are six expressive dimensions: religion, family, education, culture, interpersonal relationships, and political orientation. All statements comprising the ASC Scale reflect some beliefs, opinions, and attitudes of Black people which are relevant to important aspects of African-American life and survival requirements. Statements in the ASC Scale are scored as: strongly disagree (1-2), disagree (3-4), agree (5-6), and strongly agree (7-8). The final ASC Scale scores can be computed as either the total score (sum) or the mean total score (sum of score/number of items). The validity estimate for the ASC Scale is $r = .70$, and the reliability estimate is $r = .90$ (Baldwin & Bell, 1985).

Black Heterosexual Relationship (BHR) Survey. This measure was designed to assess the subjects' perceptions (values, attitudes, and beliefs) concerning heterosexual relationships. The structure of the BHR Survey is similar to the Black Male-Female Relations Survey developed by Fairchild (1985). The BHR Survey consists of four parts:

Ideal Mate (Part 1). This part of the BHR Survey consisted of personal qualities and social traits of an ideal mate that were pre-rated by three expert judges as representing either the Euro-American or the African-American worldview. The qualities and traits pre-rated as representing the African-American worldview derived from Asante's model (1981) of Black heterosexual relationships. These were emotional and intellectual stimulation, commitment to the Black community, mutual respect and sharing, cultural awareness, unconditional love, and being family-oriented. The qualities and traits pre-rated to represent the Euro-American worldview were: physical attraction, competition and control, independence, sexual compatibility, financial status, educational status, sexual conquests, and professional status. The latter items were taken from Fairchild's survey (1985) of Black heterosexual relationships.

Both sets of descriptors were randomly organized in the list to minimize any effects that might be derived from a systematic listing. A final item in Part 1 required the subjects to write in a quality or trait that they viewed as important in heterosexual relationships. The subjects rated each quality or trait on the following scale of importance: not at all (0), a little (1), some (2), very much (3).

Heterosexual Attitudes (Part 2). This part consisted of 20 statements constructed to be consistent in meaning with the four components of Asante's model. Attitudes and perceptions were pre-rated as projecting either Afrocentric or Eurocentric values in heterosexual relationships. For example, an item reflecting sacrifice was "In my personal relationship maintaining a workable (useful, positive, growing) relationship with my family and my spouse's family is important." An item reflecting inspiration was "Each spouse should be approved by both of our parents." An item reflecting vision was "For Black couples, the concept of building a family should definitely include the investment of the couples' productive and financial resources in Black institutions, or in efforts to build such institutions." Finally, an example of an item depicting victory was "In mate selection and/or evaluation, Black men and Black women should consider Black cultural beliefs and values (or cultural consciousness) as a main or primary criterion."

Eurocentric items dealt with such issues as physical attraction, competition, or control. An example of a Eurocentric item was "A person must have a substantial income before I would consider a serious/intimate relationship with him or her." These items were modeled after those in the Black Male-Female Relationship Survey developed by Fairchild (1985).

Responses were rated on a 4-point Likert-type scale ranging from strongly disagree (1) to strongly agree (4). On Parts 1 and 2, higher scores indexed a stronger Afrocentric cultural orientation and lower scores indexed a weaker Afrocentric orientation, or a more Eurocentric orientation.

Behavioral Scenario (Part 3). This part consisted of two hypothetical scenarios, one for male subjects and one for female subjects, involving a Black relationship dilemma. The scenarios were constructed to symbolize real-life hardships in the African-American community. The scenario for the male subjects depicted a man who is working three jobs to support his family (wife and children). The wife is unable to work due to illness, and because of the nature of her illness, she cannot actively participate in the general management of the home. For leisure activity, she usually spends several hours a day watching television and playing card games with friends. The scenario for the female subjects depicted a woman who is working two jobs to support her family (a husband and three children). The husband is unemployed and remains at home. He has not been able to contribute any financial support to the maintenance of the family but helps his wife with child care and the general duties of managing the home. For leisure activity, he spends a few hours three to four days a week at a local bar talking and drinking with friends.

For each scenario, the subjects were asked to indicate their most likely course of action, from among four choices, if they were the employed partner in the situation described. One of the four courses of action was pre-rated Afrocentric and the other three were pre-rated as Eurocentric in value projections. The Afrocentric alternative involved being totally supportive of the mate in hardship, while the Eurocentric alternatives ranged from partial to total withholding/withdrawing of support.

Personal Background Information (Part 4). This last section of the BHR Survey was used to obtain background data on the subjects relative to their age, sex, social class status, educational level, and occupational-professional status, where appropriate.

Procedure

The ASC Scale and the BHR Survey were hand-delivered simultaneously to the subjects by the researcher. The subjects were instructed to complete the ASC Scale and the BHR Survey. They were told that the questionnaires would be collected in five days at the same place where they were delivered. The college students received and returned both instruments in their psychology classes. All of the elderly subjects and some of the professional and unskilled workers received and returned the instruments in their homes. Some other professionals and unskilled workers received and returned the instruments at their places of employment. Some of the unskilled workers and elderly subjects indicated that they would have difficulty reading and comprehending the ASC Scale and the BHR Survey. These subjects were assisted by the researcher in their homes. On two separate occasions, the researcher assisted these subjects with the completion of the ASC Scale and the BHR Survey, respectively.

Results

The primary data in this study consisted of the total scores obtained on the ASC Scale, and on Parts 1 and 2 (Ideal Mate and Heterosexual Attitudes) of the BHR Survey. The frequency of Afrocentric versus Eurocentric responses to Part 3 (the Behavioral Scenario) of the BHR Survey and responses to the background data section were included as primary data in these results.

Correlational and chi-square analyses were used to evaluate the data. The Pearson product moment correlation coefficient was computed to assess the magnitude of the relationship between ASC scores and scores on the Ideal Mate and the Heterosexual Attitudes measures. A significant positive correlation was obtained between ASC scores and Ideal Mate scores, $r = .44$, $p < .001$. High ASC scores tended to be associated with high Afrocentric Ideal Mate scores. The analysis of ASC scores and Heterosexual Attitudes scores also yielded a significant positive correlation, $r = .53$, $p < .001$; high ASC scores correlated with high Afrocentric Heterosexual Attitudes scores.

The chi-square test was computed to compare the frequencies of high and low ASC Scale scores with the frequencies of high and low scores on the Ideal Mate and the Heterosexual Attitudes measures. Scores that were 1 standard deviation above the mean on each of these measures were designated high scores, while scores that were 1 standard deviation below the mean were designated low scores. Table 4.1 summarizes the means and standard deviations for these measures.

The chi-square analysis for the ASC and Ideal Mate scores yielded a significant value, χ^2 (1, $N = 22$) = 14.67, $p < .001$. Ninety-two percent of the students with high ASC scores obtained high Ideal Mate scores. Also,

TABLE 4.1   Means and Standard Deviations for the ASC, Ideal Mate,
and Heterosexual Attitudes Scores

Measure	N	Mean	Standard Deviation
ASC	177	240	48
Ideal Mate	177	46	9
Heterosexual Attitudes	177	59	13

NOTE: ASC refers to the African Self-Consciousness Scale developed by Baldwin and Bell (1985).

TABLE 4.2   Frequency and Percentages of High and Low ASC Scores,
by High and Low Ideal Mate and Heterosexual Attitudes Scores

	ASC			
	High		Low	
Ideal Mate[a]				
High Afrocentric	11	92%	1	8%
Low Afrocentric	1	10%	9	90%
Heterosexual Attitudes[b]				
High Afrocentric	14	100%	0	
Low Afrocentric	0		10	100%

NOTE: ASC refers to the African Self-Consciousness Scale developed by Baldwin and Bell (1985).
a. χ^2 (1, N = 22) = 14.67, p < .001.
b. χ^2 (1, N = 24) = 24.00, p < .001.

90% of the subjects with low ASC scores obtained low Ideal Mate scores. The chi-square value for ASC scores by Heterosexual Attitudes scores was also significant, χ^2 (1, N = 24) = 24.00, p < .001. This analysis indicated that all of the subjects with high ASC scores also obtained high Heterosexual Attitudes scores. These results are summarized in Table 4.2. Overall, both the correlational and chi-square analyses indicate that a significant relationship exists between Afrocentric cultural consciousness and an Afrocentric values orientation in perceptions of Black heterosexual relationships.

To further substantiate the role of cultural values in heterosexual relationships, additional chi-square analyses were computed to assess the relationship between scores on the Behavioral Scenario measure, scores on the ASC, Ideal Mate, and Heterosexual Attitudes measures, and several background factors (age, sex, socioeconomic status, and educational status). For this analysis, subjects who selected the Afrocentric alternative

TABLE 4.3   Frequency and Percentages of Afrocentric vs. Eurocentric
Behavioral Scores, by High and Low ASC, Ideal Mate, and
Heterosexual Attitudes Scores

| | Behavioral Scenario Measure | | | |
	Afrocentric		Eurocentric	
ASC[a]				
High	27	100%	0	
Low	2	8%	22	92%
Ideal Mate[b]				
High Afrocentric	26	96%	1	4%
Low Afrocentric	6	16%	31	84%
Heterosexual Attitudes[c]				
High Afrocentric	22	92%	2	8%
Low Afrocentric	2	8%	22	92%

NOTE: ASC refers to the African Self-Consciousness Scale developed by Baldwin and Bell (1985).
a. χ^2 (1, N = 51) = 43.52, p < .001.
b. χ^2 (1, N = 64) = 40.04, p < .001.
c. χ^2 (1, N = 48) = 33.33, p < .001.

in the Behavioral Scenario were designated high-scoring subjects and those who selected one of the Eurocentric alternatives were designated low-scoring subjects.

The results of the chi-square analysis between ASC Scale, Ideal Mate and Heterosexual Attitudes scores, and the Behavioral Scenario measure are summarized in Table 4.3. The ASC × Behavioral Scenario analysis indicates that all of the high-ASC subjects chose the Afrocentric response to the Behavioral Scenario measure: χ^2 (1, N, = 51) = 43.52, p < .001. Contrastingly, 92% of the low-scoring subjects on the ASC Scale did not choose the Afrocentric response. The analysis of the relationship between the Behavioral Scenario measure and the Ideal Mate measure was also significant: χ^2 (1, N = 64) = 40.04, p < .001. This analysis indicated that 96% of the subjects who obtained high Ideal Mate scores chose the Afrocentric alternative on the Behavioral Scenario measure. The chi-square value for the Behavioral Scenario measure and the Heterosexual Attitudes scores was significant as well: χ^2(1, N = 48) = 33.33, p < .001. This analysis indicates that the subjects with Afrocentric Heterosexual Attitudes scores also chose the Afrocentric alternative on the Behavioral Scenario measure.

The chi-square analysis was also computed for the demographic data in relation to performance on the Behavioral Scenario measure. These

TABLE 4.4   Frequency and Percentage of Demographic Data Related
to the Behavioral Scenario Measure

| | Behavioral Scenario Measure | | | |
	Afrocentric		Eurocentric	
Age[a]				
Nonelderly	17	41%	24	59%
Elderly	34	79%	9	21%
Occupational status[b]				
Students	19	43%	25	57%
Unskilled	58	70%	25	30%
Professional	19	37%	32	63%
Educational level[c]				
Primary/secondary	56	71%	23	29%
College/college graduate	38	40%	58	60%
Socioeconomic status[d]				
Lower	73	66%	38	34%
Middle/upper	23	36%	41	64%

a. $\chi^2 (1, N = 84) = 12.44, p < .001$.
b. $\chi^2 (2, N = 178) = 16.25, p < .001$.
c. $\chi^2 (1, N = 178) = 17.08, p < .001$.
d. $\chi^2 (1, N = 178) = 14.58, p < .001$.

results are presented in Table 4.4. The age × Behavioral Scenario measure analysis generated a significant chi-square: $\chi^2 (1, N = 84) = 12.44, p < .001$. This indicates that 79% of the elderly subjects as compared to 41% of the nonelderly subjects chose the Afrocentric response to the Behavioral Scenario measure. The chi-square value for occupational status (student, unskilled, and professional) and performance on the Behavioral Scenario measure was also significant: $\chi^2 (2, N = 178) = 16.25, p < .001$. This analysis reveals that 70% of the unskilled subjects chose the Afrocentric response, as compared to 43% of the students and 37% of the professionals. Additionally, educational level and the Behavioral Scenario measure generated a significant chi-square value: $\chi^2 (1, N = 175) = 17.08, p < .001$. Seventy-one percent of the subjects with a primary/secondary education, as compared with 40% of the subjects with a college education, chose the Afrocentric response. Finally, the chi-square value for socioeconomic status and performance on the Behavioral Scenario measure was also significant: $\chi^2 (1, N = 175) = 14.58, p < .001$.

This analysis indicates that 66% of the subjects with a lower socioeconomic status, as compared to 36% of the subjects with a middle-upper socioeconomic status, chose the Afrocentric response to the Behavioral Scenario measure. The chi-square analysis did not indicate a significant relationship between sex and performance on the Behavioral Scenario measure.

Discussion

It was hypothesized in this study that Afrocentric cultural consciousness is significantly related to perceptions of heterosexual relationships among African-Americans. The present findings support this prediction. The correlation analysis indicated a positive and stable relationship between Afrocentric cultural consciousness and an Afrocentric value orientation in perceptions of heterosexual relationships. The chi-square analysis also supported this finding in terms of frequency (or percentage) of subjects.

Specifically, these findings suggest that subjects with high Afrocentric cultural consciousness tended to prioritize their ideal mate in terms of emotional and intellectual stimulation, commitment to the Black community, mutual respect and sharing, Black consciousness (awareness), unconditional love, and family orientation. In contrast, subjects who manifested low Afrocentric cultural consciousness prioritized such ideal-mate qualities as physical attraction, competition and control, independence, sexual compatibility, financial status, emotional status, sexual conquests, and professional status.

Additionally, subjects with high Afrocentric cultural consciousness tended to place more value on heterosexual attitudes (or perceptions) that were consistent in meaning with Asante's four components of healthy Black relationships. That is, the subjects were more inclined to endorse the idea that partners should relate to each other in a reciprocal manner, as well as family-community building and recognition and respect for each partner's achievements, aspirations, and development. On the other hand, those with low cultural consciousness were more in favor of attitudes and perceptions reflective of Eurocentric cultural values in heterosexual relationships (e.g., competition, physical-material gratification). Overall, then, these findings strongly suggest that Afrocentric cultural consciousness is positively related to an Afrocentric value orientation in Black heterosexual relationships.

The present findings also support the position that Afrocentric values play an affirmative role in Black heterosexual relationships. This contention is strongly supported by the performance of the subjects on the Behavioral Scenario measure. All of the subjects with high ASC scores indicated that they would remain with and be totally supportive of their mate when the latter was ill or without employment. The same alternative was chosen by subjects who manifested an Afrocentric orientation on the Ideal Mate and the Heterosexual Attitudes measures. The exact reversal of this response pattern occurred for the subjects who manifested a less Afrocentric or more Eurocentric cultural orientation. Less Afrocentric subjects indicated that they would withhold either partial or total support of the mate suffering hardship. Thus, the highly Afrocentric subjects reflected a stronger commitment to the relationship during a hardship or crisis involving the other partner.

This consistency in performance on the Behavioral Scenario measure by the high and low groups on ASC, Ideal Mate and Heterosexual Attitudes measures strongly suggests that Afrocentric values may constitute a much more reliable predictor of stable and affirmative Black heterosexual relationships than the prominent literature has indicated. Regarding this point, it should be emphasized that only one of the four response alternatives on the Behavioral Scenario measure indexed an Afrocentric cultural orientation. The subjects were provided with more opportunities (three) to choose a Eurocentric alternative. Therefore, the strong preference for the Afrocentric alternative among the Afrocentric subjects tends to further support the affirmative nature of Afrocentric values in Black heterosexual relationships. In this regard, the present findings are consistent with Asante's (1980) model. His model argues that the successful attainment and/or maintenance of goals related to the survival and well-being of these relationships (e.g., economical stability, personal-social adjustment) are contingent upon the mates having and maintaining an Afrocentric cultural/value base. The performance of these subjects on the Behavioral Scenario measure, in particular, seemingly provides good support for Asante's contention.

With the exception of sex, all of the other background factors (age, socioeconomic status, educational, and occupational ranks) differentially affected performance on the Behavioral Scenario measure. The elderly subjects and the low-ranking educational, occupational, and socio-economic subject groups indicated a stronger preference for the Afrocentric alternative than did their younger or higher-level counterparts. This result may be linked to the fact that the elderly and low-ranking groups share a more peripheral or marginal status in (i.e., social and psychological distance from) Euro-American-controlled institutions than the latter groups. For example, the elderly subjects experienced their formative socialization and received their education, at least the early part of it, during the segregation era of American social policy. The younger subjects, most of whom are college students, are products of the more recent desegregation/integration era of American social policy. The elderly subjects' education and socio-cultural experiences in general are probably products of a more Afrocentric experience than the younger subjects (Billingsley, 1968; Nobles, 1974, 1978). Thus, the difference observed in this finding may have been influenced to some extent by the sociohistorical factors of American life. The present findings might also be interpreted as supporting the notion that Euro-American institutions (education, employment) tend to have a culturally alienating effect on Black heterosexual relationships.

Implications of the Study

As discussed earlier, previous research on Black heterosexual relation-ships, for the most part, has been governed by the cultural deficit perspec-tive (Asante, 1981; Baldwin, 1985). Such research tended to be guided by the erroneous assumption of the dominant culture that Black heterosexual relationships are governed by the same Eurocentric values, beliefs, and life-styles that govern Euro-American relations (Allen, 1978; Baldwin, 1980; Nobles, 1974; Staples, 1971). Therefore, most of the previous assessments of African-American heterosexual relationships emphasized the deviations from Euro-American norms and standards for healthy relationships (Cazenave, 1983; Fairchild, 1985; McAdoo, 1983). Since a cultural deficit perspective has dominated this area of research the obser-vations generated have mostly reflected the influence of racial and cultural oppression on Black heterosexual relationships rather than the role of African-American culture as a legitimate system of values and standards governing such relationships. In contrast to the deficit-oriented literature, it is important to reiterate that the present findings suggest an entirely different research focus by documenting the importance of Afrocentric cultural consciousness and Afrocentric values in Black heterosexual rela-tionships. Thus, the findings of this study help to broaden the knowledge base related to a fuller understanding of Black heterosexual relationships.

The findings relating background variables to Afrocentric vs. Eurocen-tric value orientations on the Behavioral Scenario measure suggest that these orientations may vary consistently with age and occupational, educational, and socioeconomic ranks. Afrocentric value orientations in heterosexual relationships may be moderated to some extent by these kinds of background factors. In light of this suggestion, it seems that future research should focus on comparing the relative contributions of background factors, such as those in this study, to variance in cultural values regarding heterosexual relationships. Such research could strengthen the knowledge base undergirding intervention strategies (therapeutic and educational programs) that are directed toward fostering healthy Black relationships.

The present findings also direct attention to the socialization process, especially as the latter relates to sex-role definitions in the Black community. In this regard, one implication appears to be that it might be more healthy, at least from the vantage point of heterosexual relationships, for Black males and females to internalize sex-role definitions that are consistent with African-American culture rather than Euro-American culture (Harper-Bolton, 1982; Nobles, 1974). It seems that future research in this area might also be designed to investigate the nature of heterosexual relationship patterns in Black youth as a function of socialization factors (e.g., child-rearing patterns, parental heterosexual relationship values, family structure) in African-American families. Seemingly, additional research such as this is needed to strengthen our knowledge base relative to the impact of socialization on the development of heterosexual cultural values. It should also help to generate models for fostering healthy relationships among African-American men and women.

Conclusions

The findings of this study support the major prediction that Afrocentric cultural consciousness is positively related to perceptions (values, attitudes) that prioritize an Afrocentric value orientation in Black heterosexual relationships. Additionally, the findings support the contention that Afrocentric cultural factors may be a sustaining and affirmative force even during difficult times in Black heterosexual relationships. In this regard, the findings are supportive of Asante's model of culturally based Black heterosexual relationships.

The analysis involving background factors may magnify the potential importance of culturally affirmative experiences in cultural values preferences related to Black heterosexual relationships. That is, as an explanation for the stronger Afrocentric cultural orientation manifested by the elderly subjects and low-ranking educational, occupational, and socioeconomic groups, it was speculated that these groups may be more psychosocially distant from the European-American sociocultural reality than the younger and higher-ranking subject groups. The latter groups manifested a more diffuse or more Eurocentric cultural orientation. In contrast to the deficit-oriented thrust of previous research related to Black heterosexual relationships, the present findings reflect support for an alternative paradigm for conceptualizing such relationships, one which emphasizes the importance of Afrocentric cultural consciousness and Afrocentric cultural values to healthy Black heterosexual relationships.

Given the reality of the experience of racial and cultural oppression among African-Americans, it is suggested that a continued research effort is needed in this area to further refine our understanding of the role of cultural variables and related factors in Black heterosexual relationships. Such research should result in more culturally valid intervention planning geared toward fostering healthy African-American relationships in general, and healthy male-female relationships in particular.

References

Akbar, N. (1981). Reconciliation of the African American woman and man. *Black Male/ Female Relationships, 5*, 60-64.

Akbar, N. (1984). Africentric social sciences for human liberation. *Journal of Black Studies, 14*(4), 395-414.

Allen, W. (1978). The search for applicable theories of Black family life. *Journal of Marriage and the Family, 35*, 117-128.

Amini, J. (1972). *An African frame of reference.* Chicago: Institute of Positive Education.

Asante, M. (1981). Black male-female relationships: An Afrocentric context. In L. Gary (Ed.), *Black men.* Beverly Hills, CA: Sage.

Asante, M. K. (1980). *Afrocentricity: A theory of social change.* Buffalo, NY: Amulefi.

Astin, H. (1975). *Women and work.* Paper presented at the Conference for New Directions for Research on the Psychology of Women, Madison, WI.

Baldwin, J. (1979). Education and oppression in the American context. *Journal of Inner City Studies, 1*(1), 62-83.

Baldwin, J. (1980). The psychology of oppression. In M. K. Asante & A. Vandi (Eds.), *Contemporary Black thought: Alternative analyses in social and behavioral science.* Beverly Hills, CA: Sage.

Baldwin, J. (1981). Notes on an Africentric theory of Black personality. *Western Journal of Black Studies, 5*(3), 1972-1979.

Baldwin, J. (1984). African self-consciousness and the mental health of African Americans. *Journal of Black Studies, 15*(2), 177-194.

Baldwin, J. (1985). Psychological aspects of European cosmology in American society. *Western Journal of Black Studies, 9*(4), 216-223.

Baldwin, J., & Bell, Y. (1985). The African Self-Consciousness Scale: An Africentric personality questionnaire. *Western Journal of Black Studies, 9*(2), 61-68.

Basow, S. (1980). *Sex role stereotypes.* Belmont, CA: Wadsworth.

Beale, F. (1970). Double jeopardy: To be Black and female. In T. Cade (Ed.), *The Black woman: An anthology.* New York: New American Library.

Benjamin, L. (1983). The dog theory: Black male/female conflict. *Western Journal of Black Studies, 7*(1), 49-55.

Bernard, J. (1966). Marital stability and patterns of status variables. *Journal of Marriage and the Family, 28,* 358-367.

Billingsley, A. (1968). *Black families in White America.* Englewood Cliffs, NJ: Prentice-Hall.

Bird, C. (1968). *Born female.* New York: Durd McKay.

Blood, R., & Wolfe, D. (1960). *Husbands and wives: The dynamics of married living.* Illinois: The Press of Glencoe.

Braithwaite, R. (1982). Interpersonal relations between Black males and females. *Black Men,* 83-95.

Brothers, J. (1984). *What every woman ought to know about love and marriage.* New York: Ballentine.

Burgest, D., & Bowen, J. (1982). Erroneous assumptions Black men make about Black women. *Black Male/Female Relationships, 6*(Winter), 13-19.

Burgest, M. (1981). Theory on White supremacy and Black oppression. *Black Books Bulletin, 7*(2), 26-30.

Cade, T. (1970). *The Black woman: An anthology.* New York: New American Library.

Carruthers, J. (1981). Reflections on the history of the Afrocentric worldview. *Black Books Bulletin, 7*(1), 4-25.

Carter, H., & Glick, P. (1976). *Marriage and divorce: A social and economic study* (rev. ed.). Cambridge: Howard University.

Caution, G. L., & Baldwin, J. A. (1980). *Television as projection of the European worldviews.* Unpublished manuscript.

Cazenave, N. (1983). Black male-Black female relationships: The perception of 155 middle-class Black men. *Family Relations, 32,* 341-350.

Cruse, H. (1982). The crisis in Black sexual politics. *Black Male/Female Relationships, 1*(Autumn), 27-40.

Cutright, P. (1971). Income and family events: Marital stability. *Journal of Marriage and the Family, 33,* 291-306.

Dixon, V. (1976). Worldview and research methodology. In L. M. King (Ed.), *African philosophy: Assumptions and paradigms for research on Black persons.* Los Angeles: Fanon Research and Development Center.

Fairchild, H. (1985). Black singles: Gender differences in mate preferences and heterosexual attitudes. *Western Journal of Black Studies, 9,* 69-73.

Farley, W., & Hermalin, A. (1971). Family stability: A comparison of trends between Blacks and Whites. *American Sociological Review, 36,* 1-17.

Fisher, H. (1981, April). Female sex appeal an asset even in prehistoric times. *Jet,* p. 43.

Frazier, E. (1932). *The Negro family in the United States.* Chicago: The University Press.

Frazier, E. (1957). *Black bourgeoisie: The rise of a new middle class in the United States.* Glencoe, IL: Free Press.

Glazier, N., & Moynihan, D. (1965). *Beyond the melting pot.* Cambridge: MIT Press.

Glick, P., & Norton, A. (1971). Frequency, duration and probability of marriage and divorce. *Journal of Marriage and the Family, 44,* 307-317.

Hammond, J., & Enoch, J. (1976). Conjugal power relations among Black working class families. *Journal of Black Studies, 8*(1), 107-128.

Hampton, R. (1979). Husband's characteristics and marital disruption in Black families. *Sociological Quarterly, 20,* 255-266.

Harper-Bolton, C. (1982). A reconceptualization of the African-American woman. *Black Male/Female Relationships, 6*(Winter), 33-42.

Hoffman, L. (1977). Changes in family roles, socialization and sex differences. *American Psychologist, 32,* 644-657.

Houston, L. (1981). Romanticism and eroticism among Black and White college students. *Adolescence, 16,* 263-272.

Jewell, K. (1983). Black male/female conflict: Internalization of negative definitions transmitted through imagery. *Western Journal of Black Studies, 7*(1), 43-48.

Karenga, M. (1975). In love and struggle: Toward a greater togetherness. *Black Scholar, 3,* 16-28.

Karenga, M. (1978). *Beyond connections.* Los Angeles: Kawaida.

King, M. (1973). The politics of sexual stereotypes. *Journal of Black Studies and Research, 4*(4-7), 12-23.

Ladner, J. (1971). *Tomorrow's tomorrow: The Black woman.* Garden City, NY: Doubleday.

Lewis, H. (1955). *Black ways of Kent.* Chapel Hill: University of North Carolina Press.

Mbiti, J. (1970). *African religions and philosophy.* New York: Doubleday.

McAdoo, H. (1983). *Extended family support to single black mothers.* Final report submitted to National Institutes of Mental Health. Rockville, MD: U.S. Department of Health and Human Services.

McGee, D. (1973). White conditioning of Black dependency. *Journal of Social Issues, 29*(1), 53-55.

Moynihan, D. (1965). *The Negro family: The call for national action.* Washington, DC: U.S. Department of Labor.

Murstein, B., & Christy, P. (1976). Physical attractiveness and marriage adjustment in middle-aged couples. *Journal of Personality and Social Psychology, 34,* 537-542.

Nelson, C. (1975). Myths about Black women workers in modern America. *Black Scholar, 3,* 11-15.

Nobles, W. (1974). Africanity: Its role in Black families. *Black Scholar, 5,* 10-17.

Nobles, W. (1976). Black people in White insanity: An issue for Black community mental health. *Journal of Afro-American Issues, 4*(1), 21-27.

Nobles, W. (1978). The Black family and its children: The survival of humaneness. *Black Books Bulletin, 6*(22), 7-14.

Nobles, W. (1980). African philosophy foundation for Black psychology. In R. Jones (Ed.), *Black psychology.* New York: Harper & Row.

Nobles, W. (1986). *African psychology: Towards its reclamation, reascension and revitalization.* Oakland, CA: Institute for the Advanced Study of Black Family Life and Culture.

Nobles, W., & Goddard, L. L. (1984). *Understanding the Black family: A guide for scholarship and research*. Oakland, CA: Institute of Black Family Life and Culture.

Pettigrew, T. (1964). *A profile of the Negro American*. Princeton, NJ: Van Nostrand.

Podell, L. (1966). Sex and role conflict. *Journal of Marriage and the Family, 28*(2), 163-165.

Rainwater, L. (1966). Crucible of identity: The Negro lower-class family. In Lengine & Brombley (Eds.), *White racism and Black Americans*. Chicago: Schenkman.

Scanzoni, J. (1975). Sex roles, economic factors, and marriage solidarity in Black and White marriages. *Journal of Marriage and the Family, 37*, 130-144.

Sizemore, B. (1973). Sexism and the Black male. *Black Scholar, 4*(6-7), 2-11.

Staples, R. (1971). *The Black family: Essays and studies*. Belmont, CA: Wadsworth.

Tangri, S. (1972). Determinants of occupational role innovation among college women. *Journal of Social Issues, 28*, 177-199.

Thomas, A., & Sillen, S. (1972). *Racism and psychiatry*. New York: Brunner/Mazel.

Turner, B., & Turner, C. (1974). Evaluation of women and men among Black and White college students. *Sociological Quarterly, 15*, 442-456.

Turner, R. (1982). The ordeal of the ugly Black woman. *Black Male/Female Relationships, 6*(Winter), 21-29.

Wallace, M. (1979). *Black macho and the myth of the superman*. New York: Dial.

White, J. (1984). *The psychology of Blacks*. Englewood Cliffs, NJ: Prentice-Hall.

Williams, R. (1981). *The collective Black mind: An Afrocentric theory of Black personality*. St. Louis, MO: Williams & Associates.

Rethinking Organizations From an Afrocentric Viewpoint

5

Jerome H. Schiele

Although possessing widely differing assumptions about organizational and human nature, organizational theories all have one thing in common: They reflect the conceptual frameworks of Western social science, which are derivatives of Western ideology and thought. By exclusively reflecting the values and notions of Western society, these theories are circumscribable and biased and omit different conceptualizations of human beings and society found in other cultures. To this extent—and because Western social science has negated the worldview of African people (Akbar, 1984; Asante, 1987; Carruthers, 1989; Karenga, 1982)—some have argued for development of an alternative social science model reflective of the cultural background and cultural reality of African people (Akbar, 1984, 1985; Asante, 1980a, 1988; Baldwin, 1986; Baldwin & Bell, 1985; Dixon, 1976; Nobles, 1978, 1980; Semmes, 1981; Williams, 1981). This alternative model is known as the Afrocentric model. To date, most work along these lines has applied the Afrocentric model to individual and group behavior, but its application to organizational theory has been neglected.

This chapter originally appeared as an article in *Journal of Black Studies* (Vol. 21, No. 2, December 1990, pp. 145-161). Copyright © 1990 Sage Publications, Inc.

The purpose of this chapter is to reconceptualize organizational theory by employing the Afrocentric paradigm. Drawing from some of the tenets of the Afrocentric paradigm, this chapter will identify and discuss some of the characteristics of an Afrocentric organization and the extent to which these characteristics are congruent or incongruent with Western theories of organizations. Hence this chapter will offer an alternative conceptual paradigm for the study of formal organizations in general, but human service organizations in specific.[1]

A new conceptual paradigm for the study of human service organizations will contribute to the diversification—and strengthening—of the total body of human service organization theory and knowledge. In addition, the application of the Afrocentric model to organizational theory will help to broaden its conceptual knowledge base as a social science model. This chapter seeks to contribute to the study of Afrocentric concepts and issues (i.e., Afrology)[2] and to highlight the worldview of African people in the context of organizational theory.

Tenets of the Afrocentric Paradigm

The Afrocentric paradigm is predicated on traditional African philosophical assumptions that emphasize the interconnectedness and interdependency of natural phenomena. From this perspective, all modalities and realities are viewed as one, and there is no demarcation between the spiritual and material, substance and form (Asante, 1980b). Indeed, in African philosophy, "the anthropocentric ontology was a complete unity which nothing could destroy" (Nobles, 1980, p. 26). Accordingly, all natural phenomena are functionally connected, and to destroy one part is to destroy the whole universe, even the creator (Nobles, 1980). As Asante (1980b) observes, "The continuity from material to spiritual is the universal basis of the Afrocentric viewpoint" (p. 50). In addition, the Afrocentric paradigm views affect, rhythm, rituals, and symbols as valid determiners of human activity and reality (Akbar, 1984; Dixon, 1976; Nichols, 1976).

The tenets of the Afrocentric model reflect its collective, rhythmic, nonmaterial or spiritual, and affective character. The following is a nonexhaustive enumeration of the tenets of the Afrocentric paradigm which reflect the model's assumptions about human beings and human behavior. The tenets are derived from the works of several scholars (see Akbar, 1976, 1984, 1985; Asante, 1980a, 1980b, 1988; Baldwin, 1981, 1986; Boykin,

1983; Boykin & Toms, 1985; Dixon, 1976; Hale, 1982; Khatib, Akbar, McGee, & Nobles, 1979; Mbiti, 1970; Nichols, 1976; Nobles, 1978, 1980; Williams, 1981). The underlying theme of most of their works is that because traditional African philosophical assumptions continue to be a major part of the African-American's ethos, there is a need for a social science model or conceptual paradigms that reflect the cultural background and reality of African people. The tenets are as follows:

1. Human beings are conceived collectively.
2. Human beings are spiritual.
3. Human beings are good.
4. The affective approach to knowledge is epistemologically valid.
5. Much of human behavior is nonrational.
6. The axiology or highest value lies in interpersonal relations.

Before specifically addressing the applicability of these tenets to organizational theory, the next section will examine some basic distinctions between the Afrocentric model and mainstream (Western) theories of organizations.

Distinctions Between Afrocentric and Mainstream Organizational Theories

While there are similarities between the Afrocentric model and some mainstream organizational theories, a major difference lies in "organizational normality" (i.e., that which is considered the standard of acceptability for organizations). Many mainstream or Western organizational theories—with the exception of the neo-Marxist perspective—concentrate on the factors affecting organizational productivity: how fast, how plentifully, and how well something is produced or, in the case of human service organizations, how well and how efficiently people are processed, sustained, or changed. This focus underlies bureaucracy's principle of rationality (Weber, 1946), scientific management's notion of maximum productivity (Hasenfeld, 1983), the human relations assumption that increased worker satisfaction will induce increased productivity (Kaplan & Tausky, 1977), decision-making theory's concepts of "satisficing" and "performance gap" (Hasenfeld, 1983), the attributes of a "highly effective organization" identified by Lawrence and Lorsch (1967), the natural-system model's emphasis on goal displacement and how it causes the unattainment of formal, official goals (Scott, 1967), and the political economy's focus on how the distribution of power and the availability of resources both within and without organizations shape the choice of service technologies used for production. As Perrow (1978) astutely observes, even when such theories as the natural systems and human relations theories reject mechanical and rationalistic notions of organization and accept informal, humanistic, and natural characteristics, these characteristics are viewed as constraining the organization's efficiency (rationality) in achieving its announced goals—in other words, constraining its rate of production.

Another fundamental characteristic of mainstream or Western theories of organizations is the emphasis placed on the individual organization member. Even the human relations model, with its focus on the small-group process, uses this process to affect the individual's job satisfaction and productivity. Part of this individual focus is a function of manner in which "individual" is conceived in the Western tradition, especially in Western social science. In a discussion of what he calls the Eurocentric social science model, Akbar (1984) maintains that one of its salient attributes is its individualistic character. Individualism is emphasized in the Eurocentric model, according to Akbar, because human identity is conceived insularly: It is assumed that the individual can be understood separate from others. By focusing on this conception of human identity, Akbar contends that corporate identity—relationship with significant others such as family members, community members, and friends—is of secondary importance in conceiving the individual.

The limited conception of human identity found in the Eurocentric model is reflected in the way the "client" is conceived in human service organization theory. Throughout the human service organization literature, "client" is usually conceived as one individual, as if she or he lives in a vacuum and is not a part of a social group.

Unlike the Eurocentric model, the Afrocentric model conceives individual identity as collective (Akbar, 1984; Baldwin, 1981; Nobles, 1980). Although this model emphasizes collectivity, it does not reject the notion of uniqueness (Akbar, 1984; Boykin, 1983; Boykin & Toms, 1985). Rather, it rejects the idea that the individual can be understood separate from others (Akbar, 1984). For example, Mbiti (1970) uses the African adage "I am because we are and because we are, therefore I am" (p. 141) to capture the essence of this collective identity. Similarly, Cook and Kono (1977) state that in Black or African psychology, "individuality in the sense of self in opposition to the group disappears and is replaced by a common understanding and a common goal" (p. 26). Moreover, Asante's (1988) concept of the "collective-cognitive imperative" (i.e., the full spiritual and intellectual commitment to a vision by a group), Nobles's (1980) concept of "experiential commonality" or the sharing of a particular experience by a particular group of people, and Baldwin's (1981) concept of "African self consciousness"[3] are important in understanding a fundamental characteristic of Afrocentrism, which is its emphasis on discerning similarities or commonalities of a people and their condition, instead of discerning and emphasizing individual differences. Because of this, Afrocentrism gives preeminence to the group: The welfare of the group takes precedence over the welfare of the individual. Hunt (1974) asserts that the Black perspective on public management is a collective orientation, wherein the public demands and interests of Blacks as a group supplant the needs of Blacks as individuals.

An important issue that needs to be addressed if further work is to be done with the Afrocentric approach to organizations is the question of the validity of the collective orientation assumption of Blacks or African-Americans. In recent years, especially since the passage of civil rights and affirmative action legislation, a significant number of African-Americans with advanced training and education have enjoyed economic progress, while, concomitantly, the economic condition of a broad number of African-Americans has worsened (Wilson, 1980, 1987). This apparent economic class schism within the African-American community may have attenuated the collective bond and identity of African-Americans. Further conceptual work, therefore, is needed to grapple with innovative ways of responding to the effects of social class distinctions.

Assuming that the collective-orientation assumption is valid—and being mindful that the Afrocentric model is predicated on "traditional" African philosophical assumptions—the interests of the organization as a whole or collective would be the primary concern within an Afrocentric framework, although individual interests and concerns would be recognized. Thus, from an Afrocentric perspective, organizational and group survival replaces productivity as the overriding concern. Organizational normality, therefore, would not be defined by the quantity or efficiency of production, as in Western theories of organizations, but rather by the way an organization preserves itself—whether the behaviors employed by its members maintain the survival of the organization. Although this view of survival is similar to the concept found in the natural systems model, in that organizational survival is given high importance, a fundamental difference is that the natural systems model places considerable emphasis on goal attainment, as if it were synonymous with survival. The Afrocentric perspective conceives survival in itself as paramount. Though goal attainment would be important within an Afrocentric organization, survival would include more than just goal attainment. It would, for example, include the maintenance of common objectives, concerns, and sentiments among organizational members.

In addition, the Afrocentric model's concept of survival transcends the boundaries of the organization and extends into the community. This focus highlights organization-community relations more strongly than any existing human service organization theory. Just as it is unthinkable to understand the individual separate from others in the Afrocentric model, so is it unthinkable to understand the organization separate from the community which it serves. Therefore, to a considerable extent, the organization and the community are viewed as one, in that the organization's purpose is a reflection of the community's purpose. To the extent that this bond exists, it is assumed that the survival of the organization is significantly related to the survival of the community and vice versa. Hence, the collective survival notion found in the Afrocentric model involves the coalescence of individual, organizational, and community identity.

Fundamentally, the Afrocentric model differs from existing organizational theories in its view of organizational normality, its concept of human identity, and its notion of organizational survival. Further differences will be highlighted below as tenets of the Afrocentric model are applied to describe how an Afrocentric organization might look and what it might emphasize.

Afrocentric Tenets and Organizational Theory

As this section elucidates the tenets and their application to organizational theory, it will also discuss the extent to which these tenets are congruent or incongruent with tenets of mainstream, Western-oriented organizational theories. This will be achieved by presenting each tenet and discussing its applicability to the study of human service organizations.

Human Beings Are Conceived Collectively

The Afrocentric model places considerable emphasis on a collective conceptualization of human beings and on a collective survival. Hence, organizational unity would be a primary goal of an Afrocentric organization. To encourage an orientation toward organizational unity, low internal differentiation of work tasks would probably suit an organization based on Afrocentric principles. This would help constrain the emergence of well-defined organizational subunits or subdivisions, which cause members to become more committed to the goals and interests of their subunits than to the goals and interests of the organization as a whole (Selznick, 1948). Because of the Afrocentric model's emphasis on group similarities or group "oneness," superordinate and subordinate relationships would be downplayed in favor of consensus group processes. Thus, there would be a more equitable distribution of power, unlike the Weberian model.

The human relations model probably comes the closest to an approximation of Afrocentric tenets, in that it argues against a strict hierarchical power structure and extensive division of labor and encourages the participation of subordinates in the decision-making process (Kaplan & Tausky, 1977). However, the human relations model still views these persons as "subordinates," implying that they are less competent than their superiors in making decisions. The Afrocentric paradigm would carry the argument against a rigid hierarchical power structure even further.

Human Beings Are Spiritual

The Afrocentric model recognizes the spiritual or nonmaterial aspect of human beings. Akbar (1984) observes that "when men and women are reduced to their lowest terms they are invisible and of a universal substance" (p. 408) and that without the inclusion of the spiritual or metaphysical element, the human is incomplete. Hence the inclusion and recognition of the spiritual element of humans in the Afrocentric model is indicative of its holistic perspective: Mind, body, and soul are believed to be interdependent and interrelated phenomena (Akbar, 1984; Asante, 1987; Mbiti, 1970; Nobles, 1980; Weems, 1974). Thus, for example, "to have a good body means that one has a good mind, and vice versa; one cannot exist without the other" (Weems, 1974, p. 32).

As it relates to organizational theory, the Afrocentric paradigm would place much emphasis on enhancing the spirituality of organizational members. Spirituality, as defined by Boykin and Toms (1985), is "conducting one's life as though its essence were vitalistic rather than mechanistic and as though transcending forces significantly govern the lives of people" (p. 41). According to Akbar (1984), "morality and spirituality are inseparable" (p. 409).

To the degree that spirituality implies morality, there is recognition of "organizational morality" in the Afrocentric model. Organizational morality refers to a state in which organization members have the highest regard for human life and dignity and consistently display behaviors that reflect this value. This respect is not assumed to be held exclusively for fellow members but also for clients and others served by the human service organization. To this end, humanistic values, such as client and worker self-worth, worker empathy, and concern for the welfare of clients and co-workers, are moved from obscurity to the forefront of organizational priorities. This is especially relevant to human service organizations, whose purpose is to promote the general well-being of individuals in society (Hasenfeld, 1983). Further conceptual work, however, is needed to build on this notion of organizational spirituality/morality.

Nonetheless, the development and maintenance of organizational members' spirituality would be viewed as a critical factor in shaping their mental and physical performance. It would be assumed that without a well-nourished and developed spirit the performance of organizational members would be at a minimum.

▬ Human Beings Are Good

Consistent with the notions of spirituality and morality, the Afrocentric paradigm recognizes the fundamental goodness of human beings. This model rejects a pessimistic perspective of human nature and posits that humans have a proclivity toward enhancing life in a constructive manner (Akbar, 1984; Asante, 1980a, 1988).

This notion of inherent goodness is congruent with the human relations model's assumption "that man is basically good" (Kaplan & Tausky, 1977, p. 171) and is incongruent with the scientific model or McGregor's (1960) theory X, which hold that human beings must be controlled, coerced, and threatened with punishment to work, as if adults were recalcitrant children. To the contrary, the Afrocentric model believes human beings have the capacity for self-mastery, self-direction, and self-regulation (Akbar, 1984). Hence, from an Afrocentric organizational perspective, there would be no need to practice rigid supervision and control. Further conceptual work in this area is needed, especially as it relates to how an Afrocentric perspective would deal with accountability, the hiring and firing of workers, and the censure of workers.

▬ The Affective Approach to Knowledge
Is Epistemologically Valid

In the Afrocentric model, emphasis is placed on an affective epistemology. Akbar (1984) maintains that a major premise of Afrocentric social science is that "the most direct experience of self is through emotion or affect" (p. 410). Consistent with this focus on affect, Nichols (1976), in his typology of the philosophical aspects of cultural differences, shows that the epistemology or valid way of knowing for African-Americans is affective, so that one knows through symbolic imagery and rhythm. Dixon (1976) defines symbolic imagery as the use of phenomena, such as words, gestures, and objects, to convey multiple meanings, and, like Nichols, asserts that Africans throughout the diaspora generally know reality through the synthesis of symbolic imagery and affect. Other scholars have also discussed the importance of affect in the lives of African-Americans (Asante, 1980a, 1988; Baldwin, 1981; Boykin, 1977, 1983; Brown, 1978; Hale, 1982; Senghor, 1962). Indeed, feeling has been said to be a major criterion when examining the aesthetics of African-Americans (Asante, 1988). The focus on affect in the Afrocentric model does not preclude recognition and use of rationality. Instead, affect, as a means of knowing, is viewed as offsetting the use of rationality (Akbar, 1984).

As it relates to organizations, this affective, epistemological character of the Afrocentric model has a significant implication for evaluating worker performance. Instead of the considerable emphasis placed on quantifying worker performance, which is characteristic of bureaucracies (Lipsky, 1980), Afrocentric organizations would include both quantitative and subjective (qualitative) means of determining worker performance. One example of a qualitative means of performance evaluation is the use of field or naturalistic observations. By observing the worker at daily work tasks, the observer can discern the intricate attributes of the worker and the worker's immediate work milieu. These intricacies are difficult to tap and observe when exclusively relying on quantitative measures. As Lipsky (1980) states, "actual performance is virtually impossible to measure. . . . Aspects of performance can be measures . . . but the most important dimensions of service performance defy calibration" (p. 168). Thus, to fortify the validity of performance evaluations, qualitative measures would be considered appropriate and necessary for an organization based on Afrocentric principles.

▬ Much of Human Behavior Is Nonrational

Consistent with the epistemology of affect, the Afrocentric paradigm views much of human behavior as deriving from feeling, rather than reasoning (Akbar, 1984). This is to imply not that humans are without rationality but that humans are influenced by a multitude of positive and negative life experiences resulting from social interaction. The emotions elicited by these experiences can have an impulsive effect on the decisions, actions, and moods of people which sometimes obviates the exercise and use of rationality.

Moreover, this nonrationalistic perspective of human behavior refutes the assumption that human beings are invariably rational, mechanistic, and objective. Such a rationalistic perspective prevents understanding much of the human experience by omitting the influence of affect (Akbar, 1984) and values that shape human biases.

Because of the pervasive influence of the Weberian school of organizational theory, there is an implicit and, to a great extent, explicit assumption that organizations should strive for rationality or efficiency, that the organization should employ the most efficient unit of activity to attain its goals. Implied in such an objective is the need for rational people to develop and implement these efficient activities. The Afrocentric paradigm would not place so much emphasis on efficiency or rationality. It would (a) recognize the important role of affect in the lives of people, (b) realize that people are not infallible, impervious superbeings, and (c) downplay time and speed because of its de-emphasis on the rate of production.

▬ The Axiology or Highest Value
Lies in Interpersonal Relations

Nichols (1976) shows that the axiology or highest value for African-Americans lies in interpersonal relationships. Hence, the maintenance and enhancement of the interpersonal relationship is considered the most preeminent value in the Afrocentric paradigm. Such an emphasis fosters a human-centered orientation to life rather than an object or material orientation. Accordingly, the acquisition of an object or material item would not take precedence over maintaining and strengthening interpersonal ties.

The focus on interpersonal relationships in existing organizational models is best represented in the human relations model, with its emphasis on increasing interpersonal competence (Kaplan & Tausky, 1977), warm personalities (Litwak, 1978), and collegial relationships (Kaplan & Tausky, 1977; Litwak, 1978). The strengthening of interpersonal competence and relationships in the human relations model, however, is a strategy to increase worker satisfaction, through increased participation, in order to affect worker performance and increase work efforts. Thus, enhancing interpersonal relationships is viewed as a means to achieve an end. This weakens and undermines the human relations model's interpersonal character.

In the Afrocentric model, the strengthening of interpersonal relationships in an organization would be perceived as an end in itself. The major focus in Afrocentrism is not on how much of or how fast something is produced but rather the way in which the organization preserves itself. How can an organization preserve or sustain itself and remain unified without valuable, interpersonal bonds? Meaningful and indelible interpersonal bonds would help a human service organization to uniformly serve and represent its community, providing the community with a model for unity through the practice of an interpersonal, human-centered axiology.

Implications for Research and Practice

Although this chapter has described several characteristics of an Afrocentric organizational paradigm, additional conceptual work needs to be explored to fully develop an Afrocentric organizational model. For example, since organizational survival is a primary concern of the Afrocentric perspective, several research questions emerge for an Afrocentric-oriented organization trying to function in a Eurocentric or Western-oriented society: (a) How can people in an Afrocentric organization maintain a collective orientation in a society that is, to a considerable extent, antithetical to such a communal focus? (b) How would an Afrocentric organization, with its de-emphasis on efficiency, survive in a society that places substantial value on efficiency? (c) How would other external factors, such as legal and legislative mandates, affect the de-emphasis on efficiency in an Afrocentric organization? (d) How would such an organization establish a communal bond with a community that is influenced by the dominant, Western value of individualism? and (e) What role would social class and race play in shaping organization-community relations? These are just a few research questions that speak to organization-environment relations.

Other areas need exploration: (a) What techniques or methods would be appropriate for an Afrocentric, human service organization? (b) How would goals be formulated in such an organization? (c) What should be the appropriate size of an Afrocentric organization? Research efforts in these and other areas should contribute significantly to the application of the Afrocentric model in the study of formal organizations in general and human service organizations in specific.

In addition to research implications, the Afrocentric-model can be useful for African-American managers and others working in human service organizations. For example, the interpersonal, human-centered axiology found in the Afrocentric model can assist managers in strengthening the primary function of human service organizations, which is to project, sustain, and promote the personal well-being of individuals in society (Hasenfeld, 1983). This humanistic focus can also be employed to improve interpersonal relations in the organization, and it would offset the concern over efficiency.

The Afrocentric model's focus on organizational collectivity and low internal differentiation can be used by human service personnel to preclude the heavy emphasis on subunit or subdivision interests that are created by high internal differentiation. This focus will help alleviate internal organizational conflict and will facilitate greater interest among workers in the goals of the entire organization. This focus is especially needed for human service organizations that serve the African-American community. The African-American community, especially its low-income segments, faces many social problems and is in critical need of assistance. Internal conflict in organizations that serve African-American communities can impede the attainment of overall goals and keep communities from receiving adequate services and resources for social change.

The Afrocentric model's emphasis on community relations can be used by members of human service organizations to better understand the dynamics and importance of organization-community relations. Often, the needs of a community, as perceived by indigenous persons, are omitted in the planning and delivery of human services. The Afrocentric framework will help sensitize members of human service organizations to the needs, objectives, and idiosyncrasies of the communities they serve. This sensitization will not only help foster better organization-community relations; it will also aid in the planning and administering of appropriate human services—services that are congruent with the needs and objectives of a nonindigenous, organizational elite.

Summary and Conclusion

This chapter has offered an alternative conceptual framework for the study of formal organizations in general, but human service organizations in specific—the Afrocentric paradigm. Drawing from several underlying tenets of the Afrocentric model, it was argued that an Afrocentric organization would be characterized by a unified, collective membership maintaining survival; a close identification between the community and the organization; a de-emphasis on the rate of production and efficiency; low internal differentiation; an emphasis on consensus decision-making; a positive, not negative, outlook on worker behavior; a strong emphasis on enhancing members' spirituality; a balanced (i.e., qualitative and quantitative) means of evaluating worker performance; and an interpersonal, human-centered axiology.

Because of its affective, collective, metaphysical/spiritual, and humanistic character, the Afrocentric paradigm offers a more complete representation of human qualities and needs. Rational (efficient), objective, and material/object-oriented models fail to consider the humanism of people and the circumstances that preclude the use of rationality. This blind spot, found in Western organizational theories, has fostered human service organizations that concern themselves not with the human needs and concerns of their members and clients, but with becoming more efficient (rational) in achieving their announced, and often unattainable, goals. It is time that human service organizations accept a model that is more consistent with and reflective of the human experience. The Afrocentric model best represents that experience.

Notes

1. Within the study of formal organizations is the study of human service organizations. Human service organizations are organizations that process, sustain, or change individuals. Within these organizations, human beings are considered the "raw material." Some examples are welfare organizations, hospitals, schools, mental health agencies, and churches. For a detailed discussion, see Hasenfeld (1983) and Hasenfeld and English (1974).

2. For a detailed discussion on Afrology, see Asante (1988).

3. Joseph Baldwin defines "African self consciousness" as the consciousness level process of communal phenomenology. He also views it as a basic core of Black personality. For a detailed discussion, see Baldwin (1981).

References

Akbar, N. (1976). Rhythmic patterns in African personality. In L. King, V. Dixon, & W. Nobles (Eds.), *African philosophy: Assumptions and paradigms for research on Black people.* Los Angeles: Fanon Center.

Akbar, N. (1984). Afrocentric social sciences for human liberation. *Journal of Black Studies, 14*(4), 395-414.

Akbar, N. (1985). Our destiny: Authors of a scientific revolution. In H. P. McAdoo (Ed.), *Black children.* Beverly Hills, CA: Sage.

Asante, M. K. (1980a). *Afrocentricity: The theory of social change.* Buffalo: Amulefi.

Asante, M. K. (1980b). International/intercultural relations. In M. K. Asante & A. S. Vandi (Eds.), *Contemporary Black thought: Alternative analyses in social and behavioral science.* Beverly Hills, CA: Sage.

Asante, M. K. (1987). *Afrocentricity.* Trenton, NJ: Africa World Press.

Asante, M. K. (1988). *The Afrocentric idea.* Philadelphia: Temple University Press.

Baldwin, J. (1981). Notes on an Africentric theory of Black personality. *Western Journal of Black Studies, 5,* 172-179.

Baldwin, J. (1986). African (Black) psychology: Issues and synthesis. *Journal of Black Studies, 16*(3), 235-249.

Baldwin, J., & Bell, Y. (1985). The African Self-Consciousness Scale: An Africentric personality questionnaire. *Western Journal of Black Studies, 9*(2), 62-68.

Boykin, W. (1977). Experimental psychology from a Black perspective: Issues and examples. *Journal of Black Psychology, 3*(1), 29-50.

Boykin, W. (1983). The academic performance of Afro-American children. In J. Spence (Ed.), *Achievement and achievement motives.* San Francisco: Freeman.

Boykin, W., & Toms, F. (1985). Black child socialization: A conceptual framework. In H. P. McAdoo (Ed.), *Black children.* Beverly Hills, CA: Sage.

Brown, I. (1978). *Psychology of the Black experience: A cultural integrity viewpoint.* Unpublished manuscript.

Carruthers, J. (1989, February). *Towards the development of a Black social theory*. Paper presented at the Howard University Graduate Student Council's Distinguished Lecture Series, Washington, DC.

Cook, N., & Kono, S. (1977). Black psychology: The third great tradition. *Journal of Black Psychology, 3*(2), 18-20.

Dixon, V. (1976). World views and research methodology. In L. King, V. Dixon, & W. Nobles (Eds.), *African philosophy: Assumptions and paradigms for research on Black persons*. Los Angeles: Fanon Center.

Hale, J. (1982). *Black children: Their roots, culture, and learning styles*. Provo, UT: Brigham Young University.

Hasenfeld, Y. (1983). *Human service organizations*. Englewood Cliffs, NJ: Prentice-Hall.

Hasenfeld, Y., & English, R. (1974). *Human service organizations*. Ann Arbor: University of Michigan Press.

Hunt, D. (1974). The Black perspective on public management. *Public Administration Review, 34*(6), 520-525.

Kaplan, H., & Tausky, C. (1977). Humanism in organizations: A critical appraisal. *Public Administration Review, 37*(5), 171-180.

Karenga, M. (1982). *Introduction to Black studies*. Inglewood, CA: Kawaida Publications.

Khatib, S., Akbar, N., McGee, D., & Nobles, W. (1979). Voodoo or IQ: An introduction to African psychology. In W. D. Smith, K. H. Burlew, M. H. Mosley, & W. M. Whitney (Eds.), *Reflections on Black psychology*. Washington, DC: University Press of America.

Lawrence, P. R., & Lorsch, J. W. (1967). *Organization and environment: Managing differentiation and integration*. Cambridge, MA: Harvard Graduate School of Business Administration.

Lipsky, M. (1980). *Street level bureaucracy*. New York: Russell Sage.

Litwak, E. (1978). Organizational constructs and mega bureaucracy. In R. S. Sarri & Y. Hasenfeld (Eds.), *The management of human services*. New York: Columbia University Press.

Mbiti, J. (1970). *African religions and philosophy*. Garden City, NY: Anchor Books.

McGregor, D. (1960). *The human side of enterprise*. New York: McGraw-Hill.

Nichols, E. (1976). *The philosophical aspects of cultural differences*. Unpublished manuscript.

Nobles, W. (1978). *African consciousness and liberation struggles: Implications for the development and construction of scientific paradigms*. Unpublished manuscript.

Nobles, W. (1980). African philosophy: Foundations of Black psychology. In R. Jones (Ed.), *Black psychology* (3rd ed.). New York: Harper & Row.

Perrow, C. (1978). Demystifying organizations. In R. S. Sarri & Y. Hasenfeld (Eds.), *The management of human services*. New York: Columbia University Press.

Scott, R. (1967). The factory as a social service organization: Goal displacement in workshops for the blind. *Social Problems, 15*, 160-175.

Selznick, P. (1948). Foundation for the theory of organization. *American Sociological Review, 13*, 25-35.

Semmes, C. E. (1981). Fouadations of an Afrocentric social science: Implication for curriculum-building, theory, and research in Black studies. *Journal of Black Studies, 12*(1), 3-17.

Senghor, L. (1962). What is Negritude. *Negro Digest, 6*, 3-6.

Weber, M. (1946). *From Max Weber: Essays in sociology*. New York: Oxford University Press.

Weems, L. (1974). Black community research needs: Methods, models, modalities. In L. E. Gary (Ed.), *Social research and the Black community: Selected issues and priorities.* Washington, DC: Institute for Urban Affairs.

Williams, R. L. (1981). *The collective Black mind: An Afro-centric theory of Black personality.* St. Louis: Williams & Associates.

Wilson, W. J. (1980). *The declining significance of race: Blacks and changing American institutions.* Chicago: University of Chicago Press.

Wilson, W. J. (1987). *The truly disadvantaged: The inner city, the underclass, and public policy.* Chicago: University of Chicago Press.

Understanding African   6
American Oratory:
Manifestations of Nommo

Janice D. Hamlet

On July 17, 1984, following a serious bid for the nation's highest position, the Reverend Jesse Louis Jackson climaxed his historic political campaign by electrifying the audience as a keynote speaker at the Democratic National Convention. Speaking before the largest audience of his career, the self-styled politician offered the American public words of healing, humility, and unity. It was considered his greatest oratorical triumph.

Although Jackson's speech was effective, White communication scholars, political commentators, and journalists had difficulty analyzing Jackson's rhetorical style. Techniques such as deviating from the text, the use of rhyme and rhythm, repetition, and other nuances left them bewildered, and because they did not understand it they chose to label it deviant.

Jackson's seemingly deviant style suggested that mainstream society had not yet grasped an understanding of cultural differences in public address.

In his revolutionary work on Afrocentricity, Molefi Asante notes that attempts to understand and evaluate African American oratory solely from a Eurocentric perspective have failed because mainstream society misconstrues the nature of African American oratory. Seemingly ignorant of African and African American constructs, scholars and commentators have imposed Western constructs on discourse that grows out of a coherent, albeit contrasting, tradition. The inability to see from different cultural perspectives has resulted in the implementation of one standard, developed by the dominant culture, by which all communication patterns are evaluated. And when this standard is applied to groups outside the dominant culture, they are assessed as being deviant or substandard (Asante, 1987, pp. 3-5). To this end, this chapter explains the nature of African American oratory from an Afrocentric perspective.

An Afrocentric perspective views African Americans as centered and should be examined and interpreted from a centered rather than a marginal position. This means that any examination and discussion of African Americans should be based on African American values, culture, history, and motifs rather than on imposed ones (Asante, 1988). Asante (1987) notes,

> All cultural systems are responsive to the environment; ours [African Americans] is no different but it is better for us because it is derived from our own historical experiences while maintaining fidelity in its best form to the African cultural system. (p. 36)

An Afrocentric perspective celebrates and gives deference to a rich African heritage when seeking to explain and understand African Americans (Asante, 1988). This perspective has great significance in observing and attempting to understand African American oratory.

To begin, African Americans do not consider a public speech an act—words articulated in the presence of an audience followed by a response at the end. A public speech in the Afrocentric perspective is "a happening," a dynamic activity that springs from the attitude of the speaker, the attitude and responses of the audience, and the outcomes both accomplish. Also, in contrast to Eurocentric discourse in which the speaker attempts to persuade the audience, in Afrocentric discourse it is not so much persuasion that motivates a speaker but the attainment of common ground, harmony, and stability with the audience. The commentator, critic, or theorist grounded in Afrocentricity uses the filter of African culture to understand African American discourse.

To attempt an understanding of African American oratory as well as some of the general components of African American oratory, one must understand African American culture, beginning with the lives of Africans before their enslavement in America.

The Roots of African American Oratory

The myth that Africans attained their highest level of culture when they were brought to America and civilized by Whites negates the idea of a Black cultural heritage.

Prior to enslavement in America, Africans lived in societies developed around a worldview that was predicated on highly sophisticated religious systems and an impressive oral communication style. The heart of traditional African religions was the emotional experience of being filled with the power of the spiritual. Religion permeated all aspects of their lives as every phase of life in some way related to their journey to the spirit world. Thus, everything was functionally connected. They were one with nature. To destroy one category of their existence would cause the destruction of their total existence. As a result, there was no formal distinction between the sacred and the secular, religious and nonreligious, spiritual and material areas of life (Mbiti, 1970).

Another important element that existed was the interaction between the individual and the group. One of the similarities of the distinct African community was the belief in tribal survival, which was reflected in and sustained by a deep sense of kinship. Africans believed that the community made, created, or produced the individual. Thus, unless the individual was corporate or communal, he or she did not exist (Mbiti, 1970).

Above all, the Africans believed in *nommo,* which means the generative power of the spoken word. The function of nommo is generative because it leads to a sense of collectivity, the essence of African American spirituality (Smith [Asante], 1972, p. 297). Nommo was believed necessary to actualize life and give people mastery over things. All activities of men and all movements in nature rest on the productive power of the word. Nommo was not restricted to the spoken word in a public forum. It encompassed all communication situations. The Africans found power in dance, the rhythm of the drums, and the mysticism and dramatism of stories.

Nommo operated as a spiritual force that helped Africans achieve harmony and balance, known in traditional African culture as *Ma'at* (Mbiti, 1970). Ma'at was seen in ancient Egyptian society as the spirit and method of organizing and conducting the relations of human society. As a humanizing factor, Ma'at stood for truth, justice, righteousness, balance, order, and reciprocity. It was also an appeal to create an improved life for all members of the society. As such, it adhered to liberation and healing and surpasses all other concerns (Okur, 1995, p. 138).

Culture was transmitted through this oral tradition. The people's cultural mores, values, histories, and religions were transmitted from generation to generation by elderly individuals known as griots, who were considered excellent storytellers. These storytellers gave to their listeners narratives that contained elements of realism and magic in situations and characters with which they were familiar. They infused their storytelling with dramatic power that appealed to the emotions; it satisfied inner cravings, cloaked signs of unrest, evoked laughter, provided solace, and fostered a temporary release from the misery of chaotic experiences (Faulkner, 1977).

These factors comprised some of the cultural baggage the Africans brought to America when they were enslaved.

During the Africans' transportation to America, their language, primarily their dialect, was one of the first overt African cultural traits the slave traders tried to suppress. On the slave ships, members of the same community were deliberately separated from each other, thereby restricting their oral communication. Even though the Africans came from diverse backgrounds, the specific vocabularies and cultural traits that could have separated them from each other were overcome by the similarity in the basic structure of their languages and cultures. Because they were unable to use their indigenous languages to talk freely among themselves, the enslaved developed a different form of communication that was part African, part American (Gay & Baker, 1989, pp. 77-78).

This fusion produced a language that was rich in allusion, metaphor, and imagery and prolific in the use of body gestures and nonverbal nuances. Also, the communication patterns of the enslaved stemmed from their creativity and will to survive. Language became not only a means of communication but also a desire for personal presentation, verbal artistry, and commentary on life's circumstances.

In effect, "the slave was essentially a poet and his language was poetic" (Bennett, 1971, pp. 44-56). Because it was illegal to teach the enslaved how to read and write, they compensated by using sophisticated and effective patterns of verbal and nonverbal communication (Kempler, 1985, p. 99).

Manifestations of Nommo

From this oral tradition, African Americans have developed a strong and distinct form of communication—the manifestations of the African concept of nommo. The dynamism and creativity in African American language and delivery revitalizes and reenergizes bland Euro-American talk. The metaphors, images, and poetry in "Black talk" make the ordinary extraordinary (Smitherman, 1994, p. 19). Some of these characteristics of African American oratory, or manifestations of nommo, are the following:

- Rhythm as a frame of mentality
- Soundin out as a verbal artifact
- Repetition for intensification
- Stylin as a quality of oration
- Lyrical approach to language
- Improvisational delivery
- Historical perspective
- Use of indirection to make a point
- Reliance on mythoforms
- Call-and-response pattern of participatory communication

Each of these components is discussed, using examples from a diverse selection of African American speakers.

Rhythm as a Frame of Mentality

A significant feature in African American oratory is rhythm. How well a speaker can regulate his or her flow of words with the proper pauses becomes the standard for the African American speaker before a predominately African American audience (Asante, 1987, p. 38).

In traditional African culture, words were expressed in a musical, rhythmic structure called the *toneme,* the rise and fall in pitch and reflection used to convey and determine meaning. The African Yoruba tradition, in particular, has been described this way:

> From the very earliest stages of development of Yoruba speech, rhythm had come into it. . . . Usually words are spoken in a running fashion without an attempt at rhythm. But sometimes, under certain conditions, such as rocking a child, hawking, oration, or ecstatic outburst, certain words are stressed or prolonged or hurriedly excited. This is probably the origin of rhythm. . . . When tones are raised under stress of excitement, what has been termed speech music or speech tones is produced. . . . It was the

combination of raised tone and rhythm that produced speech music. Rhythm was, therefore, the essence of speech music. (Curtis, 1988, p. 25)

Rhythm in spoken discourse is a basic measure of the successful speech (Asante, 1988, p. 38). Reverend Henry Mitchell (1979) refers to this technique as establishing "a kind of intimate fellowship with the audience."

One example of the use of rhythm is illustrated in the following excerpt from a sermon delivered by the Reverend Adam Clayton Powell, Jr., who, as pastor of Abyssinian Baptist Church in Harlem during the 1960s, preached to the largest Protestant congregation in the world. From this religious base he rose to become one of the most powerful politicians in America. Powell's rhetorical vision was to bring African Americans to a realization that they had the potential to be powerful people. As Reverend Powell said in this excerpt from one of his sermons,

> *It's not the color of your skin, brother*
> *it's what you have in your hearts and in your minds*
> *that makes you a man or a woman. Remember that.*
> *And if you will stand together there's nobody in*
> *this world that can stop a united mass of people*
> *Moving as one . . .*
>
> *Standing together*
> *Working together*
> *Picketing together*
> *Loving together*
> *Worshipping together*
> *You'll win together*
> *Walk together, children, don't you get weary.*
> *There's a great camp meeting in the Promised Land.*
>
> (Powell, 1967, excerpted in
> PBS 1990 documentary)

Rhythm moves the speaker's message in the direction of the audience, bringing both the speaker and the audience to a shared understanding.

▬ Soundin Out as a Verbal Artifact

"Soundin out" refers to a speaker's manipulation of volume but also may incorporate a musical quality. When a speaker views delivery of a message as a performance, certain constraints and possibilities are placed on the speaker. As a result, it is not just the linguistic code that a speaker must be concerned with but also presence as a speaker. Presence is integrally related to how a person chooses to argue, contend, affirm, or entertain (Asante, 1987, p. 53).

Scholar and orator Cornel West, focusing on the topic "Race Matters" in a speech delivered at Shippensburg University in Pennsylvania, September 4, 1994, provided excellent examples of "soundin out" throughout his message. In discussing the problem of racism in America, West articulated,

> *One can begin with the great text of William E. B. Du Bois,* The Souls of Black Folk. *In that text, Du Bois provides a paradigmatic characterization of what it means to be a Black person of African descent in the U.S.*
>
> *And the question is,*
> How does it feel to be a problem?
> How does it feel to be a problem?
> Which is in part to say,
> How does it feel to be a problem people
> rather than
> p-e-o-p-l-e w-i-t-h p-r-o-b-l-e-m-s   *spoken very slowly*
> because
> for a problem people
> it makes you part of
> one d-i-f-f-e-r-e-n-t-i-a-t-e-d blob
> one homogeneous conglomerate
> which makes each and every black person
> interchangeable
> and
> substitutable
> you only have to ask one
> what the rest of them think.
>
> You may recall when Jesse Jackson
> ran for president. I think it was *Newsweek*
> who raised the question,
> What does Jesse want?
> What does Jesse want?   *spoken very rapidly*
> What does Jesse want?
>
> If we could just figure out
> what does Jesse want?
> We would know what
> they a-l-l want.   *spoken very rapidly*

Spoken with the cadence of a poet, West created dramatic effects by using his voice as an instrument manipulating volume and sound. The vocal tempo of the speaker enlivened his pace and added vigor and variety to his presentation.

═══ Repetition for Intensification

Repeating phrases for impact and effect is commonly used among African American speakers. The use of repetition can be noted in the following excerpt from a speech by Minister Louis Farrakhan, addressing African Americans in government in Washington, D.C. in 1989. Urging the audience to develop self-interests, Farrakhan said,

> *When you know self*
> *then you can take anything to learn*
> *and relate it to self*
> *and coming through self*
> *you can build institutions for self*

> (Farrakhan, 1989)

Significant statements are restated not only to draw attention to a point but also to uplift and stir the audience as they become involved in the presentation. By means of repetition, the speaker ensures that the gist of what he or she is trying to communicate is not lost in the emotionalism of the audience.

═══ Stylin as a Quality of Oration

"Stylin" refers to the conscious or unconscious manipulation of language or mannerisms to influence favorably the hearers of a message. By using language common to the audience, a speaker is not merely understandable but credible (Asante, 1987, p. 39). This explains the success of some charismatic preachers, politicians, community activists, and academicians.

For example, during the struggles of the historic civil rights movement, a number of people working with the movement and voter registration would go to the South and try to get people to register and to mobilize for social change, but their messages were not effective. But when Dr. Martin Luther King, Jr. went to these same places and addressed these same people and talked about leaving "the slavery of Egypt and wandering in the wilderness of separate but equal and moving into the Promised Land of full citizenship," that made sense to the people. It perked them up and motivated them. And when they heard that language, they responded (Hamilton, 1972, p. 23).

Without a doubt, the most stirring and memorable of King's speeches is his "I Have A Dream" speech delivered in Washington, D.C. in 1963. The speech provides an excellent illustration of many of the manifestations of nommo; however, the use of "stylin" is particularly noteworthy, as indicated in the following excerpt:

> In a sense we have come to our nation's capital to cash a check. When the architects of our republic wrote the magnificent words of the Constitution and the Declaration of Independence, they were signing a promissory note to which every American was to fall heir. This note was a promise that all men, yes, black men as well as white men, would be granted the unalienable rights of life, liberty, and the pursuit of happiness.
>
> It is obvious today that America has defaulted on this promissory note insofar as her citizens of color are concerned. Instead of honoring this sacred obligation, America has given the Negro people a bad check, which has come back marked "insufficient funds." (King, 1967)

The speaker who can "style" knows how to effectively use words to manipulate for the common good, triggering emotional responses that can result in motivation and harmonious relationships.

Lyrical Approach to Language

The African American approach to language is principally lyrical, and this is the basic poetic and narrative response to reality. To be lyrical means to express feelings or emotions in a direct and affecting manner (Asante, 1987, p. 44). Among the organizing patterns for platform speaking, narration is the most consistent form for a lyrical attitude.

African American speakers have always understood that poetry is the language of emotion and imagination, and their messages have appealed to both of these as well as to reason.

Addressing an audience in the Grand Hall of the Swedish Academy in 1993, Nobel prize winner Toni Morrison communicated her message in the following style:

"Once upon a time . . ." visitors ask an old woman a question. Who are they, these children? What did they make of that encounter? What did they hear in those final words: "The bird is in your hands?" A sentence that gestures toward possibility, or one that drops a latch? Perhaps what the children heard was "It's not my problem. I am old, female, black, blind. What wisdom I have now is in knowing I can not help you. The future of the language is yours."

They stand there. Suppose the visit was only a ruse, a trick to get to be spoken to, taken seriously as they have not been before? A chance to interrupt, to violate the adult world, its miasma of discourse about them, for them, but never to them? Urgent questions are at stake, including the one they have asked: "Is the bird we hold living or dead?" Perhaps the question meant: "Could someone tell us what is life? What is death?" No trick at all, no silliness. A straightforward question worthy of the attention of a wise one. An old one. And if the old and wise who have lived life and faced death cannot describe either, who can? (Morrison, 1996)

In utilizing a lyrical approach, sentences are short, crisp and clear. Verbs are filled with energy. Sentences build up to a climax. Lyrical approaches use symbolic words and presentative words and set up a musical structure of alliterative expressions.

▰ Improvisational Delivery

To improvise means to invent, create, or recite without preparation. An improvisational delivery also invites the use of the dramatic in vocal quality as well as in body movements. As noted earlier, in oratory the individualistic, the improvisational, is the soul of the presentation.

During Professor West's presentation at Shippensburg University in 1994, he had to compete with the heavy rainfall that pounded on the roof of the auditorium where he spoke. At one point, he looked up at the ceiling and asked the audience, "Is that rain?" He then very creatively and eloquently incorporated the weather into his discussion on race and diversity:

> *What is distinctive about those raindrops*
> *is that they are actually quite unique and*
> *distinct like each and every one of us but*
> *they appear to be interchangeable and*
> *substitutable.*
> *All of them are the same.*
> *No, that's wrong.*
> *But it appears that way.*

That's why the great metaphor is in vogue.
So many raindrops,
why even bother about individual ones?
So many common folks,
why bother about individual ones?

(West, 1994)

One of the unique features of African American oratory is the beauty and power of improvisation. It is common among many African American speakers to speak without a prepared manuscript or notes, or if they have a prepared manuscript, to deviate frequently from it as relevant examples and other information come to mind. Charismatic African American speakers realize that a manuscript is a handicap to effective vocal quality, forceful gestures, and dynamic eye contact. Speaking extemporaneously allows the speaker to have more of an intimate conversation with the audience. In addition to extemporaneous speaking, the vocal tempo enlivens the pace of the speech and adds vigor and variety.

Historical Perspective

The use of illustrations from African and African American history serves to motivate African Americans to look within their own culture for wisdom and strength, role models, and heroes needed to ensure survival and growth and to make social changes, as illustrated in the following excerpt from a speech delivered by Susan L. Taylor, editor of *Essence* magazine. Taylor spoke at an African American women's conference focusing on critical issues affecting African American women:

I need to go to the Motherland.
I'm preparing to go again,
It's my spiritual journey.
It's where I go to refill my cup.
And every time I go I try to go
through those slave castles
to remind myself of who we are
and what we have survived,
and what we have survived.

You see, if you don't know your history,
you think this is hard.
You think we can't get crack out of
our communities, that we can't make our

relationships work, that we can't fix our
schools, that we can't feed the hungry
and house the homeless.
But, we can do that.

When you walk through those tombs
in Ghana or in Senegal, you know that, Oh,
this we can do because this comes from a people
who refuse to die. That's what you have to
remember everyday. That we come from a
people who refuse to die.

I walked through those tombs.
I saw how we scratched and tried to dig the
cement, the stones out of those walls.

I saw those dungeons we were held
in waiting for those slave ships to come back
to transport us throughout the Caribbean,
South and Central America and North America.
In order for you to be,
somebody had to survive that.

(Taylor, 1994)

Using a historical perspective in a speaker's message is effective because the examples from history tend to stick very close to the gut-level issues that intimately affect listeners' lives. And in the process of making a point clear, the current experiences of the people are lifted up and celebrated and identity is enhanced (Mitchell, 1979, pp. 112-147).

▰ *Use of Indirection*
to Make a Point

The African American speaker often approaches the central issues in a roundabout fashion. By "stalking" the issues, or what we commonly refer to as "beating around the bush," the speaker demonstrates skill and arouses the listeners' interest (Asante, 1987, p. 51). Indirection is essential to understanding African American oral discourse. Indirection is characterized by a speaker's use of innuendoes, insinuations, inferences, implications, and suggestions to make a point (Garner, 1994, p. 82). Indirection is usually a matter of deduction as the speaker toys with related ideas and concepts before focusing on his or her major point.

Normally, indirection has been traced as a function of the speeches and not as a rhetorical strategy in oral discourse. Mitchell-Kernan (1973) observes the following about indirection:

> Meaning conveyed is not apparent meaning. Apparent serves as a key which directs hearers to some shared knowledge, attitudes, and values or signals that reference must be produced metaphorically. The words spoken may actually refer to this shared knowledge of contradicting or by giving what is known to be an impossible explanation of some obvious fact. The indirection, then, depends for its decoding upon shared knowledge of the participants. (p. 35)

The value of indirection lies in the ability of the speaker to be creative. Proverbs, cultural slang, folktales, scriptures, poetry, song lyrics, and personal anecdotes are some of the art forms that have been used to provide indirection.

The use of indirection can be noted in the following excerpt from the sermon titled "Back-door Divinity," preached by the Reverend William A. Jones, Jr. (1979):

> He came by way of the back door to avoid and to assault the arrogance of power. . . . It is conspicuous in corporate boardrooms, at command levels in the military, in the halls of academia, in the chambers of government, and among the so-called princes of the church. This craving for power is also present at lower levels.
>
> He came that way for another reason. That was the only door that would bid Him "welcome." A soul in beggar's apparel, although a King, would elicit no warm response at the front door of sinful humanity. Herod, you remember, was a member of the front-door crowd; and as soon as he heard of His arrival, he sought to kill Him. How vivid is my own memory of the absence of front-door hospitality in this land, that shameful period when certain of us on account of color were considered fit only for back-door divinity. (pp. 122-123)

The use of indirection by African Americans is often irritating to Whites who become impatient and wish African Americans would hurry up and "get to the point." What they fail to realize is that the narrative is "the point" if they would just listen.

Reliance on Mythoforms

Mythoforms consist of a body of stories that appeals to the consciousness of a people by embodying its cultural ideals or by giving expression to deep, commonly felt emotions. Mythoforms communicate basic values and attitudes, preserving links to the past, thereby providing a cultural history. These stories offer motivation, encouragement, and sustenance, as noted in the following excerpt from a 1965 sermon titled "Handicapped Lives." Upon visiting the gravesite of scientist George Washington Carver, the preacher said he noted,

> Not only was Carver a creative scientist but a blessed saint. I thought of his sickly body. I thought of how he was expected to die. I thought of how he was stolen and later swapped for a horse. I thought of how he made a garage laundry more popular than the college president's office. I thought of how he earned a master's degree at Iowa. I thought of Booker T. Washington bringing him to Tuskegee. I thought of the first time I met Carver. He wore greasy, ragged clothes. I thought of how he painted pictures with the ends of his fingers. I thought of how those same fingers played a piano. I thought of how he surmounted every obstacle in his path, climbing higher and higher until his recognition reached international proportions. I said to myself as I left that cemetery, "A handicap can be a blessing." (Borders, 1965, reprinted in Philpot, 1972)

Call-and-Response Pattern of Participatory Communication

Finally, it is not uncommon for African American speakers to receive some kind of response from their African American audiences during their presentations. As an art form, the speech may be frequently interrupted by vocal responses from the audience with careful attention to effect. This technique has been ritualized in the traditional African American church (Smitherman, 1994, p. 8). African American preachers may call out for a specific response, such as "Can I get a witness?" and "Somebody ought to say Amen," thereby soliciting a response. Oftentimes, the response may come voluntarily from members of the congregation as an affirmation of the presence of "the spirit" and/or as an act of affirmation and encouragement to the preacher. Such responses like "Amen," "Preach!" "Tell it!" and "Well?" are commonplace and essential in the African American worship service. Still, other African American preachers may specifically ask for a specific response, as in the following illustration from Reverend Jackson's "I Am Somebody" message. For nearly two decades, Jackson opened his speeches to students and his weekly address at Operation PUSH's Saturday morning community forum with this chant:

> Jackson: Nobody
> Audience: Nobody
>
> Jackson: Will save us
> Audience: Will save us
>
> Jackson: For us
> Audience: For us
>
> Jackson: But us.
> Audience: But us.
>   —Jackson, 1978, p. xvii

However, it is also common to hear audiences respond to African American speakers in secular settings. This interactive process, commonly referred to as call-response, provides audiences the opportunity to react favorably to the message. The participants are responding not only to what is being said but also to the impact of the delivery of the message.

The participatory style combines rhythm and language to create a dialogue between speaker and audience.

Conclusion

All of these manifestations of nommo have always had usefulness both within and outside the African American community—in interpersonal interactions, small group settings, and public communication settings. African American communication also crosses boundaries of gender, age, region, religion, and social class because the language and the delivery styles come from the same source—African American culture and experiences (Smitherman, 1994, p. 2).

From this discussion on African American communication it should be clear that an oratory grounded in an Afrocentric perspective differs from oratory in the European American tradition. Therefore, in evaluating African American speakers, the critic should use the lens of African

American culture to understand African American discourse. African American culture is dynamic, highly artistic, and emotional. Emotions move people and are therefore effective and meaningful to them. This is not to suggest that all African Americans utilize these characteristics when they communicate. They do not. The dynamics of African American communication allows for individuality. But these characteristics are common among speakers within the culture, especially when communicating to other African Americans.

By accepting the constituents of African American communication patterns, we extend our understanding of human communication (Asante, 1987, p. 56). In other words, the communication patterns of African Americans as well as other cultures should be aligned alongside Western Eurocentric communication patterns rather than one being considered the superior pattern by which all other cultures are judged and must aspire to emulate.

References

Asante, M. K. (1987). *Afrocentricity*. Trenton, NJ: Africa World Press.

Asante, M. K. (1988). *The Afrocentric idea*. Philadelphia: Temple University Press.

Bennett, L. (1971). The world of the slave. *Ebony, 26*, 44-56.

Borders, W. H. (1972). "Handicapped Lives" sermon [delivered 1965]. In W. M. Philpot (Ed.), *Best Black sermons* (pp. 18-30). Valley Forge: Judson Press.

Brown, T. (1993, October 6). "African Americans in the Media" speech delivered at the Twentieth Anniversary of the National Black Coalition Media Conference, Washington, DC. Broadcast through C-Span Public Affairs Programming.

Curtis, M. (1988, October). Understanding black music. *Music Education Journal*, pp. 23-26.

Farrakhan, L. (1989, August 20). "The Lessons of Patience" speech delivered at the 11th Annual Conference of Blacks in Government Conference, Washington, DC. Broadcast through C-Span Public Affairs Programming.

Faulkner, W. J. (1977). *The days when the animals talked: Black folktales and how they came to be*. Chicago: Follett.

Garner, T. (1994). Oral rhetorical practice in African American culture. In A. Gonzalez, M. Houston, & V. Chen (Eds.), *Our voices: Essays in culture, ethnicity and communication* (pp. 81-91). Los Angeles: Roxbury.

Gay, G., & Baker, W. (Eds.). (1989). *Expressively Black*. New York: Praeger.

Hamilton, C. V. (1972). *The Black preacher in America*. New York: William Morrow.

Jackson, J. (1978). "I Am Somebody" speech. In R. Hatch & F. Watkins (Eds.), *Jesse L. Jackson: Straight from the heart* (p. xvii). Philadelphia: Fortress.

Jones, W. A. (1979). "Back-door Divinity" speech. In W. A. Jones (Ed.), *God in the ghetto* (pp. 122-124). Elgin, IL: Progressive Baptist Publishing House.

Kempler, D. (1985). *Effective preaching*. Philadelphia: Westminister Press.

King, M. L., Jr. (1987). "I Have a Dream" speech [delivered 1963]. In J. Williams (Ed.), *Eyes on the prize: America's civil rights years, 1954-1965* (pp. 203-204). New York: Penguin Books.

Mbiti, J. (1970). *African religions and philosophy*. New York: Anchor Books.

Mitchell, H. H. (1979). *Black preaching*. San Francisco: Harper & Row.

Mitchell-Kernan, H. (1973). Signifying as a form of verbal art. In A. Dundes (Ed.), *Mother wit from the laughing barrel: Readings in the interpretation of Afro-American folklore* (pp. 310-328). Englewood Cliffs, NJ: Prentice Hall.

Morrison, T. (1996). Nobel prize acceptance speech [delivered 1963]. In D. G. Straub (Ed.), *Voices of multicultural America: Notable speeches delivered by African, Asian, Hispanic, and Native Americans, 1790-1995* (pp. 892-896). New York: Gale Research.

Okur, N. A. (1995). Ma'at, Afrocentricity and the critique of African American drama. In D. Ziegler (Ed.), *Molefi Kete Asante and Afrocentricity: In praise and in criticism* (pp. 137-151). Nashville, TN: James C. Winston.

Powell, A. C. (1967). Transcript from *Adam Clayton Powell* [Documentary, February 1990]. Public Broadcasting System.

Smith, A. [Asante, M.]. (1972). Socio-historical perspectives of Black oratory. In A. Smith (Ed.), *Language, communication, and rhetoric in Black America* (pp. 295-305). New York: Harper & Row.

Smitherman, G. (1994). *Black talk*. New York: Houghton Mifflin.

Taylor, S. (1994, July 8). "Issues Affecting Black Women" speech delivered at the Black Women on Tour Conference, Washington, DC. Broadcast through C-Span Public Affairs Programming.

West, C. (1994, September 26). "Race Matters" speech delivered at Shippensburg University, Shippensburg, PA.

Culture, Communication, and Afrocentrism 7

Some Rhetorical Implications of a New World Order

John W. Smith

Our reality is a product of our symbol-making, symbol-using, and symbol-misusing behavior. Each of us only experiences a tiny slither of reality, and our whole overall picture is but a construct of our symbol systems. In fact, all of our social behavior is grounded in symbolism. It is through language resulting from our human symbol-making capacity that human action occurs and our perceptions of the world around us are most affected.

According to theorist Kenneth Burke (1966), the use of language "is a symbolic means of inducing cooperation in beings that by nature respond to symbols" (p. 31). Our use of language is the best way for us to convey our sense of reality to other human beings. Our environment fuels our choice of words that describe experiences that affect us on a daily basis. Our words reveal our reality and dictate our actions.

Our worldview—that is, how we as human beings make sense of the order of things and people in our lives—is essential to how we view ourselves. It is my contention that many African Americans fail to understand how and where they fit in the American culture and in the world at large. Many African Americans relegate themselves to a reality that is inhibiting at best and degrading at worst.

Communication is the most important means by which to achieve social order, for within communication lies the power to create and to control the images that legitimize authority. Theorist Hugh Duncan (1962) asserts,

> Images, visions and all imaginations of the future are symbolic forms. When the future becomes the present and things become real, new futures are created to guide our search for solutions to problems in the present which emerge as we try to create order in our relationships. (p. 105)

Essential to the creation of any world order is access and control to the powers that aid in image and vision making. Some African Americans are attempting to create a New World Order that places their *kind* and their *dreams* at the center of its existence. Some African American parents and grandparents are rejecting the traditional literature and Eurocentered value system and social prescriptions about life in the education of their children. This opting for a more Afrocentered view of life is more than a fad; it is a way to create a New World Order through culture and communication.

Rosemary Bray (1990), in her article "Reclaiming Our Culture," extracts the essence of several African Americans' attempts to realize their Afrocentered existence: "From generation to generation, there have been those of us who have claimed a larger worldview—an African worldview— and joined it with our American experience" (p. 84). In a profound statement, one of the interviewees in the article comments,

> That's the hardest thing, our next level of development: to finally become African. We can't just be "Black" all our lives, whatever that is. The question you always get is "Where in Africa?" My attitude is, first of all, let it be Africa. (p. 84)

The purpose here is to elucidate the values and cultural nuances that underlie Afrocentrism. I contend that the African American community must continue to gain an understanding of and develop an appreciation for the rich African heritage that pulses through our blood.

Afrocentrism: A New World Order

Grounded in a traditional African worldview, Afrocentrism refers to the underlying thoughts, patterns, beliefs, and values that explain how a community, in this case the African American community, should view the world. Africa and "things African" are purposefully placed at the center of the New World Order. African Americans as extensions of their African heritage must learn to view themselves and things African as "the subjects" and not merely as subjects on the fringes of the European culture and experience. This New World Order maintains that our reality and culture must begin with our African heritage and value system. It gives members of the African American community a new way of looking at themselves and those around them.

Although the perspective is still evolving, when it is juxtaposed with the Eurocentered and American philosophies, the contrast in the value-based way of knowing and doing reveals the incongruencies and inconsistencies in our society. This worldview describes the ethos of Africans and African Americans and the values that guide the way African Americans interact with the world around them. Joyce Everett (1991) maintains that this worldview or New World Order "illicits a proactive viewpoint toward the behaviors, beliefs and attitudes of African Americans by emphasizing their strengths" (p. 15).

Deborah Atwater Hunter (1984) describes "Afro-centricity" as a social movement (p. 239). She postulates that social movements are a form of collective behavior organized to produce a change in that they usually include a shared value system, a sense of community, and norms for actions (p. 239). She further contends that any social movement must seek to influence the social order and be oriented toward definite goals. Finally, those goals must be conveyed to a group of individuals and the message of togetherness conveyed through rhetoric (p. 240).

Hunter contends that Molefi Asante is the leader of this social movement. Undoubtedly, Asante's four books, *Afrocentrism: The Theory of Social Change* (1980), *The Afrocentric Idea* (1987), *Afrocentricity* (1988), and *Afrocentricity and Knowledge* (1990) are the foundation for the Afrocentric prospective. Asante (1980) defines Afrocentricity as "the belief in a centrality of Africa in a post modern history. It is a testimony of NJIA, the ideology of victorious thought" (p. 9).

The development of the Afrocentered approach as a theory and philosophy is a product of the 1980s and of diasporian African writers. The theoretical conceptualization of the approach is the handiwork of Isheloane Keto and Maulana Karenga in addition to Asante's work. The need to create the perspective stemmed from the nature of the Eurocentered paradigm that was used in previous African studies (Oyebade, 1990, p. 234). In the history of intellectual thought, the Eurocentered paradigm assumed a hegemonic universal character and European culture was placed at the center of social structure, thereby becoming the reference point by which every other culture was measured (Oyebade, 1990, p. 234). The Eurocentered worldview attempted to overshadow all other worldviews. The Afrocentered prospective attempts to liberate a worldview from the monopoly of scholarship and to assert an objective worldview by which Africans and African Americans can be studied. It does not seek to replace one universal worldview with another; its aim is "pluriversal" (p. 234).

Afrocentrism is concerned with the various ways in which people perceive their relationships to nature, institutions, other people, and objects. A person's worldview constitutes his or her psychological orientation to life and in part determines the way he or she thinks, behaves, makes decisions, and defines events.

Culture and the New World Order

Hatch (1985) defines culture as "the way in which any group has constructed solutions to the universal problem of how to live" (p. 178). The cultural context is an important variable affecting human behavior and perceptions of human behavior and communication. Afrocentrism as an alternative worldview for the African American community is foreign to most African Americans because we have been raised in a culture that emphasizes Eurocenteredness and Americanized values. Our community must learn and thus be taught how to shape our reality, but it may also cloud it.

The placement of African ideas at the center of analysis that involves African culture and behavior is the essence of culture and is inseparable from place and time. The following comments by Asante are illustrative of the chaining out of Afrocentricity into African America culture:

> People have begun to internalize these concepts. If you go into our homes you'll see African paintings and sculpture, books about Africa—I'm sitting at my desk right now wearing a Kente-cloth tie. It reflects me. A little part of the continent is with me. (cited in Bray, 1990, p. 86)

According to Asante, the African American culture is never static, it's always alive:

But for men and women who live an Afrocentric life, the larger choice—the more important one—has already been made. They have embraced a long diminished often denied Africa, and the power of that acknowledgement has changed them. (cited in Bray, 1990, p. 119)

As discussed earlier, language allows for the construction of reality. Our ability to use language is the vehicle by which cultures and subcultures flourish and promote their value systems on other cultures. How we label a phenomenon is to some extent a function of the implicit assumptions of our culture.

From a communication and linguistic viewpoint, the African American community continues to have a profound effect on the overall American culture. For example, words that have an African linguistic foundation have become intricate parts of the American psyche and rhetorical fabric. The word "yaka" became "okay," "goy" became "guy," and "hipe" became "hip" (Turner, 1991, p. 36). If these language variations can survive the continental divide, the African value system that underlies the African American communication modes will continue to influence the African American community. Despite cultural ignorance and willful neglect, the African American community continues to be enriched as a result of the continued staying power of things African.

The African Value System

Mbiti (1969) identifies eight principles that influence all of African communication. Middle-class Europeanized African Americans will probably be least influenced by this value system. Turner (1991) categorizes these principles in the following manner: (a) the interconnectedness of all things, (b) oneness of mind, body, and spirit, (c) collective identity, (d) extended family structure, (e) consequential morality, (f) analogue thinking, (g) time, and (h) spirituality (pp. 45-54).

The African way of viewing things is inclusive and hierarchical. In the African way, the hierarchy of the world and universe is structured as follows: (a) Gods, (b) humans, (c) animals, (d) plants, and (e) inanimate objects. All have their place and are significant in maintaining harmony and balance. Anything and/or anybody that upsets this sense of harmony and balance must be dealt with seriously and quickly. Being out of balance can cause physical, emotional, and spiritual illness. What some may count as psychosomatic is to the African worldview a reality (Turner, 1991, p. 45).

This view of being out of step with nature and others was driven home to me when I heard an African American minister exclaim, "Things will never be right with you and your God until you get it right with your brothers and sisters."

Tightly related to this principle is the view of mind, body, and spirit as one. This view allows the community to promote a wholeness approach to life. The mind can only be strong if the spirit is strong and likewise the body. The African worldview values spiritual things and therefore places a great deal of emphasis on spiritual healing. It is very common to find a healer in many African communities. These healers concentrate on healing the mind, body, and soul. Even in many African American communities today, most people in the community are aware of at least one person that professes to possess the ability to heal. The radio is full of prophets and healers who purport to have access to potions, prayers, or powers that can bring about miraculous results (Turner, 1991, p. 46).

Reverend Isaiah of Stone Mountain, Georgia is one of those community healers who has chosen to communicate his message of healing via the medium of radio. His nightly liturgy on 1500 AM, WLAC, Nashville, Tennessee often includes the following statement:

> If you are sick in mind, body, or soul, if your man has left you, and your women can't be found, call for a bottle of my blessed oil. If you feel like somebody is working evil magic on you, maybe they've got some stuff around your house. Just call me, and by the help of God we can figure it out.

The reverend claims to heal all manner of ailments, including sexual dysfunction and emotional concerns.

Collective identity refers to the shared belonging felt by every African child. An Ashanti proverb best summarizes the principle:

> I am because we are. Without we, I am not. I am because we are and because we are, therefore I am. Whatever happens to the individual happens to the whole group and whatever happens to the whole group happens to the individual. The bigger we are the bigger I am. (Turner, 1991, p. 47)

From childhood, most African Americans are taught verbally and nonverbally just how their actions influence and impact the whole community and ethnic race. I do not think most cultures understand and/or appreciate this collective identity, but adherence to this principle can be overwhelming at times. The typical African American is always concerned about how his or her actions will reflect on other African Americans.

This rhetorical and cultural dilemma was evident during the Thomas-Hill sexual harassment circus. Mainstream America saw the hearings as one middle-class African American male doing battle with a middle-class African American female—that is, one individual against another individual. However in the African American community, many saw the hearings as an indictment of the community. In the view of some, Anita Hill was seen as a traitor at worst and as a useful pawn in the hands of White conspirators at best. To many African Americans, she was viewed as a "community laundry lady" whose dirty laundry made the community look bad.

The positive side of this principle is evident when African Americans band together to protect one another. Many in the African American community, in the aftermath of the Rodney King beating, used the opportunity to convey the message that King's beating was felt by every African American. In essence, for many, King's beating was symbolic of a community beating.

The concepts of the extended family structure and consequential morality might serve to explain some of the underlying motivations of some of our people in urban America. To an African, the extended family structure means that all kinship matters and that there are "no illegitimate children." The African proverb "It takes a whole village to raise a child" symbolizes the importance of family life and community (Turner, 1991, p. 47). It also may explain why so many of our brothers and sisters in these communities choose to join gangs.

This extended family concept includes the living and the dead. In fact, Asante argues that it is not unity that Blacks need but collective consciousness—that is, an awareness of their destiny and a respect for their ancestors (Hunter, 1984, p. 240). Asante states, "I have a 9-year-old son, and when I wake him in the morning, I say to him, 'You call upon your ancestors today and you thank them for who you are'" (cited in Bray, 1990, p. 86).

The connection to those who came before is strong for those who place Africa at the center of their world, and the reverence for their ancestors make ties to their living family more vital and more precious. The oral tradition serves as the thread that binds the extended family together.

The emphasis on consequential morality might explain what some label and report as "senseless violence." There are no absolutes of right or wrong in the African culture. A person's moral judgment depends on the situation. Whether an act is right or wrong depends on its consequences to one's self and to others. For example, killing for family honor could be right, whereas in other situations it might be wrong, but killing itself is not wrong (Turner, 1991, p. 49).

This concept is not as controversial as it sounds. Despite the tremendous influence of Puritanism and the Judeo-Christian philosophical and theological way of life, Western culture makes allowances in this area as well. The allowances best known as situational ethics, justifiable homicide, and "the just war" are classic examples of the use of African-based principles in Western culture.

African culture and thus African Americans tend to think differently than the European culture; it is an analogue versus binary thought process. Westerners are taught to think binarily: dividing concepts into mutually exclusive polar opposites. Analogue thinking allows an individual to see things in terms of shades of gray rather than black and white. In the African thought process, a negative component of a whole that is primarily positive does not negate the whole (Turner, 1991, p. 49).

Time is a valuable commodity in Western cultures. In America we are taught that time is something that can be wasted and that it is both futuristic and mathematical. Our lives for the most part in this culture are ordered by our clocks and watches. In Africa, time is present and most concerned with the here and now. As a matter of fact, there are no words in most African cultures that allow for a futuristic concept of time. The verb tenses simply do not exist, and for African culture "being in time is not wasting time" (Turner, 1991, pp. 51-53).

Finally, spirituality is a part of everyday life for the African. Mystical experiences, spontaneous swaying, motions and commotions in sacred and secular context are natural as well as a belief in an acceptance of the supernatural.

Implications of the New World Order

To reiterate, the study and development of an Afrocentric perspective is an attempt to treat African Americans as subjects and not merely as subjects on the fringes of the European experience. It rightfully locates Africa and "things African" to a place of value and cultural awareness. With this in mind, let us take a second look at some of the principles that underlie this perspective in an attempt to ascertain some implications for this new way of thinking and doing.

The oral tradition is a key component of the concept of interconnectedness. The African culture and thus African Americans are more influenced by oral than written communication. African Americans are influenced by what Asante (1980) labels *nommo,* the power of the spoken word. Nommo was an effective communication power used by the enslaved Africans to protest their incarceration. This power was often conveyed in drumming, storytelling, and praise singing (Oyebade, 1990, p. 236). As a professor of speech communication, I have often heard my African American students discuss their willingness to "do a speech" rather than write a paper. As our universities begin to reflect and encourage diversity, our pedagogy must be geared to maximizing a student's strengths. For example, small group assignments might be a more effective teaching tool for African Americans who are influenced by the principle of collective identity. Taking advantage of this cultural collaborative tendency could prove to be quite effective, certainly in our field.

Those texts that preach individuality and self-sufficiency might cause some ambivalence in the African American student. The American educational system has been designed to reward those who strive for individual accomplishments rather than tribal ones. This conflict is at the heart of understanding and educating African Americans.

With regard to morality, I find it hypocritical that White America glorifies and in some cases deifies its 19th-century heroes who tamed the wild west and vilifies young inner-city Black males for operating within the same value system. The late-night westerns are filled with White honorable men defending their honor and/or community by killing the bad guys. Yet when young African American males, popularly known as gang members, purport to defend their turf and honor, it is viewed quite negatively by most of Western society. This is not an endorsement of my brother's behavior, but is not violence violence? How does the principle of consequential morality differ from the concept of a just war and the Monroe Doctrine?

The view of time obviously has serious implications for those of us as African Americans. The concept of time in Western culture is used to assess everything from motivation level to competence. I faced this conflict of the use of time for the first time at the university level when I taught a class titled "Communication in Black America." Because only 5% of the school's population was African American, I erroneously concluded that the bulk of my class would consist of well-meaning but, at best, curious White students. After preparing an ABC syllabus, I was surprised to find that 10 of the 13 students on the class roster were African American. I quickly discovered that preaching to the choir would be unacceptable, and therefore I adjusted and adapted the course throughout the semester. The issue of time caused me distress and soul searching throughout the semester. My African American students would arrive at class late and turn in their assignments late. At first I found myself responding to them in a strictly European mode. I had been trained by Europeans to teach other Europeans. I soon resolved my conflict by reacquainting myself with things African. I used my conflict with this issue as fuel for discussions about cultural differences. This allowed me the opportunity to educate even those 10 African American students on the "why" of many of their actions. If I had continued to try to relate to the majority of those African American students strictly in a European mode of communication, the communication process would have been inhibited.

Conclusion

America is a great nation and, despite its various cultural and ethnic diversity, has persevered and created an educational system that is to be commended. However, America must continue to allow for cultural diversity within its educational system. Many ethnic and cultural groups are rediscovering their roots and making conscious choices to operate from a New World Order, which ultimately influences and impacts all of society.

The purpose of this chapter has been to urge mainstream America to continue to gain an understanding of the values and principles that guide the African American culture. Although understanding is not enough, it is a beginning. However, if one gains an understanding, the next two steps in the process, appreciation and accommodation, may be easier to negotiate. Acceptance of this New World Order is thus predicated on these three legs: (a) understanding, (b) appreciation, and (c) accommodation. Finally, if we want to maximize the potential of all African Americans, we must agree that this is not a choice but a necessity.

In the words of Asante, "We are on a pilgrimage to regain freedom. This is the predominant myth of our life" (cited in Bray, 1990, p. 119). If we cannot change our educational system, let us educate ourselves and thus change our destiny.

References

Asante, M. K. (1980). *Afrocentricity: The theory of social change.* Buffalo, NY: Amulefi.

Asante, M. K. (1987). *The Afrocentric idea.* Philadelphia: Temple University Press.

Asante, M. K. (1988). *Afrocentricity.* Trenton, NJ: African World Press.

Asante, M. K. (1990). *Afrocentricity and knowledge.*Trenton, NJ: African World Press.

Bray, R. (1990, December). Reclaiming our culture. *Essence, 21,* 84-119.

Burke, K. (1966). *Language as symbolic action.* Berkeley: University of California Press.

Duncan, H. (1962). *Communication and social order.* Oxford, England: Oxford University Press.

Everett, J. C. (1991). *Child welfare: An Afrocentric perspective.* New Brunswick, NJ: Rutgers University Press.

Hatch, E. (1985). Culture. In A. Kuper & J. Kuper (Eds.), *Social science encyclopedia* (pp. 178-179). Boston: Routledge.

Hunter, D. A. (1984). The rhetorical challenge of Afro-centricity. *Western Journal of Black Studies, 7,* 239-243.

Mbiti, J. S. (1969). *African religion and philosophies.* New York: Praeger.

Oyebade, B. (1990). African studies and the Afrocentric paradigm: A critique. *Journal of Black Studies, 21,* 233-238.

Turner, R. (1991). Afrocentrism: Affirming consciousness.In J. C. Everett (Ed.), *Child welfare: An Afrocentric perspective* (pp. 32-49). New Brunswick, NJ: Rutgers University Press.

PART III

AFROCENTRICITY AND THE BLACK AESTHETIC

Part III celebrates the Black aesthetic and its Afrocentric influences. Addison Gayle, Jr., in the introduction to his edited volume, *The Black Aesthetic* (1971, p. xxxii), argues that the Black aesthetic is a means of helping African Americans out of the polluted mainstream of Americanism and offers logical, reasoned arguments as to why African American artists should not desire to meet the standards of White European artists, but, instead, their world should be judged based on their own social, political and economic history. A critical methodology has no relevance to the African American community unless it aids in helping the people become better than they are. The five chapters in Part III offer Afrocentric discussions and analyses of various African American art forms.

African American literature is the focus of Chapter 8 by Abu Abarry. He reviews African American contributions as seen in the works of a few significant writers from the earliest times until the death of Langston Hughes in 1967.

Gale Jackson, in Chapter 9, proposes that the Africanness in African American culture is often deeply embedded in the conceptual framework out of which acts of cultural performance come.

Barbara and Carlton Molette examine characters from the African American oral tradition in Chapter 10, which they title "Afrocentric Heroes in Theater," suggesting that there are specific characteristics that cause

African Americans to regard such characters as heroic. The authors draw analogies about those characteristics and the values and heroic ideals that African Americans seek to instill.

The portrayal of African American women continues to be subjugated in Hollywood movies. The stereotypical representation of African American women from older movies has been replaced by modern versions. M. Patricia Hilliard-Nunn's Chapter 11 is an African-conscious critique of how three selected aspects of African American female identity—physical appearance, sexuality, and African consciousness—are typically represented in Hollywood movies.

In Chapter 12, Alice Tait and Robert Perry examine the underrepresentation and stereotypical portrayals of African Americans in television programming, suggesting that the strongest impact of positive African American portrayals can be achieved when African Americans have some influence in the media at the program conception and selection levels.

The African-American Legacy in American Literature

8

Abu Abarry

Since their enforced and brutal emigration to North America about 400 years ago, African Americans have forged rich and dynamic literary forms that today have become an important and unique aspect of American literature and culture. The sound literary qualities, interesting thematic range, and social significance of this variety of American literature notwithstanding, it has remained largely unknown to the general African American reading public, including even students of literature. We are, of course, aware of the presence of books by and on African Americans in our libraries and African American literature courses in the curricula of African colleges and universities. But such books are generally limited to those of well-known authors, such as Langston Hughes, Richard Wright, and James Baldwin, and the courses are offered by only a few privileged institutions and even then on an irregular basis.[1]

The aim of this chapter, then, is to help acquaint more African-American readers, particularly students of literature, with the ways in which the meanings, beauty, and power of African-American literary creations have

This chapter originally appeared as an article in *Journal of Black Studies* (Vol. 20, No. 4, June 1990, pp. 379-398). Copyright © 1990 Sage Publications, Inc.

evolved to enrich American literature and culture. However, due to its time span, generic variations, stylistic complexity, and content range, it would be presumptuous and preposterous to attempt to treat the whole literature here. What follows, then, is a modest effort to review mainly African-American poetic contributions, as seen in the works of a few significant writers, from the earliest times until the death of Langston Hughes in 1967. General statements, however, will be made, where relevant, regarding other personalities and events of literary significance in African American history.

Any meaningful discussion of the literary creations of Africans in America must, of course, begin with their orature. African-American orature is the corpus of oral discourse created by African peoples in a variety of forms to deal with various exigencies and rhetorical situations (Asante, 1987: 83-95). It ranges from the spirituals, the blues, and the work songs to the sermons, proverbs, and tales. The literary significance of these forms seems to surpass anything written by African-Americans until modern times. The songs, especially the spirituals, have sublime themes, powerful imagery, and special vocabulary. These were the qualities that moved Du Bois (1903: 225) to say that such songs constitute probably America's most important contribution to world culture.

The blues, the spirituals, and the work songs have historically reflected the collective woes, outlook, courage, aspirations, and humor of their creators in their encounter with an alien and hostile culture. While the secular songs portray major episodes in mundane individual and communal lives, the spirituals express the spirituality, inner strength, and collective unconscious of the people. These special songs have always held importance, especially during periods of enslavement, persecution, or hardship, for they provide ecstatic visions of an alternate world of solace and hope. The spirituals also have functioned as an efficient system of communication, bearing concealed messages of inspiration, insult, or revolt as well as instructions and directions for escape and freedom of enslaved or persecuted Africans in America.

The tales, on the other hand, contain interesting ideas enriched with symbolic and allegorical materials and expressed with rhetorical vehemence. Acknowledging the qualities and significance of such tales, the well-known folklorist Richard Dorson had this to say:

> One of the memorable bequests by the Negro to American Civilization is his rich and diverse store of folktales. . . . Only the Negro, as a distinct

element of the English speaking population, maintained a full blown story-telling tradition [quoted in Chapman, 1968: 21].

This rich and interesting orature was kept from the reading public until the publication of *Uncle Remus Stories* in the 19th century by Joel Chandler Harris, a White southern journalist (Chapman, 1968: 21-26). And the spirituals and the poetic songs did not appear in print until the 1860s. In spite of neglect and woeful circumstances, the African-American genius was able to create yet another genre of orature, the sermon, by harmonizing brilliantly the dramatic, emotional, and rhetorical qualities of the spirituals and tales. These oral literary forms have, in one way or another, affected the minds and hearts of Americans of all races. They have become a common pool of emotional experience on which contemporary American writers of African descent draw according to their idiosyncracies, talents, and vision.

There was, however, another variety of African-American literature which evolved during the era of slavery. Unlike the orature, however, such early, written literary creations did not reflect the collective unconscious of the African peoples in America. These were largely personal creations, bearing the marks of individual imagination, style, concerns, and orienta-tions. A review of some of this literature now becomes imperative. Al-though Lucy Terry, an enslaved girl from Deerfield, Massachusetts, is on record as the first African-American poet, not much is available concerning her life and work beyond "Bars Fight," the title of a heroic poem about an Indian raid on a White settlement that she wrote in 1746 but which was not published until 1893. Jupiter Hammon, a Long Island enslaved African who published his 88-line religious poem in 1760, is therefore regarded as the first African-American published poet. Thirteen years later, Phillis Wheatley became the first African-American to publish a volume of verse, followed in 1837 by George Moses Horton whose work, *Poems by a Slave,* appeared that year (Long, 1972: 10-19). Hammon, however, does not seem to have benefited much from any formal instruction beyond what he had acquired in basic reading and writing. But he gained something in his own way from the tutoring he had received on the Bible, hymn books, and English religious poetry. The preaching and lectures in which he was allowed to engage also helped to improve his oratorical skills. His poetry frequently reflects didacticism, the New Testament, and slavery which he was reluctant or unable to condemn. Poems like "An Evening Thought: Salvation by Christ" and "A Winter Piece" reflect a rustic piety typical of

Euro-American writers' talents and temperament at the time. As noted by Long (1972), the expectation initially raised by probably Hammon's best poem, "An Address to Phillis Wheatley," was, however, crushed by the poem's metered preaching and open moralizing:

> O, Come, you pious youth! adore
> The wisdom of thy God,
> In bringing thee from distant shore,
> To learn His holy word,
> Come, you, Phillis, now aspire,
> And Seek the living god,
> So step by step thou mayst go higher
> Till perfect in the word.
> Now glory be to the most High,
> United praises given,
> By all on earth, incessantly,
> And all the host of heaven.

Although Hammon's poetry is occasional, otherwordly, and repetitive, its sharp phonological sense and originality make it a unique contribution to American poetry in the 18th century. To other critics, however, he remains more of a colonial curiosity than a genuine monument of African-American literature (Long, 1972: 21).

George Moses Horton had an edge on Hammon. Born in 1800 in North Carolina, he lived in the vicinity of the university at Chapel Hill. Recognized for his gift at versifying, young, amorous undergraduates frequently sought his services to compose poems of dalliance. But he also had more serious thematic concerns, his liberty being the most important, which were often expressed in stilted syntax and abstract language. Prolific and indefatigable, Horton produced three volumes of poems: *Poems by a Slave* (1837), *Poetical Works* (1845), and the *Naked Genius* (1865). Although he tried unsuccessfully to gain his freedom by the sale of his poems, this talented African remained enslaved until the Emancipation.

We now turn to Phillis Wheatley, easily the best of the slave poets. Phillis Wheatley was about 7 years old when she was sent to America in 1761. She was bought by the Wheatleys, a wealthy religious family in Boston, who treated her as a daughter. Phillis was never assigned menial work nor granted the liberty to socialize with the other enslaved Africans in the Wheatley home. Being precocious, she quickly acquired literacy and began to read. With the encouragement of the Wheatleys, she read vora-ciously, developing her poetic talent. Putting together pieces from psalms and neoclassical poetry, she churned out verses that quickly brought her wide acclaim. In 1773, she accompanied the Wheatleys to London, England, where her first volume, *Poems on Various Subjects, Religious and Moral,* was published. She was also received by the Lord Mayor of London who gave her a copy of Milton's *Paradise Lost* as a gift.

Phillis Wheatley's poetic themes range from the religious, consolatory, and celebrative to the didactic and intellectual. Witness the following lines from the poem she addressed to General Washington, Commander-in-Chief of the American Liberation Army who eventually became the first president of the United States:

> *Celestial choir! enthroned in realms of light,*
> *Columbia's scene of glorious toils I write.*
> *While freedom's cause her anxious breast alarms,*
> *She flashes dreadful in refulgent arms.*
>
> *Muse! how propitious while my pen relates*
> *How pour her armies through a thousand gates,*
> *As when Eolus heaven's fair face deforms,*
> *Enwrapp'd in temperest and a night of storms.*
>
> *Shall I to Washington their praise recite?*
> *Enough thou know'st them in the fields of fight.*
> *Thee, first in peace and honors,—we demand*
> *The grace and glory of thy martial band.*
>
> *Proceed, great chief, with virtue on thy side,*
> *Thy every action let the goddess guide.*
> *A crown, a mansion, and a throne that shine,*
> *With gold unfading, Washington! by thine.*

It is ironic that Phillis Wheatley should ask the American people to show gratitude to their illustrious warrior by giving him a mansion, a crown, and a shining golden throne—all powerful symbols of the monar-chical system that he had just led his people to overthrow. She also wrote on abstract and difficult subjects, such as the following on the nature, expressions, and achievements of the human intellect:

> *Thy various works, imperial queen; we see*
> *How bright their forms! how deck'd with pomp by thee!*
> *Thy wondrous act in beauteous order stand,*
> *And all attest how potent is thine hand.*

> *Imagination! Who can sting thy force?*
> *Or who describe the swiftness of thy course?*
> *Soaring through air to find the bright abode?*
> *Th' empyreal palace of the thundering God,*
> *We on thy pinions can surpass the wind,*
> *And leave the rilling universe behind*
> *From star to star the mental optics rove,*
> *Measure thy skies, and range the realms above,*
> *There is one view we grasp the mighty whole,*
> *Or with new worlds amaze th' unbounded soul.*

Many of her poems, however, are sentimental, religious, consolatory, and otherwordly as evidenced by the following lines from a letter she wrote to a copatriot and fellow slave:

> *Till we meet in the region of consumate blessedness,*
> *let us endeavour, by the assistance of divine grace,*
> *to live the life, and we shall die the death of the righteous.*

This reference to the hereafter recurs several times in her writings. Note the lines from the poem she wrote to console a couple on the death of close relations, including a child named Avis:

> *But Madam, let your grief be laid aside,*
> *And let the fountain of your tears be drop'd.*
> *The glowing stars and sliver green of light*
> *At last must perish in the gloom of night:*
> *Resign thy friends to that Almighty hand,*
> *Which gave them life, and bow to his command:*
> *Thine Avis give without a murm'ring heart,*
> *Though half thy soul be failed to depart.*
> *To shining guards consign thine infant care*
> *To waft triumphant through the seats of air.*

And a few works express her joy and gratitude to God for causing her departure from dark and heathen Africa to the saving, divine light of love of America where the knowledge of a true Christian God is self-evident:

> *Let us rejoice in and adore the wonders of God's infinite love*
> *in bringing us from a land semblant of darkness itself, and where*
> *the divine light of revelation (being obscured) is in darkness.*
> *Here the knowledge of the true God and eternal life are made*
> *manifest; but there profound ignorance overshadows the land.*

Although her poems hardly reflect her racial identity and were not directed toward militant action against slavery, the literary and and intellectual efforts of Phillis Wheatley achieved positive results in other directions. She was a much more original and gifted poet than either Jupiter Hammon or George Moses Horton. Her poetry reveals an interesting and innovative blend of Christian and neoclassical features, even if she does not use such elements very skillfully. In her exploitation of the Muse, classical symbols, and extended metaphor, Milton's influences are unmistakable. She equally reminds one of Alexander Pope and Thomas Gray in her handling of wit, nature, and heroic couplets. In reference to Pope, Gloria Hull (in Bell and Parker, 1979) had this to say of Phillis:

> Her poetry is not as imitative and moribund as most commentators make it sound. Some of her images and conceits display an originality which shows that many of her thoughts are fresh ideas of her own even if her rhythm is almost always Pope's [p. 71].

In spite of her deeply religious worldview, her poems are often interspersed with musical qualities that make them delightful and memorable. Apart from the solace, comfort, and delight that her poetry brought to many people, both Black and White, her fine sentiments, imaginative power, and artistic sense endeared her to many influential, contemporary American leaders, such as General Washington who helped to initiate government policy enabling African-Americans to enlist in the Continental Army that fought the British in the Revolutionary War. The abolitionists eventually found in her poems an effective weapon with which to attack White misconceptions and prejudice concerning the nature and quality of the African mind. Her life and works were exploited to prove that African-Americans, like Euro-Americans, could also possess a benign soul and intellectual and social graces given favorable human conditions, such as the abolition of slavery. As noted by Frazier (1957), in another environment, she might have been an ornament in American literature.

Though literary activity of a wide variety was carried on by African-Americans long after Phillis Wheatley's death, no real, significant breakthrough was achieved until the 1890s. That decade ushered in the modern period in Afro-American literature when writers began to master literary craftsmanship and articulate pertinent ideas on specific literary and cultural issues of African-Americans in the United States. One of the most significant poets in those literary beginnings was Paul Laurence Dunbar (1913). Others include W. E. B. Du Bois and Charles W. Chestnut.[2]

Born to former slaves in 1872 in Dayton, Ohio, Dunbar began writing verse as a youth in high school where he was the only African-American. But after graduation, the only job that this gifted youth could get was that of an elevator operator in his native city. Undeterred, he persevered and eventually published privately two volumes of poems, *Oak and Ivy* and *Majors and Minors* in 1893 and 1895, respectively. Here, too, the marketing and the distribution of the books were done by the author himself. Through public readings of his work, he built up a following of a predominantly White audience. After a favorable review of *Majors and Minors* by the famous literary critic of the period, William Dean Howells, Dunbar was able to secure a reputable publisher for his third volume, *Lyrics of Lowly Life,* which contains the best poems from his initial two volumes and Howells's introduction. *Lyrics of Lowly Life* established Dunbar in the United States and England as the first African American to give lyric expression to a truly aesthetic feeling for the life of Americans of African ancestry.

Nearly every scholarly work on Dunbar recognizes the two fields which his poetry basically embraced: conventional English and dialect. In his conventional poems, Dunbar generally tends to express his anguish, frustrations, and sorrow concerning the status and dilemma of African-Americans trapped in a hostile and unresponsive European culture. Haunted by the distorted image of African-Americans which White audiences loved, Dunbar expresses his anger and frustrations in poems such as "We Wear the Mask," "Sympathy," and "Ethiopia." The first two poems subtly articulate the manner in which African-Americans are forced by racism to conceal their genuine fears, feelings, and frustrations behind a mask in order to get by or stay alive. This protest, however, appears less subtly and much stronger in "Ethiopia." Here, the poet also exhorts African-Americans to be proud of their African heritage, to love and respect their ancestral continent. However, poems in this assertive strain are rare in Dunbar's works. The more typical are the poems in which the anguish and lamentations are clearly articulated through ambivalent language and universal imagery:

> *I know what the caged bird feels, alas!*
> *When the sun is bright on the upland slopes;*
> *When the wind stirs soft through the springing grass,*

And the river flows like a stream of glass;
When the first bird sings and the first bud opens;
And the faint perfume from its chalice steals—
I know what the caged bird feels!

I know why the caged bird beats his wing
Till its blood is red on the cruel bars;
For he must fly back to his perch and cling
When he fain would be on the bough a-swing;
And a pain still throbs in the old, old scars
And they pulse again with a keener string—
I know why he beats his wing!

I know why the caged bird sings, ah me,
When his wing is bruised and his bosom sore,
When he beats his bars and he would be free;
It is not a carol of joy or glee,
But a prayer that he sends from his heart's deep core,
But a plea, that upward to Heaven he flings—
I know why the caged bird sings!

In the dialect poems, however, Dunbar attempts an artistic representation of the life, behavior, attitudes, and sentiments of rural African-Americans. As such these poems tend to reflect the imagined simple pleasures and sorrows of a childlike people, capable mostly of comic or pathetic conduct. These dialect poems to which Dunbar's reputation is always latched have angered many African-Americans largely because of their negative stereotypical content. Eurocentric critics would encourage him however, to believe, in spite of himself, that the dialect poetry accurately portrays the Americans as well as his own poetic genius. Witness the words of William Dean Howells in praise of Dunbar's dialect poems on the publication of *Lyrics of Lowly Life*:

> The precious difference in temperament between the races is best preserved and most charmingly suggested by Dunbar in those pieces of his where he studies the woods and traits of his race in its own accents of English. . . . They are really not dialect so much as personal attempts and failures for the written and spoken language. He reveals in these finely ironic perception of the Negro's limitations with a tenderness for them which I think so very rare.[4]

Viewed from a contemporary perspective, Howells's introduction reflects the dingy vision of a Eurocentric critic concerning African-American realities. Ironically, his exaggerated praise could destroy rather than en-hance the possibility of Dunbar's acceptance as a serious artist. This notwithstanding, Dunbar went on to achieve fame and fortune. The more serious point, however, is the genuineness of the claims made for Dunbar in that introduction. The dialect poems, as noted by Long (1972: 19), are not all that true. In fact, they are an artificiality which Dunbar composed to reach a wider audience, following in the footsteps of such Eurocentric apologists for slavery as Thomas Nelson Page and Joel Chandler Harris. Dialect was, in fact, unnatural to Dunbar whose trip to the South came long after the publication of his dialect poems. It seems that he drew on folk speech that he had heard in his native Ohio and successfully con-structed a patchwork dialect similar to the idea of African-American folk speech in the conception of northern Whites. These so-called dialect poems of Dunbar have conventional literary rather than folk oral poetic form. By replacing classic English with "funny spelling," Dunbar succeeded in producing quaint, graceful poems which reflect the White man's image of "the watermelon-stealin', possum-eating', banjo-thumpin', dancing and laughin' negra" (Rexroth, 1971: 152).

In contrast, many of his conventional poems tend to laud notable people and celebrate nature and attractive women. Despite his popular success, Dunbar felt restive and unfulfilled. He was harassed by a feeling of failure owing to the prominence and significance given to his dialect poems over his conventional ones. Indeed, during his lifetime, his conven-tional poems appeared sparingly. According to Turner (1969: 80-92), the very format of the 1901 edition of *Lyrics of the Heartside,* which contains most of his nondialect poetry, suggests this. *Heartside* was the least publi-cized of all of Dunbar's poetry. The reason for this may be seen in the following lines:

> He sang to love when earth was young,
> And love itself was in his lays,
> But, ah, the world it turned to praise
> A jingle in a broken tongue.

Witness how one such "jingle," "A Negro Love Song," tries to capture a plantation scene of African-American dalliance in the rural South:

> Seen my lady home las' night,
> Jump back, honey, jump back.

Hel' huh han' an' sque'z it tight,
Seen a light gleam f'om huh eye,
An' a smile go flittin' by—
    Jump back, honey, jump back.
Hyeahd de win' blow thoo de pine
    Jump back, honey, jump back.
Mockin'-bird was singin' fine,
    Jump back, honey, jump back.
An' my heart was beatin' so,
When I reached my lady's do,
Dat I couldn't ba' to go,—
    Jump back, honey, jump back.

Put my ahm aroun't huh wais,
    Jump back, honey, jump back.
Raised huh lips an' took a taste,
    Jump back, honey, jump back.
Love me, honey, love me true?
Love me well ez I love you?
An' she answe'd "Cosc I do"—
    Jump back, honey, jump back.

Judgment on the work of Dunbar oscillates between Vernon Loggins's view that the publication of *Lyrics of Lowly Life* is the "greatest single event" in the history of American literature (in Long, 1972: 214) and the feeling among some contemporary African-American writers that he was an Uncle Tom. The latter categorization is certainly unfortunate. Dunbar was an exceptionally gifted lyricist whose work reflected the limitations imposed by his environment and the need to survive in a Eurocentric literary world. He was the first African-American poet to earn national recognition in mainstream America. As James Weldon Johnson (1931) said, Dunbar was "the first to demonstrate a high degree of poetic talent combined with literary training and technical proficiency (p. xxxiii).

However, another very significant literary contribution that was made in Dunbar's time came with the publication of James Weldon Johnson's "Lift Ev'ry Voice and Sing" in 1961. The poem, a collaborative effort of Johnson and his brother, was written for Jacksonville, Florida schoolchildren's anniversary celebration of Abraham Lincoln's birth. In this poem, Johnson endows the African's enslavement in America and struggle for freedom with a special nobility. It expresses both an acceptance by African-Americans of their past and confidence in the future. It can be asserted that Johnson's poem helped to cultivate a sense of history among African-

Americans. This standpoint is supported by the fact that "Lift Ev'ry Voice and Sing" has now become a national hymn of sorts for African-Americans and is often sung at the opening of their public gatherings.

In the wake of the mass migrations to northern cities during and after World War I, there began what is now known as the Harlem Renaissance. The "first fruits" of this renaissance appeared in 1925 in *The New Negro,* edited by Alain Locke. One of the contributors to this volume was James Weldon Johnson, who wrote of Harlem as the "cultural capital" of the Negro in the United States.[5] The creative work of James Weldon Johnson forms a watershed separating the fame of the Harlem Renaissance from an earlier period when African-Americans began to write about their history with more sophistication. Johnson's book, *Fifty Years and Other Poems,* appeared in 1917 when the migration of African-Americans from the South to northern cities was at its highest. His poem "O Black and Unknown Bards" (in Locke, 1925: 30) asks:

> *How came your lips to touch the sacred fire?*
> *How, in your darkness, did you come to know*
> *The power and beauty of the minstrel's lyre?*

In this poetic fashion, he strongly urged a reevaluation of the spirituals as an aspect of the African-American's past. The dominant spirit of the Harlem Renaissance, whether expressed in poetry or in the novel, was seeking a new definition of values. This fresh examination of the African's experience in American life "shows that the younger generation has achieved an objective attitude toward life" (Locke, 1925: 304). "Race for them," Locke continued,

> is but an idiom of experience, a sort of added enriching adventure and discipline, giving subtler overtones to life, making it more beautiful and interesting, even if more poignantly so. . . . Our poets no longer have the hard choice between an over-assertive and an appealing attitude. By the same effort they have shaken themselves free from the minstrel tradition and the fouling nets of dialect, and through acquiring ease and simplicity in serious expression, have carried the folk gift to the altitudes of art. There they seek and find art's intrinsic values and satisfaction—and if America were deaf, they would still sing.

As we understand the poems and fiction of the writers included in *The New Negro,* the sociological implications of the modified outlook of African-American writers toward the African experience in America become obvious. Rudolph Fisher's two short stories, "The City of Refuge" and "Vestiges," are pertinent citations in this regard. Both stories treat the urbanization of the Southern African-American masses with understanding and objectivity. This approach is an index to the African-Americans' new attitude toward their history in American culture. In a similar vein, Countee Cullen offers no apology in his poetry for the "brown girl's swagger," and he captures the beaming faces of Hellenic angels as they greet the African girl of "dancing feet."

In Langston Hughes's poetry, however, we are offered a vision of the African-American's rise to civilization through reference to the world's great rivers—the Euphrates, the Congo, the Nile, and the Mississippi. In America, the African was the "dark" brother who ate in the kitchen but the future would see him welcomed to sit at the table when company comes. Many of the writers who were included in *The New Negro* are today counted among the meaningful contributors to American literature.

Although African-American poetry of that period was dominated by Claude McKaye, Countee Cullen, and Langston Hughes, only the last-named poet is still thriving. McKaye and Cullen seem to have consistently utilized early 20th-century poetic style which makes their passionate and powerful poetry probably difficult for contemporary tastes. Born in Joplin, Missouri, in 1902, Langston Hughes lived most of his childhood life with his grandmother in Lawrence, Kansas. Later, he moved to Cleveland, Ohio, where he began writing poetry as a student at Cleveland Central High School. After graduation, he spent a year with his father in Mexico, studied Spanish, and wrote "The Negro Speaks of Rivers" (Hughes, 1963: 3-66) which reads as follows:

> *I've known rivers:*
> *I've known rivers ancient as the world and older than the glow of human blood in human veins.*
> *My soul has gone deep like the rivers.*
>
> *I bathed in the Euphrates when dawns were young.*
> *I build my hut near the Congo and it lulled me to sleep.*
> *I looked upon the Nile and raised the pyramids above it.*
> *I heard the singing of the Mississippi when Abe Lincoln went down to New Orleans, and I've seen its muddy bosom turn all golden in the sunset.*
>
> *I've known rivers:*
> *Ancient, dusky rivers.*
>
> *My soul has grown deep like rivers.*

Hughes's traditional and symbolic treatment of the Mississippi River is very effective. The river, profound, enigmatic, and persistent, becomes a powerful religious symbol of eternity. As Huggins (1976: 66-68) and other writers have pointed out, this symbolic treatment is reinforced by the mention of the other great world rivers, the Euphrates, the Congo, and the Nile. Apart from life, nurture, and civilization, these rivers are also linked with the African, free or enslaved, who has observed and known them for centuries, therefrom imbibing a sense of inevitability and eternity. No matter where he is, the African will therefore survive, persist, and persevere because he has attained harmony with the great streams of life. The identification of the persona with eternal forces that may help in the transcendence over worldly life conditions reflects the force and beauty of the spirituals.

After working at different times as a seaman and a waiter, Hughes settled down to write poetic pieces that eventually won the admiration of Vachel Lindsay, a leading critic of the time. With encouragement from him and others, Hughes won his first literary prize for *The Weary Blues* in 1925 (Hughes, 1963). He then steadily moved on to become a major figure of the Harlem Renaissance, as was noted earlier. He resumed his college education at Lincoln University in Pennsylvania where his first novel, *Not Without Laughter,* was written in 1932. During his lifetime, 12 volumes of his poems were published; a last collection, *The Panther and the Lash,* came out posthumously in 1967.

For about 40 years, Langston Hughes wrote poetry on different themes and experimented with a variety of techniques. But the recurring themes include those on Harlem, the African-American's African roots, protest and social commentary, and orature. Harlem, the predominant theme, refers not only to the suburb of New York City of that name but alludes metaphorically to all places typical of African-American communities in the United States. His treatment of this theme is complex because it is variously stated, implied, or used as a subject, protagonist, or background in his poetry. He always tries to portray the changing moods of Harlem residents whose colorful language he loves, and whose interests and problems he considers his own. This theme is so important to him that it recurs in every major volume he has written from his earliest beginnings to the publication of *The Panther and the Lash* in 1967 when he died. In *The Weary Blues,* he depicts Harlem as the swinging, joyous "cultural capital" of "jazzonia," where "shameless gals" "strut and wiggle" in a whirling cabaret, and "sleek haired black boys blow their hearts on silver trumpet" (in O'Daniel, 1971). But the volume also portrays Harlem as having its full share of sorrow even in that auspicious period. As Hughes says, the rhythm of this "gay and cabaret world" is "a jazz rhythm" but it eventually brings "the Broken heart of love/The Weary, weary heart of pain." Gradually, Hughes's portrait of Harlem becomes gloomy. By 1949, when *One Way Ticket* was published, race riots and the Depression had turned the city into a disillusioned "edge of hell," although it could still be, as portrayed in the poem "Negro Servant," a heaven to downtrodden folk after slaving all day for Euro-Americans. Hughes's best treatment of this theme, however, may be seen in "Montage of a Dream Deferred." Originally an 85-page poem, it exploits a "jam session" technique that enables the poet to give a vivid picture of Harlem's frustrations. The central piece of the poem consists of a powerful question:

> *What happens to a dream deferred?*
> *Does it dry up*
> *like a raisin in the sun?*
>
> *Or fester like a sore—*
> *And then run?*
>
> *Does it stink like rotten meat?*
> *Or crust and sugar over like a syrupy sweet?*
>
> *Or does it explode?*

In the treatment of the African theme, Hughes's work shows similar maturation. Initially, it colored his early poems, suggesting the African-American tendency to make Africa the spiritual home of creative artists, a popular theme during the Harlem Renaissance. The poems "Afro-American Fragments" and "Danse Africaine" portray African-Americans as aliens in America, permanently estranged and profoundly nostalgic about their sunny and beautiful African home. In such poems, the superiority of African beauty and wisdom are highlighted together with the "foolishness and the pale washed-out looks" of Euro-Americans. The poems speak of "jungle joys," but in "Lament for Dark Peoples," we hear protest from the persona who has been snapped from one's African roots to be "caged in the circus of civilization." The African's experience in America is then shown in the poem "Afraid" to be just as bad:

We cry among the skyscrapers
As our ancestors
Cried among the palms in Africa
Because we are alone.

Although Hughes's treatment of the African theme led to a charge of sentimental idealism, his poetry gradually matured to reflect Africa much more realistically. It began to probe serious issues of politics, leadership, and meaningful intercultural exchange.

The subject of protest and social commentary permeates the whole body of Langston Hughes's poetry. Instances of this may be seen in his earlier works, *The Weary Blues* and *Fine as Clothes to the Jew*. And since the publication of *One Way Ticket* in 1949, his works have always featured aspects of protest and social commentary. In such poems, lynching is the recurrent symbol of injustice against the African-American. Significantly, a section of *One Way Ticket* called "Silhouette" is reserved for various descriptions of and comments on this terrible crime. It is interesting to recall that in 1967 a White schoolteacher in Boston was dismissed for daring to teach his students one of Langston Hughes's poems in this vein—"Ballad of the Landlord" (Chapman, 1968: 25).

By the time of his death in 1967, Langston Hughes had distinguished himself as the most prolific and probably the best-known African-American writer. His prodigious literary achievements are documented in libraries and other institutions all over the world. An eloquent testimony to this attainment may be seen in the numerous awards and honors that he won in his lifetime: the *Opportunity* Magazine poetry prize (1925), the Witter Bynner undergraduate prize for poetic excellence (1926), the Rosewald and Guggenheim fellowships, and a grant from the American Academy of Arts and Letters. In spite of his sound social educational background, wide travels, and prodigious talent, he became the first African-American poet to submerge himself totally in African-American folk speech and culture, writing for and about ordinary folks. Appropriately, he was always introduced as "the Poet Laureate of Harlem" to audiences. Initially, he was even rejected by the African-American elite for "portraying the worst aspects of race" (Rexroth, 1971: 155-158). The tables, however, were turned after World War II. By this time, he had begun steadily to achieve popularity with all shades of the African humanity in the United States. And by the time of his death, Langston Hughes had become accepted all over the world as one of the truly gifted poets of our time.

Notes

1. The University of Jos, Nigeria, has regularly offered courses in American and African-American literatures since 1978 when this author first introduced them into the English department's curricula.

2. Aspects of their significant works appear in *Black Voices* (Chapman, 1968) and other anthologies.

3. Quoted in *Harlem Renaissance* (Huggins, 1973: 38).

4. This and subsequent quotes have been taken from *Afro-American Writing* (Long, 1972: 214-215).

5. See "Harlem: The Cultural Capital" in *The New Negro* (Locke, 1925: 301-311).

References

Asante, M. K. (1987) The Afrocentric Idea. Philadelphia: Temple Univ. Press.

Bell, R. A. P. and B. J. Parker [eds.] (1979) Sturdy Black Bridges. Garden City, NY: Anchor/ Doubleday.

Chapman, A. (1968) Black Voices. New York: Mentor.

DuBois, W. E. B. (1903) The Souls of Black Folk: Essays and Sketches. Chicago: McClurg.

Dunbar, P. L. (1913) The Complete Poems of Paul Lawrence Dunbar. New York: Dodd, Mead.

Frazier, E. F. (1957) The Negro in the United States. New York.

Hughes, L. (1963) The Big Sea. New York: Alfred A. Knopf.

Huggins, N. I. (1976) Harlem Renaissance. New York: Oxford Univ. Press.

Johnson, J. W. (1917) Fifty Years and Other Poems. Boston: Cornhill.

Johnson, J. W. (1931) "Preface," in J. W. Johnson (ed.) Book of American Negro Poetry. New York: Harcourt, Brace.

Locke, A. (1925) The New Negro: An Interpretation. New York: Alfred & Charles Boni.

Long, R. A. (1972) Afro-American Writing: An Anthology of Prose and Poems, Vols. 1-2. New York: New York Univ. Press.

O'Daniel, T. [ed.] (1971) Langston Hughes, Black Genius: A Critical Evaluation. New York: Modern Language Association of America.

Rexroth, K. (1971). American Poetry in the Twentieth Century. New York: Herder & Herder.

Turner, D. (1969) Black American Literature: Essays. Columbus, OH: Charles E. Merrill.

The Way We Do 9

A Preliminary Investigation of the African Roots of African American Performance

Gale Jackson

> Speak to me so that I may speak to you. By our voices we
> recognize each other in the darkness.
>
> *—Ifa divination*

> Once Spider came to have a calabash filled with all the
> knowledge in the world. . . .
>
> *—Ashanti tale*

In the performance of storytelling, we reconstruct and perpetuate the history of a mythic past in order to better understand both that past and our own time in a historic and ritual continuum. In the performance of storytelling, we participate in pure celebration, in ritual, in imparting the moral or the lesson of the story, and in creating the "stage" on which that story can be told.

This chapter originally appeared as an article in *Black African Literature Forum* (Vol. 25, No. 1, Spring 1991, pp. 11-22). Copyright © Gale Jackson. Adapted with permission.

This storytelling is an attempt to reconstruct a detail of Spider's calabash—its voice, its wisdom, its theater or symbol—in order to illuminate the African philosophical base of African American theater and cultural performance. The black church—its "theater," its pomp, its ceremony—is a signpost on the epic cultural journey of African sacred and secular ritual into the diaspora. This storytelling attempts to reconstruct part of that epic in a juxtaposition of voices and acts, in call and response, along a continuum of African to African American performance—to talk about performance through performance.

> Night falls and we lay our sleeping mats. Day breaks and we roll them up.
> The one who lays the warp threads must walk back and forth. (Ifa divination)

This is a collage or weaving of story in a preliminary journey towards meaning and recognition. This telling looks to illustrate the steps from African sacred and secular performance through to the oral traditions, folkways, religion, and theater of the diaspora. This telling is itself an investigative "performance" which attempts to examine the uses of specific symbolic patterns—of actions and words—in the telling and recording of history, in moral instruction, in expressing and coping with a world view which acknowledges duality, in acts of cultural survival, and in the communal creation of the stages on which we are, by all these attributes, regenerated, recreated, and transformed.

> *If you want to find Jesus,*
> *Go in the wilderness,*
> *Go in the wilderness,*
> *Go in the wilderness.*
>
> —African American traditional

This telling begins with, and gathers refrains from, ritual verse from the Yoruba divination text, the *Ifa*. Subsequently I look at other African performance, both sacred and secular, and at cultural continuity in performance rituals across the continents. From there I look at our holidays and holy days, at blues and spirituals, at autobiography and folklore, and at the neo-African theaters in which these forms are created and shared as they are performed. The juxtaposition reveals a cultural philosophy rich in symbolic text and act, and with an ordinal, grammatical, and ritual structure of its own. Across the African continent and in the Americas; in old-time religion and Southern burial markers; in carnivals, pinksters, jubilees, susus, and secret orders; in the linguistic "dozens"; and in the religious witness which prefigures black literature in black performance are African symbol systems. And these symbols encode a philosophy of life that is circular, a correlative understanding of divinity and creativity as activated by community, and an understanding of ritual as an ordering and empowering force.

> *Orunmilla, carry me in your bag.*
> *Carry me in your purse so that*
> *We may go together slowly, so*
> *That wherever we may be going we*
> *May go there together.*
>
> —*Ifa* divination

Back and forth along the four winds and into the wilderness, where the pieces of the calabash have fallen, are the routes of migration of African peoples and their cultures, beginning in the "prewritten" history of the Sudanese regions, thousands of years before the forced migrations of the Atlantic slave trade. From this regional and cultural genesis, I draw a working definition of African performance.

In this pan-African context, and perhaps in line with true folk meaning, the term *performance* refers to a broad spectrum of cultural acts—from religious ritual, to playing mass at carnival, to children's circle games. These cultural performance acts are all, at root, a defined series of symbolic gestures, done in a set manner, having set meanings, and performed with a particular end in mind (even if the meanings and ends have been lost or forgotten over time and nothing but the gestures and their ontological "spirit" have survived). These performance acts, in the African context, create a discrete ritually potent and potential moment, a theater, in time.

> *Hambone, Hambone where you been?*
> *All 'round the world and back again.*
> *Hambone, Hambone what'd you do?*
> *I got a chance and I fairly flew.*
>
> —African American folk game/song

A pan-African poetics of performance is potentially a basis on which memory and reconstruction happen in the diaspora. William Bascom reminds us that the Yoruba priests brought the entire text of Yoruba history, mythology, and divination intact in their memories to the "New World." In addition to the professional performers of music, story, dance, and song, laypersons also brought with them a distinctively African world view. Consequently, the Africanness in African American culture is often deeply embedded in the conceptual framework out of which acts of cultural performance come. My focus here is on specific shared aspects of these "theaters."

Witness and History

> *Go tell it on the mountain*
> *Over the hills and everywhere.*
> *Go tell it on the mountain . . .*
>
> —African American spiritual

For the African, the overriding collective truth to be publicly told in the early history of this country was the story of journey, oppression, slavery, and liberation. In thousands of work songs, blues songs, and spirituals; in thousands of instances of oral witness and written narratives; in the early publication of black drama (e.g., William Wells Brown's *The Escape*), African Americans voiced a communal desire to tell their story and to have it passed on. This outpouring of witness often used mythological forms which prefigured the formal religious "witness" of the Afro-Christian church, but are consistent with its passion, its sense of mission, and its urgency. Over time, and whether in oral or written narrative, whether in the sanctified church or on a formal and informal dramatic stage, the meaning and performance of witness would remain much the same. Sacred or secular, it has been an articulation wrought from the heart of African American oral performance. As such, it is a wielding of the power of remembered and performed history. It is the spiritual. It is the work song. It is the sermon and the narrative which arise from them.

> *Dis ole hammer*
> *Huh!*
>
> *Kill John Henry*
> *Huh!*
>
> *Laid him low, buddy*
> *Huh!*
>
> *Laid him low.*
>
> —African American work song

The African American performance of history charts the actual and the mythic journeys of thousands who tell the same tale in strikingly similar ways. In hundreds of autobiographical recollections of antebellum life, in song and story, African Americans of the early generations wrote a communal text of their own story, imbued with a mission urgent and holy. It is a story of day-to-day, backbreaking labor and how it was expressed in the field holler. It is a story, a historical drama, of how the individual and the community moved to a moment of revelation which swept them into actual and metaphorical wilderness and flight. It is a story of how, against the odds, they escaped the physical and the spiritual clutches of slavery, and how they survived. And the witness, the telling of that story, is a ritual, a performance which remembers, encodes, and perpetuates the possibility of that survival . . . through the valleys of slavery's inhumanity and despair; across the wilderness, the rivers—the byways of escape which tested both strength and faith in the journey north. Finally, by their witness, that journey is transformed, just as it is transforming. The stark reality of a community's history became, in time, a shared mythological drama.

> *I know, I know, Lord.*
> *Believer, I know, I know, I know, Lord.*
> *Believer, I know, I know, the road so thorny.*
> *Believer, I know . . . I done cross Jordan.*
> *Believer, I know.*
>
> —African American religious traditional

Similarly, in traditional Yoruba society, ritual marks individuals' progress within the community from birth to death. Ritual accompanies us in successfully achieving our predestined journey with fate; it intercedes and negotiates with faith and the ancestors as we go along. A ritual text, the *Ifa,* is revealed by a system of symbols. That ritual text gives both proverb and proscription, divine performance and divine "writing" to assist in ordering the chaos of incomplete knowledge of the world. *Ikin,* or palm nuts, are thrown in a ceremony which reveals the symbolic writing of our history and our fate. When we read the palm nuts, we are guided to an *Ifa* verse, which in turn points our way on the road of life. But before and after the actual ceremony, the priests and petitioner(s) must circle the community, must take a symbolic communal walk. Their "parade" symbolizes both the totality of community involvement in a life and the journey that the individual must take toward faith. The history of the *Ifa* begins with a story of journey. The history of *Ifa* is the history of a community witnessing its fate. The history of the *Ifa* in America begins with the journey embedded in the remembered text. When, it is reasoned, people see into their own fate, they remember to mark their ancestors in history. When the people were enslaved, Legba, among the gods, shared their slaveship journey.

> O great one, I pay obeisance. The young child does not confront the powerful one. I pay obeisance to Elegba Eshu, who is on the road. (Brazilian cult song to Legba)

The Moral Lesson

The narrative act of witness has its parallels and prefigurations in both African and diaspora lore. Here instruction and documentation go hand in hand. Oral history performance is particularly suited to giving social/political/moral instruction, overt or covert. Folk songs and tales, particularly, provide a performance vehicle of extraordinary social possibility and are very useful in the diaspora—small animal tales, for instance. In African societies, and later in the Americas, these tales have passed down the imagination of causality and revolution in nature. In them, small and oppressed animals suffer their oppression (mirroring the condition of races and classes of people) but also use aspects of their oppression to their advantage.

> *Didn't my Lord deliver Daniel?*
> *Deliver Daniel deliver . . .*
> —African American religious traditional

Sermons and spirituals utilize the same moral methodology and aesthetic play by structuring the performance of witness, with its myth and grandeur, into a complex duet with the parable. Examples abound in African American public performance: The papier-mâché dreams of the carnival artists, for instance, resonate with the power, beauty, rhetorical seduction, and righteous witnessing of this duet. Even in strictly sacred "performance," in religious rites across the African American spectrum, the spirit will "move you" and the congregation will "bear you up," since performance and possession are the moral responsibility of those who know. In the telling of this story, sacrifice is not seen solely as tragedy but as an aspect of transformation and, if the truth has survived to be told, as a symbol of actual or potential spiritual power. Here the masks represent not only pathos and bathos but the deep-set duality of Legba: its two-colored face, its two-colored hat.

The Two Sides/The Circles

> *Orunmilla, carry me in your bag.*
> *Carry me in your purse so that*
> *We may go together slowly, so*
> *That wherever we may be going we*
> *May go there together.*

Africans, separated by generations of geographical differentiation, came together under the common oppression of the Atlantic slave trade, consciously and unconsciously forming and reforming a neo-African aesthetic built on African conceptual retentions which were masked. From this shared, subversive, and reconstructed base came a system for reading/improvising or signifying within a theater of communal performance. The masked meanings of African American performance are still very much hidden in their own structures. Africanisms in African American performances are as often hidden as they are evident, and this seems somewhat by design. The conceptual framework, the stage on which dual but nonoppositional systems of symbols or meanings are encoded, by virtue of their masked nature, was built to survive a period underground. Masking, a pervasive element in African performance, has equal weight and meaning in the social history of the diaspora. The masked performances of carnival, jonkonnu, cakewalks, and creole balls play, as do folktales and even slave narratives, between concealment and revelation, between joy and sorrow, between light and dark like a child's circling song. Like them, the religious "performance" is both an act of public affirmation and a rite of cloaking, of creating a safe space for believers.

> *Sometimes I feel like a motherless child.*
> *Sometimes I feel like a motherless child.*
> *Sometimes I feel like a motherless child*
> *Such a long long way from home.*
>
> —African American traditional

Sometimes I feel like an eagle in de air.
Some of these mornings bright and fair
I'm going to lay down my heavy load
Going to spread my wings and cleave the air.

—African American traditional

The established church standardized the spiritual and took it on the road, where it has been performed as popular theater since the late 1800s. Black and white musical writers put the spiritual and the sermon—something of black song, black dance, and black talk—on the American musical stage, which has, since its inception, been informed, if not by African content, then by the African form. Of course, for African Americans the tension between identity and social constructs has remained (think of Dunbar's "We Wear the Mask," of Du Bois's "double-consciousness," and of Washington's conceptual "Veil." Minstrel theater, for example, parodied observations of black performance in both sacred and secular forums. Subsequently, it brought to the American stage an "original" American form built on a mockery of African performance. When African Americans first began to perform on the mainstream stages of this country, they, in turn, improvised and, in some cases, signified on the black-faced mockery of white minstrel men. As African American theater has developed as an autonomous genre, it has increasingly pulled on the signifying potential of what has become a contemporary enactment of masking. And the festivals of masking remain as well, operating on many public and less public levels—perhaps now driven, in addition, by a new need for catharsis. Beside them, the church has also remained as a stage for a "theater" of revolutionary rhetoric and rebellion, as well as a resource for popular culture.

The Alter/The Stage

The mortar will testify that I see room in which to settle.
The teteleaf will testify that I see room in which to stretch out.
The gbebe leaf will testify that I see room in which to dwell.

—*Ifa* divination

When the Bakongo of Southern Zaire perform a traditional ritual oath, the petitioner stands on a Greek cross drawn into the earth. The vertical line is a line of entrance: a path that crosses into the next world and on which we symbolically gain wisdom and age. The horizontal line is the division between this world and the next. Together, these lines mark a point of intersection between this, the world of the living, and the other, that of the ancestors before and beyond. The Bakongo write this meaning. The cross is in fact understood as given or written by the ancestors, who are our gods. Cuba descendants of the Bakongo call their neo-African cuniforms *la firma* "the signature of the spirits." The performance of this ritual is set on a continuum from ancient time. On this point, we sing ritual words (*yimbila ye sona*), according to tradition. On this point, the petitioner draws a point and sings proscribed words in a meditation. This meditation on the oath on the symbolic crossroads creates the power of god, and brings it—creativity, power, possibility—to the point where we stand. In Bakongo belief, the meditation on the oath on the symbolic crossroads remembers the relationship between the living and the dead, individual and community, communion and continuity. The rite of mediation on the oath retains its power in the diaspora in specific speech acts of witness, in the use of rhyme and repetition (within the very language structures of African Americans), and in the knowledge that what goes around (even if we don't know from where) still comes around.

> Ogbe sprouts firm. It enters into the belly of the forest. Ogun sprouts long and slender. It reaches the road. (*Ifa* divination)

What stands out in the parallel between African and African American ritual performance is the way in which the performance itself, be it sacred or secular, involves communally creating a moment of potentiality and regenerative possibility—a theater on which to act out existential drama or a stage on which to put potentiality and regenerative possibility into play in both the social and spiritual universe. When stories are told in most of the Francophone Caribbean, the storyteller begins, ends, and punctuates the tale with the call *crick* or *yea crick,* to which audience members respond *crack* or *yea crack.* Similarly, in most traditional African American churches, the sermon and the service are created by the entire community, participating in a communal performance of worship. Like the African rituals which prefigure them, these African American sacred performances involve the creation of sacred space (or "black space"). In an act of choral movement, shouting, clapping synchronization, and/or call-and-response, which recalls the bond between individual and community, these neo-African performances remain percussive, mythic (or allegorical), circular, improvisational, and double-edged in the African theatrical mode.

Wade in the water.
Wade in the water, children.
Wade in the water.

—African American traditional, Sea Islands

Bakongo, Ibo, Mendi, and Yoruba rituals of community interaction, vodun *vere,* Balkongo cosmograms—all speak to the idea of created space between the realms of the living and the realms of the dead. It is a ritual space that sings of trouble with a powerful voice and soars toward the sacred with the verve and sensuality of gutbucket blues or sings gutbucket blues with a voice that recalls to the listener his or her higher self. The ritual space is, in the African American case, an alternative stage. In the context of the diaspora experience, it is a needed stage or place for affirming and recreating the drama of existence.

Eye of secret unseen by evil
Eye of secret unseen by evil
The diviner's eyes will not see evil
The diviner's eyes will not see evil.

—*Ifa* divination

We stand on a point of infinity. We circle the compound. The party circles the compound in a parade toward the divination ceremony. Carnival circles the parish. The spirit circles the room. The song rises up from the totality. The storyteller rises up out of the communal circle and weaves another circle of enclosure with the tale. The Spider in Ashanti lore spins a web to the heavens to bring to the people all of history in story. Legba takes a journey to the places where he will find the ingredients of prophecy, a journey written before Legba began. Legba learns this from Earth's animals and teaches Orunmilla. Orunmilla carries us in his bag. And we bring Orunmilla to the Americas—preserving, carrying, concealing, encoding, and protecting ourselves in a journey, never ending, in the rituals of living we perform.

Members, plumb the line.
Members, plumb the line.
Plumb the line.
If you want to get to Heaven, you got to
Plumb the line.

—African American traditional

These are performances which move toward the mythological in the recreation of an African universe, performances which are self-consciously ritualistic and which play off the "mainstream" idea of text, performances which increasingly, along this continuum, seek to establish place and order in chaos through symbolic gesture, action, and words. Implicit in all this is the root of oral witness, a statement about the importance of the story of a people, about the circle embracing us in an African cosmology of meaning. African performance throughout the diaspora recalls the Yoruba emphasis on becoming gods ourselves, on meeting Legba at the crossroads (in any of his incarnations), of molding the mutability of fate, of becoming, like vodun and santeria practitioners, empowered to "make the gods." These performances of cultural sustenance, survival, and liberation draw on a communal creativity. This cultural community has invested the wilderness or, more vernacularly, the edge with a potentiality for transformative action. This is the place used to generate power. Whether the physical place is the wilderness, the pulpit, or the state matters little. Here the performance can be mounted by the actual and symbolic power of the ritual itself. It doesn't matter whether the rites are acted, spoken, danced, sung, or written down. The internal rhythm is the same. The intent, the call to power, is the same.

> Ogbe closes very generously, was the one who cast *Ifa* for head, who had knelt and chose his destiny. (*Ifa* divination)

This is about the way we do culturally—about the drama of dance, about the writing of divination, about the musical telling of tales, about the ordinary and mystical oral conjuring of space, and about the identification marks and road signs to the heavens on hennaed hands.

Works Consulted

Abrahams, Roger D. *African Folktales*. New York: Pantheon, 1983.

Abrahams, Roger D., et al. *After Africa: Extracts from British Travel Accounts and Journals of the Seventeenth, Eighteenth and Nineteenth Centuries Concerning the Slaves, Their Manners and Customs in the British West Indies*. New Haven: Yale University Press, 1983.

Baldwin, James. *The Amen Corner*. New York: French, 1968.

Bascom, William. *Ifa Divination: Communication between Gods and Men in West Africa.* Bloomington: Indiana University Press, 1969.

Barnes, Sandra, ed. *Africa's Ogun: Old World and New.* Bloomington: Indiana University Press, 1989.

Bernal, Martin. *Black Athena: The Afro Asiatic Roots of Classical Civilization.* New Brunswick: Rutgers University Press, 1987.

Cabrera, Lydia. *El Monte: Notas sobre las religiones, las magla, las supersticiones y el folklore de los Negros Crillos y el Pueblo de Cuba.* Miami: Daytona, 1986.

Counter, S. Allen, and David Evans. *I Sought My Brother.* Cambridge: MIT Press, 1981.

Courlander, Harold. *Afro-American Folklore.* New York: Crown, 1976.

Dalphinis, Morgan. *Caribbean and African Languages.* London: Karia, 1985.

Deren, Maya. *Divine Horsemen: The Living Gods of Haiti.* Kingston: McPherson, 1953.

Diop, Cheikh Anta. *The African Origins of Civilization: Myth or Reality.* New York: Hill, 1974.

———. *Black Africa.* New York: Hill, 1978.

Dixon, Melvin. *Ride Out the Wilderness: Geography and Identity in Afro-American Literature.* Urbana: University of Illinois Press, 1987.

Douglass, Fredrick. *Narrative of the Life of Fredrick Douglass, An American Slave, Written by Himself.* Boston: Anti-Slavery Office, 1845.

Galeano, Eduardo. *Memory of Fire: Faces and Masks.* New York: Pantheon, 1987.

Gates, Henry Louis, Jr. *The Signifying Monkey: A Theory of Afro-American Literacy Criticism.* New York: Oxford University Press, 1988.

———, ed. *"Race," Writing, and Difference.* Chicago: University of Chicago Press, 1986.

Harrison, Paul Carter, ed. *Totem Voices.* New York: Grove, 1989.

Herskovits, Frances, and Melville Herskovits. *Surinam Folklore.* New York: AMS, 1968.

Herskovits, Melville. *Dahomey: An Ancient West African Kingdom.* Evanston, IL: Northwestern University Press, 1967.

Hill, Errol, ed. *The Theater of Black Americans: Roots & Rituals/Image Makers.* Englewood Cliffs, NJ: Prentice Hall, 1980.

Holmberg, Carl Bryan, and Gilbert D. Schneider. "Daniel Decatur Emmett's Stump Sermons: Genuine Afro-American Culture, Language and Rhetoric in the Negro Minstrel Show. *Journal of Popular Culture* 19, 4 (1986): 27-38.

Hull, Richard W. Munyakare. *African Civilization before the Banturee.* New York: Wiley, 1972.

Hurston, Zora Neale. *Mules and Men.* 1935. Bloomington: Indiana University Press, 1978.

———. *The Sanctified Church.* Berkeley: Turtle Island, 1981.

———. *Tell My Horse.* 1938. Berkeley: Turtle Island, 1981.

Johnson, James Weldon, and J. Rosamond Johnson. *American Negro Spirituals.* 1928. New York: DeCapo, 1985.

Lucas, J. O. *Religion of the Yoruba.* Lagos: n.p., 1948.

Moore, Lillian. "Moreau de Saint-Mery and 'Danse.' " *Dance Index* 5 (1946): 232-59.

Neff, Robert, and Anthony Connor. *Blues.* Boston: Godine, 1975.

Omedele, Oluremi. "Traditional and Contemporary African Drama: A Historical Perspective." Dissertation, University of California at Berkeley, 1989.

Ositola, Kolawole. "On Ritual Performance: A Practitioner's View." *Drama Review* 32, 2 (1988): 31-41.

Parrish, Lydia. *Slave Songs of the Georgia Sea Islands*. Hatboro: Hatboro Folklore Association, 1965.

Patewonsky, Isidor. *Eyewitness Accounts of Slavery in the Danish West Indies*. St. Thomas: Author, 1987.

Scale, Lea, and Marianna Scale. "Easter Rock: A Louisiana Negro Ceremony." *Journal of American Folklore* 55 (1942): 212-18.

Sobel, Mechal. *Trabelin' On: The Slave Journey to an Afro-Baptist Faith*. Princeton, NJ: Princeton University Press, 1988.

Sofola, Adeymi. *African Culture and the African Personality*. Lagos: African Resource Publishers, 1973.

Stuckey, Sterling. *Slave Culture*. New York: Oxford University Press, 1987.

Thompson, Robert Farris. *Flash of the Spirit: African and Afro-American Art and Philosophy*. New York: Random, 1973.

Wippler, Migene Gonzalez. *Rituals and Spells of Santeria*. New York: Original, 1974.

———. *The Santeria Experience*. Englewood Cliffs, NJ: Prentice Hall, 1982.

———. *Tales of the Orisha*. New York: Original, 1985.

Afrocentric Heroes in Theater   **10**

Barbara J. Molette
Carlton W. Molette

Heroes and the standards of heroism that a culture projects are important techniques for informing a society of behavioral ideals and expectations. One of the most important functions of heroism is identity bonding by the members of a culture that produce a particular hero. People must be able to connect their own identities to that of the hero in a manner that is consistent with the values of their culture. The linking or transfer of one's identity to another is closely associated with the concept of empathy. But the concept of identity bonding is much broader in scope than the emotional connections associated with the Eurocentric concept of empathy, although the group members must also have empathy with the hero. The bonding of identities is simultaneously emotional and cognitive. It can operate on a personal level, on a nationalistic level, or on a number of other subnationalistic levels. In an Afrocentric framework, the hero's actions and the outcome of his or her actions must transcend his or her individual needs. The hero must be a prototypical manifestation of the hopes, aspirations, and values of the group. Other people who belong to the group for which the character is heroic must believe that they have a vested interest in the hero's actions and in the consequences of those actions.

The subtle ironies of being Black and living in the United States are often missed by White theatergoers and White theater critics when they witness a great deal of the African American theater that is most meaningful to African American theatergoers. The missed perceptions occur because Afrocentric values are significantly different from Eurocentric values. The differences in values cause differences to exist between African American heroes and European American heroes. Many of the differences between Afrocentric and Eurocentric heroes grow out of differences in values that promote or reject notions about inherent superiority because of aristocratic birth and male gender. A hero must be an important person. In other words, a hero must have magnitude. Moreover, the concept of magnitude in a hero can and does exist outside the context of a White-male-dominated political aristocracy. Over time, this political aristocracy has evolved into what White males claim is a democratic meritocracy. However, the transfer of wealth, and, therefore, also political power, remains from White father to White son. This economic fact has not changed from the earliest examples of European theater to the present day. Thus, a nonracist, nonsexist concept of magnitude is necessary in order to identify and understand African American characters who are heroic.

In some non-Europhile cultures, heroes may achieve their magnitude through means other than aristocratic breeding and the exhibition of prowess by winning military or athletic contests. Traditionally, African culture does not require the exhibition of aggression through such contests as a criterion for achieving the status of hero. Instead, the criterion might involve the use of a nonaggressive athletic skill, accompanied by the exhibition of bravery, courage, and wit, to resolve a crisis. The use of strategy, in lieu of brute force, against an adversary in a serious context and the comic use of the rhetoric of diplomacy are two of the most frequently observed forms of heroism that are used to achieve victory over one's adversary. Eurocentric popular culture in the United States disseminates very large amounts of comedy that has no apparent social value. Because of this dominant model, many well-meaning Afrocentric people have concluded that comedy, even when performed by African Americans for African Americans, has no significant social or aesthetic value. In Afrocentric terms, art must be useful in order to have aesthetic value. Thus, we have chosen to focus first on Afrocentric comic heroes in order to establish that presentations of such heroes disseminate information that encourages beneficial behavior.

Wit can be exhibited in a number of ways. Rhetorical skill is an attribute of great value in African American culture. At the very least, rhetorical ability is a survival mechanism, particularly as a means of avoiding hostile and aggressive behavior. Besides its pragmatic value, the ability to use the language imaginatively and effectively may also function to create an art form when synthesized with other elements requisite to the generation of a work of art. The ability to perform certain word games is characteristic of heroes in Afrocentric ritual drama. Verbal diplomacy that is regarded in African American culture as heroic can be exemplified by a mythological hero called the Signifying Monkey, who is the main character in a poem of the same title. Many versions exist of *The Signifying Monkey* (see Abrahams, 1970; also Hughes & Bontemps, 1958). The poem is intended to be performed orally, rather than written down and read silently. In a very real sense *The Signifying Monkey* is designed to be a theatrical performance. *The Signifying Monkey* is not a play in the Eurocentric literary sense; nevertheless, it is a dramatic experience. The traditional method of performing such African American poems as *The Signifying Monkey* involves a definite ritual form. The first step in this ritual form is to cajole the reluctant storyteller into performing. This first step is essential. The principal performer must not begin to perform *The Signifying Monkey* until he or she has provoked a virtually unanimous and relatively demonstrative communal request to do so. Prior to the storyteller's making a final commitment to actually perform the work, overt participation by the audience must be assured.

The story of *The Signifying Monkey* is a simple one, as is the entire structure (plot, character, and theme) very simple. The complex subtleties of the work grow out of the texture—the ritual theater performance techniques and the verbal appeal of the words used to elaborate upon the story as directly experienced by the audience. The scene opens with the Signifying Monkey high in a tree with nothing to do. For no particular external reason, he decides to "start some shit." About this time the "King of the Jungle" happens to pass by. The Monkey calls out to the Lion and relates to him a fallacious, malicious story about how the Elephant has recently degraded the Lion.

The individual storyteller has a certain amount of freedom to ad-lib in this segment of the presentation in order to exhibit his own virtuosity as a player of "the dozens." In this context, the storyteller must exhibit such traditional characteristics of African American performance as asymmetry of rhythm and movement and the use of repetition and empathetic response to emphasize the importance of rhythm. Also, he must stay within the rhyme scheme of the poem but is free to add to or subtract from the list of negative things that the Monkey claims the Elephant has said about the

Lion. However, the performer must necessarily make some mention, within the context of the poem, of the Lion's alleged cowardice and his inability to fight. Of course, the storyteller ought to have some pointedly negative things to say about the Lion's mother and grandmother and about the uncertainty of the identity of the Lion's father. The performer is expected to follow traditional Afrocentric performance aesthetic as exemplified by jazz and gospel musicians and preachers. Thus, the performer lengthens or shortens each segment of the performance as a direct outgrowth of the amount and intensity of the audience's participation. While the performer has the freedom to expand or abridge the details of the story, this freedom carries with it a necessity to master the material and certain performance techniques so that the behavior of the audience may significantly impact not only the style of the performance but its content as well.

The story continues with the Lion going off in a rage after the Elephant. When the Lion meets the Elephant face-to-face, the Lion confidently tells the Elephant how badly he (the Lion) is going to beat him (the Elephant). The Lion then attacks the Elephant. The Elephant wins the fight easily, beating the Lion unmercifully for some time and with considerable flamboyance. The Lion, beaten and humiliated, drags his battered and bloody carcass back through the jungle, where he is once again greeted by the Signifying Monkey from high atop a tree where he can safely "signify." The Monkey makes fun of the Lion by describing in great detail the extent of the Lion's injuries. The Monkey explains how badly the Lion has been beaten by the Elephant. The Monkey also asserts that the Lion is not really the "King of Beasts" after all. Finally, the Monkey proclaims that, given the Lion's present condition, he (the Monkey) is just liable to come down out of the tree and whip the Lion some more, just on "general principle." The Monkey enumerates the various ways he will go about giving the Lion another whipping. The Monkey is so enamored with his own performance that he begins to laugh uncontrollably at the defeated and demoralized Lion. The Monkey slips from his perch in the tree and falls unceremoniously to the ground. Like a flash, the Lion has his paw placed menacingly upon the neck of our hero.

Here begins the Monkey's apology. The Monkey explains that he did not really mean any harm by the things he said. It was all in fun. Everyone knows that the Lion is the "King of the Jungle." The Monkey proclaims that he has the utmost respect and esteem for the Lion. But the Lion is not impressed with this apology. Then the Monkey tries a new tactic. The Monkey musters an attitude of enthusiastic belligerence and yells,

Get your foot off my neck,
let my head out of the sand,
and I'll kick your ass
like a natural man.
You damned well better be
holding me down,
cause if you turn me loose,
I'll stomp your ass
six feet under the ground.

And the Monkey continues to yell threats until the Lion eventually gets so angry that

The Lion jumped back,
he was ready to fight,
but the Signifying Monkey
was already out of sight.

The Monkey quickly scrambles up into the tree, returns to his perch, and continues to signify. This time the Monkey concentrates on the theme of the Lion's stupidity.

Certain key attributes make the Signifying Monkey a heroic character. First, he has heroic magnitude. He is important because he is an allegorical representative of those who are small, weak, and oppressed. Second, he has developed innovative techniques for survival. Because he is small, weak, and oppressed, his survival depends on his cleverness and innovativeness as well as his persistence and tenacity. Third, his method of survival includes the unabashed exhibition of considerable verbal skill. Further, the Monkey manages to use his verbal skill to parry the hostile aggressiveness of the Lion in a manner that appears to be almost effortless. He exhibits wit that is clearly superior to both the physical strength and hostility of the Lion. In order to be a hero, a character of this type must exhibit all three of these characteristics to some degree.

Shine, in *The Titanic,* is another example of such a hero (Abrahams, 1970, pp. 100-103, 120-129; Hughes & Bontemps, 1958, pp. 366-367). According to African American mythology, Shine is the only African American aboard a ship that is as legendary for its exclusion of Black passengers as it is for its total failure as an example of the superiority of White technology. *Titanic* was a British steamer of the White Star Line. On the night of April 14-15, 1912, it struck an iceberg and sank approximately 1,600 miles northeast of its destination, New York City. Although the ship was widely publicized as being unsinkable, it sank on its maiden voyage across the Atlantic. Only 705 persons survived, in part because there were not enough lifeboats aboard the ship. Most of the survivors were women and children. Three different investigations of the incident fix the number who died at 1,490, 1,503, and 1,517.

Our concern here is not so much the facts surrounding the sinking of *Titanic* but the perceptions of African Americans with respect to the incident. The comic irony that African Americans perceive in this Eurocentric pathos emerges from the policy of racial discrimination in booking passage aboard *Titanic* and the widespread claims that White folks' technology had created an unsinkable ship. Subsequently, when the news of its sinking spread across the United States, Black folks knew that none of the hundreds of people presumed dead were Black. Black folks further knew that White folks' technology is sometimes not as miraculous as it is reputed to be. As Leadbelly often sang in reference to the good ship *Titanic,*

> *Jack Johnson tried to get on board,*
> *The cap'n said we ain't haulin' no coal*
> *Fare thee well, Titanic, fare thee well.*

Shine, the mythological one and only Black person aboard *Titanic,* was deep in the bowels of the ship, shoveling coal. Black Americans knew that a job shoveling coal was the only possible way for a Black person to have gotten on board the unsinkable ship on its maiden voyage. So Shine represents something much greater than a shoveler of coal—even greater than a trans-Atlantic swimmer. Shine was, from a Eurocentric point of view, the lowest man aboard the ship. Nevertheless, Shine survived in a situation where large numbers of Whites did not. But mere survival would not have been enough to make him a hero. If he had simply exhibited the physical prowess necessary for his mythological swim to safety, he would deserve to be commended, but he would not be a hero. He is a hero only because he was able to exhibit other necessary attributes of heroism. First, Shine is a representative of oppressed people. Second, he exhibits the mental discipline to not be diverted from acting in his own best interest, even when the temptations included promise of great wealth and offers of sex by and with the White captain's blonde and voluptuous daughter. Third, he exhibits verbal skill in articulating his goal.

Other examples of verbal strategy are less controversial than *The Signifying Monkey* and *The Titanic.* Overpraise is such an example. One can overpraise either himself or his opponent. Mohammed Ali provides a well-known example of overpraise of one's self. Of course, one becomes a hero only if the self overpraise turns out to be a reasonably accurate statement about one's actual performance. The reverse type of overpraise is not as familiar a ritual to most segments of American society. The goal of reverse arrogance is to disarm one's adversary by telling him that he is the greatest. Overpraise of one's opponent may appear to the causal observer as "Uncle Tomming," but it is not. Rather, the underlying theme of overpraise, as expressed through comic irony, is "Not only am I confident that you are not much of an adversary, but I also have so much disdain for your intelligence that I think you are stupid enough to believe me when I tell you that I think you are better than I am." Because this disdain remains unexpressed, it cannot be attacked by the adversary.

Sometimes, Afrocentric heroes find it necessary to behave in a self-effacing manner under extremely difficult circumstances, for the purpose of achieving their own goals. They do not demean themselves for the aid, comfort, or conciliation of their oppressor. They are playing a verbal game in order to survive. And because they outwit the oppressor with a sense of comic irony, they also survive with dignity. The word we consider the most appropriate to describe the quality that must be exhibited by such African American comic heroes is *panache*. That word is applicable to African heroes as well. Chief Kwame Ansa's written response to the ranking Portuguese emissary, who attempted to establish a permanent presence in the Gold Coast in 1482, demonstrates a sense of comic irony, wit, and the use of overpraise of the enemy. A portion of the message is quoted here:

I am not insensible to the high honour which your great master the Chief of Portugal has this day conferred upon me. His friendship I have always endeavoured to merit by the strictness of my dealings with the Portuguese, and by my constant exertions to procure an immediate lading for the vessels. But never until this day did I observe such a difference in the appearance of his subjects: they have hereto been only meanly attired, were easily contented with the commodities they received; and so far from wishing to continue in this country, were never happy until they could complete their lading, and return. Now I remark a strange difference. A great number richly dressed are anxious to be allowed to build houses, and to continue among us. Men of such eminence, conducted by a commander who from his own account seems to have descended from the God who made day and night, can never bring themselves to endure the hardships of this climate; nor would they here be able to procure any of the luxuries that abound in their own country. The passions that are common to us all men will therefore inevitably bring on disputes; and it is far preferable that both our nations should continue on the same footing they have hitherto done, allowing your ships to come and go as usual; the desires of seeing each other occasionally will preserve peace between us. (deGraft-Johnson, 1986, p. 129)

Chief Ansa's eloquence and skill with words enabled him to forestall the immediate invasion of the Portuguese as they sought another tactic to accomplish their end.

Being Black and living in the United States is an experience saturated with incongruities and ironies and, not surprisingly, African American heroes often expose incongruities and ironies. Apparently some of the ironies that African American heroes expose in African American theater are clarified and intensified by an experiential frame of reference that includes being Black and living in the United States. Much of the negative reaction to Melvin Van Peebles's motion picture *Sweet Sweetback's Baadasssss Song* has been attributed by Van Peebles to a failure of the film's detractors to perceive any difference between a Black exploitation film and a film about Black exploitation. An appreciation of Afrocentric heroes frequently depends on the audience's ability to perceive subtle differences such as those required to distinguish between a film that exploits African American people and a film that presents the exploitation of African American people. An African American audience is often able to appreciate subtleties and ironies that seem to require an Afrocentric point of view. For example, a respected White drama critic who attended the opening of an African American play titled *Dr. B. S. Black* perceived that "it uses all the broad earthy cliches that banished such performers as Stepin Fetchit and Rochester from a [White] liberal's respectability list." The White critic further observed that "this play actually is a throwback to the playlets of Bert Williams and the days when sly, shiftless blacks and their womenfolk were figures of fun." The White critic was apparently puzzled by the fact that the nearly all African American "first night audience seemed to find humor in the characters" (Coe, 1970, p. D8). The White critic was especially puzzled by the audience's enthusiastic acceptance of the production because Black cultural nationalism dominated the behavior patterns on the Howard University campus in 1970—the time and place of this opening night. Had *Dr. B. S. Black* been perceived by the African American audience as a "throwback" to sly, shiftless, stereotypical Black characters, there would undoubtedly have been an enthusiastically negative response. Nevertheless, the African American audience members laughed unreservedly at the performance because they were able to differentiate between a play that exploits African American stereotypes for comic effect and a play that presents the exploitation of African American comic stereotypes.

The Stepin Fetchit and Rochester characters to which the White critic refers are scripted in a manner that African American audiences find demeaning. The dominant trait of such characters as these is their total inability (or unwillingness) to control circumstances for their own betterment. At the decisive moment, the character willingly sacrifices himself for the good of the White folks in power. The lesson is projected that the most heroic possible behavior for an African American is to sacrifice one's own best interests in order to maintain the well-being of some White person. Or, conversely, that African American people can achieve significant success in America only as a result of the magnanimous help of one or more White people. Because they are never in control of anything important, these characters are perpetual victims. Had Stepin Fetchit, for example, been in control of his destiny, he could have exhibited all of his usual clichés of language, superstition, and mannerism and still remained an acceptable Afrocentric characterization—but that was not the case. African American audiences that found the Stepin Fetchit characterization unacceptable did so primarily because he was controlled, even manipulated, by one or more White characters, often to the obvious disadvantage of Stepin Fetchit.

Rochester, the character that Eddie Anderson played on radio and in motion pictures, was relatively more acceptable (or less unacceptable) to many Blacks. But Rochester was never really in control either. The Rochester character often created the illusion of outsmarting Jack Benny and thereby controlling his situation, which represented an improvement over the usual Stepin Fetchit character. Nevertheless, the Rochester character was always portrayed as Jack Benny's servant. As such, Jack Benny controlled the situation in all the important aspects. Whenever Rochester seemed to outsmart "Mr. Jack," Rochester was in control of some situation that had no real significance. No matter how smart Rochester may have appeared to be in some situations, the audience was never allowed to forget that Jack Benny was always the boss. Moreover, the projected behavioral ideals of the modern, intelligent, "Black," African American heroes on television and in the motion pictures are seldom more than modernizations of the original Uncle Tom, who is considered a degrading character within the framework of African American culture because there is no sense of comic irony in his verbal diplomacy. He takes himself too seriously. But Uncle Tom's behavior would not be nearly so degrading if he did not possess so much inner sincerity in his willingness to subjugate his own best interests in order to better serve the needs, even the whims, of "his White folks."

An Afrocentric hero in the United States must behave in a manner that is independent and external to the expectations of the White establishment. So, as characters in plays by African American playwrights are encountered, the key question must constantly be raised: Who is really in control? Failure to control one's own destiny constitutes failure to achieve heroic proportion. However, a character may provoke laughter and still achieve the status of hero. African American playwrights have provided many important comic heroes in their plays. Some of the most memorable characters are Joe Smothers in *Strivers Row* by Abram Hill; Jesse B. Semple (Simple) in *Simply Heavenly* by Langston Hughes; Mrs. Grace Love in *Contribution* and Charlene in *Idabelle's Fortune,* both by Ted Shine; Rev. Purlie Victorious Judson in *Purlie Victorious* by Ossie Davis; and Tommy in *Wine in the Wilderness* by Alice Childress. Tommy is an African American woman, as are Grace Love and Charlene. A significant number of the heroes in plays by African American playwrights are female. This female presence is true not only of the plays that grow out of a sense of comic irony but is also true of serious plays. The comic and the serious in African American drama are not always clearly and sharply separated. Comic heroes sometimes provoke tears, and serious heroes sometimes provoke laughter. Comedies, as well as serious dramas, have important characteristics that have evolved out of African American mythology and out of the values of African American mythology. African American mythology projects heroic ideals that influence the behavior of Black people in American society.

Some of these heroic ideals are vividly presented in a comedy called *Strivers Row* (Hill, 1939/1991) that was first presented in 1940 in Harlem. Since its premiere, productions of *Strivers Row* have been staged in several cities across the United States. Throughout the 1980s *Strivers Row* continued to provide one of the most popular comic characters of the African American theater. This contention is based on the attendance and the responses of African American theatergoers for more than 40 years. Mr. Joe Smothers, better known as Joe the Jiver, makes the following speech as he enters the Van Striven home where a debutante ball is in progress:

[To the cab driver] "Scram Joe meter, you an' that gas eater can't beat me for no change, I'm no Sam from Alabam'. [To the young African American man who has answered the door] Twist that slammer, Gatemouth. That cat may be from the deep south. That nickel-snatching taxi driver. [To the guests at the Van Striven's] What's happening, folks, I'm Joe, the Jiver!"

When Mrs. Dolly Van Striven objects to his presence at her daughter's debutante ball, Joe responds with

"Don't play me cheap, I ain't no Bo Peep. Let me get you straight, 'fore it is too late. I'm here to stay, so on your way. [To the audience] That chick comes on like an Eskimo."

Joe the Jiver uses many of the tactics that are exemplary of traditional African American comic heroes. Joe has the requisite verbal skills to be a comic hero. He uses his verbal skills and his flair for comic irony to express his monumental contempt for the Eurocentric middle-class values and status symbols of the African American inhabitants of Strivers Row. Verbal skill alone does not make a comic hero. However, Joe the Jiver's verbal skills also function to encourage African American people who see the play to be less concerned with the creation of artificial barriers of social status and their symbols and to focus instead on relationships with other individuals by using traditional Afrocentric standards of human worth as the basis for those relationships. Joe's visual and verbal style as well as the magnitude of his usefulness as an advocate of Afrocentric values contribute to the enthusiastic attachment of audience identities to the character of Joe the Jiver. Joe also exhibits sufficient imperfection to avoid the general reluctance of an audience to identify with one who exhibits perfection. Even though he causes identity bonding and exhibits magnitude and verbal skill, a conclusive determination as to whether or not Joe Smothers is a legitimate African American comic hero remains a function of whether or not he is in control. Joe Smothers finds himself in a situation in which social status is regarded as necessary to survive. Joe has no social status. Nevertheless, he manages to accomplish his goals and establish his personal worth on his own terms. Joe Smothers overcomes and retains control of an environment that is structured to ensure his inferiority.

Strivers Row exhibits another characteristic that is important to a thorough understanding of the concept of control as it relates to African American heroes. The play has no White characters to provide a White frame of reference or point of view. The issues that are addressed in the play are viewed by the playwright as issues that Blacks must address for themselves and that Blacks can and must solve for themselves. An African American character cannot be a hero if his behavior never rises above the level of reacting to the behavior of Whites. African American heroes must exhibit initiative as well as control. Although some of the other plays mentioned hereafter have White characters, the African American heroes in these plays act on their own initiative in order to control their own destinies. The character Purlie Victorious Judson, in *Purlie Victorious* by Ossie Davis, is a hero that is similar to Joe the Jiver in many ways. Although his verbal skills are more characteristic of an African American preacher than of a secular African American hero, he too has the ability to use his verbal skills to control a situation that is designed to victimize him. Purlie Victorious Judson succeeds in accomplishing his goals on his own terms in an environment that is designed to make him a victim. Further, he does so with wit and with panache.

Some African American women characters succeed in accomplishing their goals, on their own terms, in an environment that is designed to make them victims. Examples of such heroines are Ted Shine's characters Charlene in *Idabelle's Fortune* and Mrs. Grace Love in *Contribution* and Tommy in Alice Childress's *Wine in the Wilderness*. These female characters differ from the males who have been discussed with regard to the way wit and panache are exhibited. The exhibition of wit and panache by these heroines is more subtle. After all, these women must overcome an environment that is sexist as well as racist. In the case of Tommy, her wit is disarmingly natural. Charlene and Mrs. Love carefully contrive their wit to disarm people. Charlene, who is a maid, and Mrs. Love, who is a cook, deliberately create the illusion that they are old-fashioned, stereotypical, "mammy" types for the benefit of the White characters who observe them. This subterfuge enables each of these women to accomplish her goals in an extremely hostile environment. Moreover, these women exhibit the same type of stereotypical characteristics that African American people often find unacceptable in such characters as Beulah of radio drama and Mammy and Prissy in the film *Gone with the Wind*. However, the characters created by Shine and Childress differ in that they possess the key factors of initiative and control. Despite their circumstances having placed them in a status that makes them extremely vulnerable to the control of others, Tommy, Charlene, and Mrs. Love control their respective situations.

An additional significant example of an African American comic hero is Jesse B. Semple (Simple), the leading character in the play *Simply Heavenly* by Langston Hughes. Prior to writing this play, Langston Hughes published several books and many articles in *Chicago Defender* that featured this character. The play is reminiscent of Langston Hughes's newspaper column and subsequent books in the same serialistic style. The play has an episodic story line held together by the Simple character and the music of David Martin, which grows spontaneously from the action and the locale of the play.

Simple is the prototypical Harlemite. His most extraordinary quality is his ordinariness. Relationships with women, the cost of living, landladies, taxes, alcoholic beverages, and the U.S. Army are Simple's catastrophes and the subjects of his frequent barroom oratory. But the thing about Simple that strengthens his identity bonding to heroic proportions is that he recognizes the ironies of American racism and how it functions as a barrier to his aspirations. As Simple explains it, "something's always happening to a colored man!" (Hughes, 1959, p. 62). Simple is not a gangster or a sports or show-business personality or a super-successful professional man. He does not drive an expensive car or wear flashy clothes. Neither is he a pathetic victim of external circumstances. These stereotypes are well known in the White world. Simple is concerned with the ordinary things of life. He is disturbed by the fact that Blacks are never mentioned in the newspapers in connection with any nonsensational, positive, or beneficial activity. "Unless we commit murder, robbery or rape, or are being chased by a mob, do we get on the front page, or hardly the back?" Simple asks. He points out that he has read about Karl Krubelowski and Giovanni Battini and Heinrich Armpriester all seeing flying saucers, but never about Roosevelt Johnson or Henry Washington, or anyone that even "sounds like a Negro," seeing one (pp. 30-31).

African American people laugh first at the things that make them different from Whites in order to eliminate or reduce the hurt and indignity that result from ridicule of those differences by the oppressor group. When African American people experience this indignity and hurt in response to negative institutional recognition of racial differences, African American people do not generally regard the differences as indicative of their alleged racial inferiority. Rather, the frequency, force, and magnitude of negative assertions by White people and White institutions become overwhelming. Simple frequently makes statements that describe the plight of African

Americans. For example, he says, "I been caught in some kind of a riffle ever since I been Black" (p. 62). But Simple is articulating an irony that functions very effectively in the identity bonding process. The irony is that the victim of the act of oppression, rather than the perpetrator, gets the blame. The "fault" that causes the victim to get the blame is that the victim is Black. No African American is completely able to escape this irony. Therefore, African Americans can readily identify with Simple in this respect. And, in his own very ordinary way, he succeeds. Despite Simple's awareness of the oppression of African Americans, he does not pity himself, and he seeks to control his own destiny—two key factors that enable African Americans to identify with Simple.

First produced as a play in 1957, *Simply Heavenly* is based on *Simple Takes a Wife,* a book published in 1953. So the social issues that are treated with such comic effectiveness are issues of the early 1950s. Within that context, Simple expresses both pride in his Blackness and confidence in himself. He asserts that in the newly integrated Army he would "rise right to the top today and be a general." Further, he insists that he wants to command a White regiment from Mississippi. He goes on to explain that he would "do like all the other generals do, and stand way back on a hill somewhere and look through my spy-glasses and say, 'Charge on! Mens, charge on!'" After his imaginary White troops have succeeded in battle under his leadership, he will assemble them to forgive them for their past racial transgressions and present them with medals for bravery. He concludes his speech by asking his White troops to stop fighting him and join him in a drink to celebrate their victory (p. 72). As with all Afrocentric comic heroes, Simple provides an illustration of how African American people can come to terms with hostile environments, control their circumstances, and achieve their goals. Comic heroes recognize the incongruities and ironies of their environment and are able to laugh at them. Thus, comic heroes enhance the abilities of those who benefit from their example to maintain a positive self-image.

Sometimes in dramatic literature we are confronted with a heroic character whose struggle to overcome a hostile environment demands the endurance of pain and suffering. These heroes are usually referred to as tragic heroes. There may be moments of comic irony and the character may exhibit wit, but the route to achieving his or her goals leads to a confrontation with the forces that are preventing the achievement of these goals. The essential differences between comic and tragic heroes are seen in the way they deal with efforts to prevent them from accomplishing their goals.

Tragic heroes confront the forces that stand in their way, whereas comic heroes successfully navigate a route to their goals that avoids the struggle and suffering that usually accompany confrontation.

A recurring phenomenon among African American people in the United States has generated a type of African American hero in theater and other art forms. This African American hero is an individual who has faced American racism all of his or her life and who suddenly and sometimes without apparent overt provocation gets tired of trying to cope with the overwhelming effects of racism. This African American hero makes a decision and takes a stand. He or she makes this commitment with the full realization that to take a stand against racism usually results in death or some barbaric form of punishment, such as castration for males or rape for females. But this hero says, "I don't mind dying," and means it. In real life, such a hero may or may not actually die as a result of taking a stand against racism. Mrs. Rosa Parks must have fully expected, if not to die, at least to be thrown in jail and subjected to physical abuse when she refused to give up her seat to a White passenger on a bus in Montgomery, Alabama, in 1955 and thereby initiated a series of events that precipitated the Montgomery bus boycott.

Most African Americans in the United States with some sanity and dignity remaining have said, on some occasion, to themselves, "I don't mind dying," and really meant it. But the sincere expression of the phrase "I don't mind dying" does not make one a tragic hero. A decision to confront the forces that stand in one's way does not, in and of itself, generate dignity. Dignity does not automatically result from pain and suffering, even when the pain and suffering are totally unjustified. However, dignity is undoubtedly easier to recognize when pain and suffering have been unjustly inflicted. One does not have to have much strength of character to maintain one's dignity in an environment of comfort and convenience. But one whose dignity prevails while enduring pain and suffering evidences a strength of character that may be regarded as heroic when it is accompanied by other elements that a hero must exhibit. Members of the audience must identify with a hero in a manner that is dictated by their values and to an extent that causes them to regard themselves as connected to the hero. A hero must have one or more characteristics that are of sufficient magnitude for his or her achievements to rise above the personal. A hero makes a decision to overcome an obstacle in an effort to control his or her destiny and to survive.

African American people in the United States exist in an environment of institutional racism that is not generally recognized as such by those who do not have to suffer its consequences on a continual basis. Institutional racism in the United States provides an environment of pain and suffering that demands considerable strength of character to simply survive with one's dignity intact. Appropriately, we reiterate that in the tradition of African American culture, finding a way to survive is an important element of heroism. When African American heroes say "I don't mind dying," they are not seeking to achieve martyrdom. They do not wish to die or to suffer for a cause. They simply recognize the inevitability of their pain and suffering within the context of a society that systematically oppresses African American people. Their strongest impulse is always to survive. But their survival includes a strong desire to achieve some reasonable degree of human dignity not only for themselves but for their group. Sometimes, the struggle for human dignity for oneself and for one's group overrides the impulse for individual biological survival.

This kind of African American hero does not want to provoke a violent reaction that causes pain and suffering. He simply recognizes that he exists within a societal structure that is programmed to inflict pain and suffering and possibly to cause a violent death to any member of his group who overtly refuses to accept subhuman status. In this context, suffering is not inflicted by the gods or as a result of some internal character flaw. The suffering is inflicted by institutional racism through White oppressors or the non-White agents of those oppressors. The African American hero's choice, then, is whether or not to assert his human dignity in an environment that has been structured to overwhelm him with denials of that dignity. When such an African American hero is presented as a character in a play, he must reflect some important priorities and values of African American culture through his actions. The simple assertion of self-worth in the face of White oppression is not enough.

Some important African American heroes are in serious plays by African American playwrights. A few of these heroes are well known by a broader American public—the Younger family in *A Raisin in the Sun,* for example. An African American play that has achieved some success before White audiences may still be an important and worthwhile play by African American standards. The fact that White audiences find a play with African American characters acceptable does not guarantee that the play is or should be unacceptable to African American audiences. However, on numerous occasions African American audiences overwhelmingly found a character to be demeaning while White audiences found the same character quite acceptable. As a result, some African American people may be suspicious of any play with African American characters that acquires the enthusiastic support of White audiences.

In the case of *A Raisin in the Sun*, African American audiences generally see a positive image of an African American family dealing with issues that are important to African American people. The central issue is the continuation of the family as a unit within an environment that is structured to oppress and exploit that unit. This central issue raises several specific questions. The playwright, Lorraine Hansberry, raises the question of abortion as it relates to African American values. The question of who should handle the family finances is discussed. But who owns the insurance money is different from the question of who is head of the household. The quest for higher education is another issue that is important to African American audiences, who often find validation for their own decisions in the Younger family's decision to sacrifice for Beneatha to become a medical doctor. Implicit in the play is the idea that both of the adult generations of the Younger family regard higher education as an important mechanism not only for the financial rewards that accrue to the recipient of the education but especially for the nonfinancial rewards associated with the delivery of desperately needed professional services to African American people. Another issue that affects the continuation of the family as a unit is security for the family. The generations differ as to the details of what constitutes security. However, all members of the household are working to achieve it. The broader theme that brings all the issues together into a significant whole is the concern of all for the progress of the race. Strategies may differ from one member of the Younger household to the next, but they all desire to see the race progress.

Walter Younger grapples with the issues facing the Younger family and, in doing so, emerges as a hero. Walter is the only character in the play who changes as a result of self-realization. He is able to rise above his personal strivings and relate to larger issues. Walter has not been generally regarded as a hero by White theater critics. The principal difficulty they have in recognizing him as both the central character of the play and as a hero seems to be that Walter, a virile Black male, poses a threat, whereas Lena does not. Lena is usually played by a woman who is visually reminiscent of the mammy stereotype, although the character is not a stereotypical mammy character. White audiences and critics seem to obtain comfort from seeing her as a mammy figure. In contrast, Walter is a young Black man who is both angry and virile. White audiences and White critics seem to assuage themselves by diminishing Walter's role in the overall scheme of things. By their viewing Lena as a bossy old woman, they are relieved of the disquieting prospect of recognizing Walter Lee Younger as a force with which to be reckoned. This avoidance of Walter as a representative of angry and virile Black males is accomplished by focusing on the "scientific discovery" by White sociologists that African American families, especially poor ones, are inevitably ruled by matriarchal figures. The tradition of matrilineal succession, and the respect and power that women enjoy as a result, is very definitely a significant part of our African cultural heritage. But to see this play from the White sociologists' point of view of "the poor Black matriarchal family" is to miss the essence of the play. Although the play is undisputedly about the entire Younger family, the central character and the head of the Younger household is Walter.

Two important factors in *A Raisin in the Sun* seem to go unnoticed by those who regard this as a play about Lena. First, Walter's father and Lena's husband, the head of the Younger household for more than 35 years, has recently died. Most families require a period of adjustment following such a trauma. Second, Walter respects his mother both as mother and as the elder of the family. Consequently, Walter's behavior is comparable to that of an African chief who must listen to the elders before important decisions are made. The African chief does not have to follow the elders' advice, but he must listen to it. Likewise, Walter must listen to his mother's advice, although he is not obliged to follow it. Even Lena Younger herself states, at the end of Act II, scene 2, "I'm telling you to be the head of this family from now on like you supposed to be." Somehow, though, the respect that Lena receives from Walter and his wife, Ruth, and demands from her daughter, Beneatha, as mother and elder is misconstrued by Whites as reducing Walter's status in the family.

The concept that Lena Younger's rule prevails in the Younger household has little to do with the content of the play and a great deal to do with prior assumptions, sometimes known as prejudices. As we have already mentioned, Walter is the only character in this play who changes as a result of self-realization. In addition, a consensus among White Americans asserts they have conclusive scientific proof that the controlling force in virtually every African American household is a Black woman. Therefore, when an African American woman is portrayed as strong of body, mind, and opinion, Whites males immediately conclude that she is the head of the household and has emasculated any and all males in that household. Any suggestion of respect by an adult male family member is assumed to be indicative of subservience. Just as White males seem to regard any assertion of strength or independence by an African American male as an implicit assertion of White male weakness, any indication of strength or independence by a woman seems to be regarded by White males as a threat to their own strength or independence.

The economic and social forces of White male oppression have caused an unfortunately large percentage of African American households in which there is no regularly employed adult male in residence. The absence of a male breadwinner in many African American homes has resulted in the inaccurate assumption that African American values generate households dominated solely by women. Although this lack of male presence is a terrible social problem rooted in the economic exploitation of African American males, it has very little to do with the content of *A Raisin in the Sun* because the Younger household does have an employed, adult male in residence. Any connection between the play *A Raisin in the Sun* and the phenomenon of African American households without an adult, male wage earner is a connection that is largely created by the prejudice of the observer.

The wording of Joseph Walker's (1973) dedication page to his play *The River Niger* suggests his concern about the stereotypical dismissal of the role of African American men in the family: "The play is dedicated to my mother and father and to highly underrated black daddies everywhere." *The River Niger* is another serious play with an African American hero who communicates positive values for African American people. The hero of the play, Johnny Williams, comes to the realization that he has accomplished just about as much as he can reasonably expect to accomplish. Further, he knows that he does not have much longer to live; therefore, he sacrifices himself to save his son. Survival of the family and progress of the race represent higher priorities for African American heroes than the "save your own skin no matter what" concept of survival. The ideal of freedom that is sometimes expressed by African artists suggests that a man does not have the "freedom" to let his brother go without food and shelter when he has enough of both to share.

A play by William Branch titled *A Medal for Willie* presents an African American woman who embodies the characteristics of heroism. Written in 1951, the play centers around the posthumous awarding of the Distinguished Service Cross to Corporal Willie D. Jackson. The act of bravery that earned Willie the medal also cost him his life. His mother goes to the

Booker T. Washington High School Auditorium to accept the medal. Mrs. Jackson is a quiet, hardworking African American woman who raised a son and a daughter in a small southern town. But Mrs. Jackson's son went off to fight in Korea because he could not get a job in his hometown. Now Willie is dead and a General has come to town to present her with Willie's medal. The Mayor and the Superintendent of Schools have come to the Black high school, too.

Mrs. Jackson is clearly in an environment that is structured to place her in a subservient role. She is expected to behave exactly as these White male figures of authority tell her to behave. They have even written an acceptance speech for her. However, as Mrs. Jackson begins to read the speech, she chokes on the hypocrisy of the words and she refuses to read the prepared speech. Instead, she eloquently expresses her anger over the injustices suffered by her son Willie at the hands of the White establishment. To show her contempt for the military symbol, she rejects the medal. She tells the General to take the medal back to Washington and "give it to the ones who send boys like my Willie all over the world to die for some kinda freedom and democracy they always gets the leavin's of!" (Branch, 1951/1971, pp. 470-471). Mrs. Jackson exemplifies many of the heroic characteristics often found in African American mythology. Her acceptance speech shows the process of soul searching that serious heroes undergo. Her actions exhibit those values and ideals that African American people regard as heroic. She summons courage to garner control over her environment. Mrs. Jackson, like other African American heroes, maintains a sense of self in the midst of a hostile environment.

From the *Signifying Monkey* to Mrs. Jackson, communication skills and exhibitions of bravery and courage are the hallmarks of heroic behavior. African American poets and playwrights who create Afrocentric heroes, both comic and serious, create characters who enable African Americans to perceive the ironies and realities of their circumstances. Additionally, these characters transmit the style, the aspirations, the values, and the survival skills of African American culture.

References

Abrahams, R. D. (1970). *Deep down in the jungle* (Rev. ed.). Chicago: Aldine.
Branch, W. (1971). *A Medal for Willie* [Play]. In W. King & R. Milner (Eds.), *Black drama* (pp. 439-473). New York: New American Library. (Original work by Branch published 1951)

Coe, R. (1970, October 30). "Soul" plays. *Washington Post,* p. D8.

deGraft-Johnson, J. C. (1986). *African glory.* Baltimore: Black Classic Press.

Hill, A. (1991). *Strivers Row* [Play]. In J. V. Hatch & L. Hamalian (Eds.), *The roots of African America drama* (pp. 359-445). Detroit: Wayne State University Press. (Original work by Hill published 1939)

Hughes, L. (1959). *Simply Heavenly* [Play]. New York: Dramatists Play Service, Inc.

Hughes, L., & Bontemps, A. (Eds.). (1958). *Book of Negro folklore.* New York: Dodd, Mead.

Walker, J. A. (1973). *The River Niger* [Play]. New York: Hill & Wang.

Representing African American Women in Hollywood Movies

11

An African-Conscious Analysis

M. Patricia E. Hilliard-Nunn

As a little girl growing up in Monrovia, Liberia, movies were a special treat for me. I believe that the first film I ever saw was *My Fair Lady* (1964), a movie about a White woman who sheds her working-class identity to integrate into the world of the British upper class. Although I was in an African country, the movies that were distributed there, like *Tarzan the Ape Man* (1932), represented Africans and Africans in the diaspora as immoral, cultureless, brainless savages. I never saw a film that presented Black people, let alone Black little girls, as humans. To this day, mainstream images of Black people have not significantly changed. After years of raping the natural resources on the African continent, one of the few things that the West has given back—motivated by a desire to earn profit—has been warped movies that support White supremacy.

Problems associated with mainstream representations of Black women have been examined by scholars, laypeople, and others. But after years of film criticism, film effects studies, and stereotype analyses, film and communication theories have not converged with Hollywood practices to foster the development of inclusive, diverse, and accurate representations of Black women. Fortunately, there are articles and books that examine, in whole or in part, movie representations and text-reading practices of Black women (i.e., Bobo, 1989; Bogle, 1989; Donalson, 1982; hooks, 1992;

Jones, 1991; Larkin, 1988; Wallace, 1992). Because these works are important, more studies addressing the many relationships between film and Black women (e.g., effects, filmmakers, employment, actresses, writers, representation) are needed.

Approach

This chapter focuses on issues related to Black female identity as presented in several Hollywood movies. I use textual analysis and situate myself as an African-conscious text reader/critic. I apply historical critical method to analyze the way that selected Hollywood movies from the past and present represent three specific aspects of Black female identity.

Definitions

Readers of this chapter should understand how I define certain concepts. These concepts are African consciousness, Black female identity, and Hollywood film.

African consciousness describes my centering as an African[1] female critic. Although born in America, I acknowledge the Black/African experience as being unique and consider African historical, political, cultural, social, and economic realities as relevant when observing and responding to people, places, and things. As an African-conscious observer, I believe that all movies are functional—whether they are considered "just entertainment" or not—and can have a positive and/or a negative influence on peoples' perceptions of and interactions in the world. I pay close attention to how movies represent Black people, Black history, and Black culture.

As an African-conscious critic, I point out where I see movies contributing to *Isfet,* a Kemetic (Egyptian) word that can be translated as "disorder," "imbalance," or "injustice," among others (Hilliard, 1993, p. 15). I feel that movies, like other forms of culture, should contribute to *Maat,* a Kemetic word that can be translated as "truth," "justice," "righteousness," or "balance," among others (Hilliard, 1993, p.15). When viewing a movie I ask,

- Given the context in which African people find themselves in our society, what does this film mean?
- Does this movie blatantly ignore, lie about, or disrespect African people, history, culture, or political realities?

- Can this movie have an effect on how African people see themselves and are treated in society?

Artists have the freedom to create what we choose, but we must remember that moviegoers have the freedom to be critical spectators.

Black female identity means Black women's healthy or unhealthy identification with themselves as Black women in a White supremacist, patriarchal society where these essentialist categories have "real" economic, social, political, and cultural consequences. There are many facets to Black female identity, but this study specifically surveys how Black women's physical appearance, Africanness, and sexuality are constructed in Hollywood films.

The final concept that must be clarified is *Hollywood film*. The body of films produced in the American film production system are often referred to as " 'mainstream films,' 'Hollywood movies,' or 'classical Hollywood cinema' " (Hilliard-Nunn, 1993). Hollywood films have a distinct style (Bordwell, Staiger, & Thompson, 1985) and the primary concern of Hollywood film communicators is making money (Jarvie, 1978; Jowett & Linton, 1989). Filmmakers use old film formulas that contain codes the majority of people in society desire and are familiar with. Garth Jowett and James Linton (1989) say,

> It is generally agreed that mass media are capable of "reflecting" society because they are forced by their commercial nature to provide a level of content which will guarantee the widest possible acceptance by the largest possible audience. Thus, there is a definite tendency to create a product which consists of familiar themes, clearly identifiable characters, and understandable resolutions. (p. 83)

In America, a wide audience means one that is White, young, and predominantly male. In an effort to attract the "wide audience," Hollywood film communicators have presented and continue to present less than desirable, and often racist, images of non-White people (Bogle, 1989; Shaheen, 1984).

African Women in Hollywood Movies

Representations of Black women in Hollywood movies have generally consisted of a few stereotypical character types that are modified to fit the social and political climate of the day. Some of the labels used to describe these character types are contented slave, mammy, sexual exotic, exotic primitive, and tragic mulatto. I find that most people can easily identify stereotypical characterizations of Black women in older movies—for example, the Stoneman's maid/mammy in *The Birth of a Nation* (1915)—but find it difficult to identify stereotypical characters in more recent movies—for example, the maid/mammy in *Driving Miss Daisy* (1989). Some of the newer characterizations are merely updated versions of older ones. People are often so happy to see any representation of Black women—or Black men—on the screen that they are not critical spectators and often accept any image, no matter how degrading.

I do not suggest that Black women must always be represented in movies as perfect, infallible people. I do suggest that Black women should be cast in more roles and that these roles should be diverse and complex. A mammy/maid character is not inherently bad but can appear so when it is one of the few roles that Black women repeatedly play in mainstream movies and because of the narrow, elementary way in which they are presented.

The Absence of African American Women in Hollywood Movies

Black women are generally invisible in mainstream films. This is one of the reasons why *Waiting to Exhale* (1995) was so popular. There were Exhale parties, Exhale discussion groups, and so on. The sad fact is that, with the exception of *Waiting to Exhale* and a handful of other movies, Black women have not been cast as lead characters in mainstream movies. This is disturbing, as 1991 marked the year of the so-called Black film explosion. At that time, article after article commented on how more Black-themed, Black-directed films would be made now that Blacks had a "foot in the door." But three years later, in 1994, they were still rarely found as main characters. In most movies that include Black women, they play supporting characters and could just as well be a part of the lighting fixtures on the production set. Their characters are important only because of how they support the White characters and, in newer movies, the Black male characters.

The absence of Black women on the silver screen reflects the institutionalized absence of Black women in other mainstream media like television, news magazines, and school texts. The Screen Actors Guild (SAG) statistics on ethnic and gender employment indicate that in 1990 Black women were cast in 619, or 9%, of all female lead performer roles, whereas White women were cast in 6,321, or 87%, of these roles (NAACP, 1991). Further, Black men were cast in 1,581, or 12%, of the male lead performer roles, whereas White men were cast in 10,806, or 84%, of these roles (NAACP, 1991). The statistics on lead performer roles for other people of color are much lower than those of Blacks (NAACP, 1991). Because these SAG statistics combine employment percentages for the areas of film, videotape, advertising, stage, and theater, the statistics on Black employ-ment in film would actually be lower.

In referring to the absence of Black females in movies, I refer to us not being seen at all, but there is another kind of "absence"—when Black women's appearance in a film is totally out of context. This lack of context occurs when Black women are present in a movie to provide a shallow, symbolic referent to set the mood or give flavor to one or more scenes. It also occurs when Black women are present as "props" to complement other characters.

One scene in Oliver Stone's skillfully crafted *JFK* (1991) provides one of the many examples of how Black women are used to symbolically set the tone and "spice up" a scene. The scene opens as the main character, attorney Garrison (who is fighting to prosecute a man that he believes to be an accomplice in the John F. Kennedy assassination) pulls up to a restaurant in his car. A Black woman standing on a corner and dressed in a tight-fitting, shiny gold dress is casually talking to some men. She spots Garrison and struts over to him as he exits his car, saying, "Mister Garrison. How are you? You remember me?" Garrison says, "I certainly do. Did you vote for me?" The woman answers, "I certainly did, sir." She then reminds him that they had sung together in the past. Garrison says, "Yeah! We sang together," and in unison they sing "you're the cream in my coffee." Garrison continues walking toward the restaurant as his assistant gently holds the woman, who is still following him, back. It is not clear where this Black woman, who has not appeared earlier in the film and does not appear again, comes from or how she contributes to pushing the story forward. Judging from the activity in the background, which includes a few cos-tumed people walking down a street, she has been watching a parade—perhaps a daytime Mardi Gras parade. To the African-conscious spectator, it appears that the woman was placed to add some color to the movie. The woman appears on a street corner dressed suggestively and is overly anxious to approach Garrison. Like the dramatic lighting, the woman is placed to set a raunchy carnival mood. This is especially likely given the movie's setting in New Orleans, one place with a history of sexual licentiousness between White men and Black women dating back to the octoroon balls of antebellum times.

The brief, symbolic presence of a Black woman as an evil force was evident in *The Golden Child* (1986), Eddie Murphy's film about a social worker who helps a Tibetan woman search for a little Tibetan boy who has been kidnapped by people eager to use the boy's magical powers for evil purposes. Eddie Murphy is the only Black character in the movie except for a Black woman who periodically appears in his nightmares. The nightmares feature a montage of disturbing images. One recurring image in the montage is a close-up of a Black woman wearing heavy makeup. The woman's face is contorted, and harsh colors on her face and behind her, combined with the sound of sinister laughter, underscore the point that she is present to represent evil, devilish forces.

Terminator 2: Judgment Day (1991), which stars Arnold Schwarzenegger and Linda Hamilton, is about a White female (Sarah) and a White male (actually a good "terminator" sent to protect Sarah's son, John Conners).

> John Conners must live to become an important military genius in the future. Another element of this movie traces the adventures of the good terminator, Sarah, and John as they locate and stop the creator of Skynet, a microprocessor that has the potential to destroy the world if it is fully developed. The creator of this microprocessor happens to be a Black man (Miles Bennett Dyson). (Hilliard-Nunn, 1993, pg. 36)

The movie includes only six Black men (mostly extras) and one Black woman.

The one Black woman in *T2: Judgment Day* is Dyson's wife. She is in a scene where the White woman, Sarah, opens fire on her house in an effort to murder her husband. When Sarah arrives at the plush house, she blows out all of the windows and wounds Dyson. The Black woman cries, "Oh Jesus, Miles!" as she runs to her husband's side. Sarah storms into the house, where we hear the only words she says to the Black woman when she yells "Get to the floor, bitch! Fucking down now!" The Black woman hustles to the floor in horror as the White woman towers over the whole Black family aiming an M16-like gun at them. Interestingly, this film places the Black male—and through him the Black family—as the symbolic destroyer of the planet or the creator of death. Conversely, it places the White woman, White man, and the White boy—the White family—as the saviors of the planet. The Black woman as individual, as wife, and as mother is presented as the partner/supporter of the creator of death. This is an ironic twist, as in America, White women, although victims of patriarchy, have historically supported and benefited from White supremacy—a system of oppression that influences sexism, environmental decay, war, racism, homelessness, and other things that threaten to destroy the world. Further, numerous Black people and specifically many unknown and known African American women have written, organized, and risked their lives in the fight to save the world.

Presenting few or no images of Black women may be more acceptable than constantly presenting the same oppressive ones. As shown above, even the small, symbolic presence of Black women in mainstream films can be degrading.

African American Female Identity in Hollywood Movies

In this section I examine how Hollywood movies represent three selected areas of Black female identity: physical appearance, African consciousness, and sexuality.

Physical Appearance

Standards of beauty have been created and reinforced by the media for years, and Hollywood films have played no small role in this process. Women and men of all races, nationalities, religions, and economic groups would, to different degrees, imitate the hairstyles, makeup, walks, and actions of their favorite stars. In our capitalistic, image-conscious society, certain "looks" for women are accepted as "beautiful," while others are considered less attractive or ugly. By Hollywood's standards, the ultimate, beautiful woman is young and White with long blonde hair, blue eyes, a thin body, and sharp facial features. With few exceptions, most Black actresses cast in Hollywood movies do not have the natural, untampered physical characteristics of most Black women: dark or medium-brown skin, short, curly/nappy black hair, thick noses and lips, full legs, full hips, and full buttocks.

Darker-skinned actresses like Cheryl Lee Ralph have, at times, found it difficult to find work (Horowitz, 1991). Ken Parrish Perkins (1992) reported that Charles Burnett, the director of *To Sleep With Anger* (1990), was asked to replace Cheryl Lee Ralph because her legs were thought to be too big: "Ralph wasn't accepted until Burnett threatened to abandon the project" (p. 53). Historically, lighter-skinned actresses with European features like Freddie Washington, Nina Mae McKinney, Dorothy Dandridge, Lena Horne, Lonette McKee, and Halle Berry have fared better—though slightly so—than their darker-skinned sisters with more African-like features. Still, neither light-skinned actresses nor dark-skinned actresses have the quantity or quality of acting opportunities that White women have.

Movies have contributed to society's devaluation of natural Black female characteristics. Both film and television communicators have participated in this process by using Black actresses, and Black and White male actors dressed in women's clothes and makeup, to misrepresent Black women. An early film titled *The Masher* (1907) is one example of Hollywood's early obsession with presenting Black women as ugly and undesirable. In this film, a White man anxious to meet a woman keeps getting rejected by them (Bogle, 1989). Finally, he meets a veiled woman (played by a White actor in blackface) willing to spend time with him. When he lifts her veil, however, he learns that she is Black. The film proceeds in slapstick fashion as the woman chases him. The film fosters the belief that Black women are so desperate to meet a man that we will go to extraordinary lengths to chase and capture one.

Some movies subtly hold up White women as models of comparison to Black women. This is shown in two different versions of the movie *King Kong*. The first version of *King Kong* (1933), a film that was significant for its use of stop-motion photography, has a scene where a group of White men and a blonde White woman, played by Fay Wray, are exploring an island when they happen on a group of Black people (some White actors in blackface makeup) in the midst of a wedding ceremony. When the Black chief spots the White woman, he is so taken by her that he offers to trade six of the Black women in his tribe for her. The remake of the film, made more than 40 years later, was no less blatant in its comment on the lack of worth of Black women and the suggestion that women are to be traded. In the 1976 version of *King Kong*, the same scene remains, but the director goes even further. This time the chief offers the White men seven Black women for the one White woman (this time played by Jessica Lange), and there is a shot of the seven Black women, adorned in their tribal dress, walking toward their chief ready to be traded. There are many problems with this scene—as well as with the whole movie—but two significant problems that stand out are these: (a) The film presents Black people as believers that women are property to be bought and sold, and (b) it suggests that one blonde woman is worth seven Black women.

Younger and older Black women viewing films like *King Kong* may feel that to be accepted in society they must look like a White woman. Many people are aware of Kenneth Clark's famous "doll" experiment where he found that most of the Black children in his study showed a preference for a White doll and rejected a brown doll (Clark & Clark, 1958). This shows that even at a young age some Blacks are socialized (not only by film) to believe that White is better. Of the Black obsession with color consciousness, clinical psychologist Na'im Akbar (1984) says,

> Even today there is an unnatural equation of Caucasian physical features with beauty, intelligence, authority, and so forth. A disproportionate number of professional, educated and so-called "beautiful" African-Americans have prominently Caucasian features. There are still vast sums of money spent yearly on skin lighteners, hair straighteners and wigs, in the frantic effort to change African-American physical features. (p. 32)

The pressure to look more Caucasian is even greater for Black actresses working in a business where having the "right look" means the difference between being employed and unemployed.

Although movies have always been filled with African cultural elements (i.e., music, dress styles, slang, etc.), in American culture, Black physical features, on Black women, have never been popular. It is now fashionable for White actresses to have full lips (i.e., Michelle Pfeiffer, Julia Roberts, Kim Basinger) just as cornrows/braided hair became more fashionable and acceptable (even among Black women) only after Bo Derek wore them in the movie *10* (1979).

African Consciousness

The few films that do present Black women in major roles usually ignore elements of Black history, Black culture, and Black social and political realities. The characters lack any basic consciousness that might make them multidimensional. When a Black female like Whitney Houston is in a movie like *The Bodyguard* (1993), she could just as easily be White. In fact, audiences are expected to identify with her as White or raceless because it makes her more acceptable.

A career manager who works for several popular actors demonstrates the resistant posture that people in Hollywood have with showing the Blackness/Africanness of actors. In a *Premiere* article about Black actresses in Hollywood, the career manager is quoted saying,

> The bottom line here is money, not sex or race. Whoopi Goldberg opens a movie. At the same time, her roles weren't about being black. You [rarely] see her with a black family or black problems. She's a character. I'm happy for her. She shows it can be done, and that opens another door. (Chambers, 1993, p. 92)

There are several problems with the manager's comment. First, she suggests that Whoopi Goldberg's success has shown that sex and race do not matter in movies and that most viewers will accept a Black actor in a story line not connected with anything Black. There is nothing revealing about this idea, as we have always known that it could be done. In fact, over the years, when Black actors appeared in most movies there were often no other Black characters, no "Black problems," or "Black family" members. In fact, Whoopi Goldberg, who became the highest paid actress for her participation in *Sister Act II,* is just the latest version of Sidney Poitier, who was the popular, nonthreatening Black actor of the 1960s. In the 1963 movie *Lilies of the Field,* Poitier presents the prototype Black person who lives with and helps a group of White nuns. Other Black actors have shown "it can be done" in many "crossover" movies like *A Member of the Wedding* (1993). If this "color-blind" typecasting opens doors for other Black actors, then thousands of doors should have been opened a long time ago. The issue is not opening the doors just to see Black faces. The issue is what the Black faces are doing.

Another problem with the manager's comment is that she seems to find something inherently wrong with presenting "Black family" and "Black problems." Of course, it is not her fault that the presentation of Black people, Black history, Black problems, Black culture, and so forth in Hollywood is not considered profitable. Still, her statement that sex or race has nothing to do with the dynamic takes this overboard. Would she suggest casting Italians as Germans, or Jews as Christians?

The pattern of placing Black film characters, female or male, in an all-White environment and ignoring their historical, social, cultural, and political context is not new. Many may believe that this is not a significant observation because, after all, these roles show the Black actors as "people"—neither Black nor White. Let us examine this concept of the "raceless" character in a different way. Picture one of the popular White actresses—say, Demi Moore or Meryl Streep—cast as the main or supporting character in a movie where she is the only significant White person. What if she has a Black husband or boyfriend, only Black friends, Black coworkers, and everything that she does in the movie is culturally Black? Would spectators not question the unreal dynamics of the relationships? The raceless/color-blind characters allow film communicators to ignore White supremacy.

Donald Bogle (1989) addresses this pattern of ignoring the Blackness of actors in his discussion of "the modern-day mulatto." He points out that light-skinned women are often presented as nonracials. These characters, who have been played by actresses like Rae Don Chong, Lisa Bonet, and Jennifer Beals, are usually placed in a White environment where no culturally symbolic or practical reference is made to their African heritage. An example of this is *Flashdance* (1983), where the main character, played by Jennifer Beals, never interacts with Blacks. By observing everyone, from her friends to her love interest, the audience does not get a hint that she might be Black. In short, Beals is passing.

Light-skinned actresses are not the only ones placed in modern-day mulatto roles. Whoopi Goldberg, who became the second Black woman to win an Academy Award for best supporting actress for her role in *Ghost* (1990), often appears as the only significant Black character in her movies. With the exception of her performances in *The Color Purple* (1985), *Sarafina!* (1992), and *Sister Act II* (1993), Goldberg's characters are often raceless and/or sexless and situated in White environments to support White characters. In *Made In America* (1993), in which Goldberg stars with Ted Danson, she is the owner of a store called "The African Queen," which sells Black books, Black art, and other items. The movie trivializes what little bit of consciousness Goldberg's character is shown to have.

Sexuality

The fact that mainstream film communicators often use women to exploit their sexuality has been examined by many scholars (Kaplan, 1983; Kuhn, 1985; Mulvey, 1989). White actresses like Mae West, Marilyn Monroe, Jane Fonda, Goldie Hawn, Demi Moore, Michelle Pfeiffer, Julia Roberts, and others have played vamps and had their bodies become the focus of movies, but they have also played other kinds of roles. Black women, however, have not been cast in a variety of roles.

One of the more common Black female character types is the sexual exotic. In this case, Black women are presented as worldly, raunchy, and always ready to have sex with anybody. Film communicators perpetuate this myth, which was partially formed in the days when Blacks were enslaved and Black women were violated by White men. On this subject, bell hooks (1981) says, "Annals of slavery reveal that the same abolitionist public that condemned the rape of black women regarded them as accomplices rather than victims" (p. 53). Thus, to this day, many spectators may subconsciously expect nothing more from Black women than to see them as the sexual exotic. Spectators, Black and other, feel comfortable watching Black women in this role that has been repeated so many times.

Hollywood helped develop the sexual exotic myth in many films, including one of the first all-Black musicals, *Hallelujah* (1929). One of the film's main characters, Nina Mae McKinney, is the first Black woman to be labeled a love goddess of the movies (Null, 1975). In *Hallelujah,* McKinney plays "Chick," a vamp who almost completely corrupts a "good" young Christian man. The man encourages Chick to turn to God, but eventually Chick corrupts him. In the end, he kills her. He then returns home to be with his family and to repent for the bad things that he did under the influence of Chick. This role of the "good-time" sexually promiscuous Black woman who loves to dance, sing, and party is repeated in other films. The actresses change, but the stereotype remains.

In 1970, Lola Falana, like McKinney and Dorothy Dandridge, played the role of a sexual exotic in *The Liberation of L. B. Jones.* Falana plays a woman married to a wealthy Black man. Her dress is sparse, she has a poor attitude, and her boredom leads her to have an affair with a racist White police officer. The police officer ultimately beats her up and rapes her, but because her character is presented as a spoiled, conniving, loose woman, viewers may feel that she deserves to be raped.

The blaxploitation movies of the 1970s are famous for subjugating Black women and men. Ira Konigsberg (1987) defines the blaxploitation film as "a film made with black performers and aimed at a black audience, though generally made by White producers" (p. 30). The success of blaxploitation films like Melvin Van Peebles's *Sweet Sweetback's Baadasssss Song* (1971) and Gordon Parks' *Shaft* (1971) showed Hollywood executives that Black movies, produced with little money, can make significant profits. But the term *blaxploitation,* as usually defined, is misleading, as other films not considered under this label because they were not released during the 1970s are just as exploitative.

Pam Grier became a sex symbol in blaxploitation movies by playing supporting and starring roles in films where she fights corrupt men and uses her sexuality to get what she wants. In one of her more popular films, *Coffy* (1973), Grier outsmarts the drug dealers, but consistent with the sexual exotic pattern, she spends a significant amount of time sparsely dressed. Although many people criticized the film for its sexual innuendo and violence, the film was praised by others. As Bogle (1988) says, some people "came to view her [Grier] image as being socially significant. When *Ms.* ran Grier's picture on its cover, some White feminists saw her as a liberated movie heroine" (p. 398). Some people suggest that Robin Givens's character in *A Rage In Harlem* (1992) was socially significant because she was a woman in control and simply used her body to get what she wanted. Still, she was exploited, as the first image viewers get of Givens's character is of her rear end as she struts through a train station.

Film director Alan Parker elevated former "Cosby kid" Lisa Bonet to sexual exotic status in the movie *Angel Heart* (1987). In this film, Bonet plays a creole "voodoo princess" who seduces her White costar, Mickey Rourke, a detective in search of a man. A notable scene in the film features the Bonet and Rourke characters violently having sex. Rourke has a surreal dream that blood is dripping onto their bodies. Bonet's facial expressions are animalistic, and they are edited into a montage of images that include a group of people participating in an orgy. Further, Rourke pounds into Bonet, feeding into the "Black sexual beast" myth. The scene ends when Rourke, consumed by the disturbing images in his dream, almost chokes Bonet to death. Bonet, however, continues to be involved with Rourke as if that was perfectly normal sex for her. There is a connection between sex and violence, and the Black woman appears to enjoy it.

Most representations of Black women as sexual exotics have been presented by White men. For this reason, it is not surprising that few films have presented sexually promiscuous White males raping or lusting after Black women. This is interesting, as historical examination shows that White men have been aggressors toward Black women since Africans were first kidnapped and brought to America. Instead of addressing this historical reality, Hollywood films have placed the label of the sexual aggressor on Black women and men.

The Black, Puerto Rican actress Rosi Perez fosters the sexual exotic stereotype in the 1992 White and Black male bonding movie *White Men*

Can't Jump. It is appropriate that Perez's character is first seen sitting on the bed in the apartment she shares with her White boyfriend, played by Woody Harrelson. The film communicators attempt to balance her character out by presenting her as a smart woman capable of envisioning complex money-making schemes. Still, most of the time she is having sex, talking about having sex, or serving as the object of sexual desire for one or more of the male characters.

One of the first arguments that she has with her boyfriend takes place the morning after a night of sex. She mentions that she is thirsty, and when he brings her a glass of water she goes off on a tangent about how men control women by solving their problems. She points out that she simply wants him to "sympathize" and "connect" with her. This conversation digresses to a discussion about how each prefers to refer to the sex act. She prefers the terms "make love" and "fuck," and he prefers the term "screw." When Harrelson's character gets tired of debating, he storms out of the apartment as she begs, "Ahh, honey, come back, I want to make love. Honey, come back, honey, I want to screw." The Black woman is so desperate, she surrenders her argument and begs the man to return and "screw" her.

Al Pacino and Sean Penn star in *Carlito's Way* (1993), another Hollywood movie that places a Black woman in the role of a sex-crazed whore. The movie is about a Puerto Rican crime lord (Al Pacino) who tries to leave the world of crime. The one Black woman in the movie, played by Ingrid Rogers, is mainly shown in the club where Pacino's character works. She flirts often with the Pacino crime lord, who is polite but does not want anything to do with her. One day she comes right out in a matter-of-fact manner and asks him, "How come you never try to fuck me?" She has an affair with Penn's character, a lawyer strung out on drugs. Because of the way Rogers's character was set up, I knew that she was going to be shown having sex with someone. I just didn't know who the person would be or when it would happen. Her heated sex scene ultimately takes place in a men's rest room stall at the club.

White people directed most of the films mentioned so far, but Black male directors—who have distributed their films through mainstream channels—copy and sometimes outdo mainstream film communicators in presenting Black women as sexual exotics. As yet, only a few Black women, such as Euzhan Palcy and Cassie Lemmons, have directed a movie that has been funded and distributed through mainstream channels.

Poetic Justice (1993), which has a Black woman as a main character, was directed by John Singleton, one of the Black male filmmakers who became known with the release of *Boyz N The Hood* (1991). Although this film has many excellent elements, too much of it is devoted to long and purposeless gazes at Janet Jackson's body (Jackson played the main character, Justice). Maya Angelou's poetry added a nice element to the movie, but it may have been too sophisticated for the story. For example, at the end of the movie, when Justice's voice is heard reciting Angelou's poem "Phenomenal Woman," the camera shows her laid out on the bed, staring at the ceiling with her blouse half open to reveal a black lace bra. I could not help but wonder what the connection was between a Black woman's opened blouse and her being phenomenal. Of course, everybody has his or her own interpretation of the scene, but I do not think that it did Angelou's poem any justice—no pun intended.

Spike Lee has played an invaluable role in paving the way for the current interest in Black films. While his movies have challenged us with their technical creativity, refreshing story lines, and by sparking discussion, they often present Black women as sexual objects. Lee's first film, *She's Gotta Have It* (1986), set the tone for his future representations of Black women. The title should hint at the film's focus. The film is about a single Black woman named Nola Darling, who enjoys her sexual freedom. She dates and sleeps with three different men, each of whom has a unique quality that she likes. Although each man would like to have a relationship with her, she does not care to be committed to any of them. When the film was released, it was praised by both men and women because it supposedly presented a liberated Black female free to be as sexually aggressive as men. Who said that there was anything progressive about men being sexually aggressive? According to bell hooks (1989), "the tendency to see liberated women as sexually loose informed the way people viewed the portrayal of black female sexuality in *She's Gotta Have It*" (p. 136).

Although Black female rape is rarely presented in movies, *She's Gotta Have It* does have a scene where Nola is raped. The rape occurs when one of her male friends, named Jamie Overstreet, gets mad at her because she will not commit to him. Some spectators may not view this scene as a rape because Nola looks like she is enjoying it. This scene suggests that Black women can be punished by men if they do not "act right." Further, Nola's seeming enjoyment with the rape reinforces the stereotype that Black women love sex so much that they cannot be raped.

In Lee's *Do the Right Thing* (1989), Rosie Perez plays a single mother living with her mother. Lee plays the Perez character's boyfriend—the baby's father—who is able to calm his girlfriend and make her forget her complaints about his irresponsible habits by pleasing her sexually. The first image in *Jungle Fever* (1991), a film that touches on interracial relationships and drug abuse, features veteran actress Lonette McKee with her screen husband, Wesley Snipes, in the middle of a passionate sexual encounter. With breasts exposed and legs spread wide, McKee's character is in a position that Black women in most of the Black-directed movies released during and since the 1991 Black film boom have been in.

An older Black filmmaker, Melvin Van Peebles, presented sexually exploitative images of Black women in *Sweet Sweetback's Baadasssss Song* (1971). The main character, played by Van Peebles, is a Black folk hero of sorts who has sex with Black women and one White woman as a means of survival. We never get to know these women. The women are present to show that the Sweetback character is a "good lover." Some people have suggested that Sweetback uses his penis as a weapon against White oppression. If Sweetback's penis or his sexual prowess is a metaphor for Black people's resistance to or liberation from White supremacy, Black people are in sad shape. Instead of going after the real oppressor when making his statement about the oppression of Black people, Van Peebles takes the easy way out and copies Hollywood's sexual exploitation formula (actually going further than Hollywood). In his film, the main character gains folk status in part because of how he manages to elude the police but mainly because of his ability to please women sexually. Van Peebles creatively incorporates elements like music, editing, and political commentary on police brutality in the Black community. These factors should not be overlooked when pointing out the sexism in the movie, but as an African-conscious spectator, I must stress that it is hypocritical to profess an interest in Black liberation when you are exploiting Black women.

Melvin Van Peebles's son Mario made his directing debut in 1991 with *New Jack City* (1991). In this movie, Tracy Camilla Johns, the same actress who plays Nola in Lee's *She's Gotta Have It,* is presented as the loose girlfriend of drug dealer Nino Brown. In a study I conducted that examined the responses of African American college students to four films, including *New Jack City,* both males and females reported that the film was particularly degrading to Black women (Hilliard-Nunn, 1993). The students also stressed that they found it ironic that Johns's sexuality was stressed in both films. Of the repeated negative characterizations of Black women in Black-directed films and of the casting of Johns in *New Jack City,* Jacquie Jones (1991) says,

It is ironic that Nola Darling should be the mother of Black female characters in contemporary mainstream Black film—and it is eerie to watch Tracy Camilla Johns stripping down to red satin lingerie in Mario Van Peebles' *New Jack City*. The significance of Johns' two major roles to date is profound because, unfortunately, they express the entire range of female representation in commercial films made by Black men. Black women are allowed to occupy two narrow categories in this cinema: that of the bitch and that of the ho. (p. 39)

Conclusion

"Nobody is interested in seeing a movie about a Black woman." This is what a Black woman—who writes and directs films independent of Hollywood—told me when I suggested that she try to get a film company to produce one of her screenplays. Still, the success of *Waiting To Exhale* and *The Color Purple* (1985) shows that people, especially Black women, enjoy seeing Black women's stories on the screen. The success of films by some Black independent filmmakers also demonstrates that people are interested in seeing films that show the humanity of Black women.

Black audiences are heterogeneous, so it would take a diverse body of films to please everyone. Further, all artists do not have orientations that enable them to or influence them to want to make every kind of film. For example, the type of person who would be excited about seeing or producing the latest *House Party* movie may not care to see or produce a movie like *Daughters of The Dust* and vice versa. Unfortunately, there is no balance in the types of movies that get made in Hollywood, as most are of the variety that subjugates Black women.

The continued production and patronage of films that subjugate Black women may suggest that moviegoers, including Black women, are not concerned. This seeming lack of concern may be more a consequence of their being conditioned not to expect diverse images. Instead of boycotting movies that subjugate Black women, we keep going to see them and, for the most part, remain silent.

Black viewers are, however, not always silent about issues of representation in movies. Often, criticism from Black women and men features each accusing the other of defamation. For example, when *The Color Purple* was released, there was an uproar over the unfavorable way that it represented Black men. Even before *Waiting To Exhale* was released, debates about how it would represent Black men began. Whether we agree with the criticism of these films or not, we must ask why the same intense criticism and discourse has not been as prevalent concerning the way that Black women are represented in movies directed by Black men. Martin Lawrence, the star and director of *It's A Thin Line Between Love And Hate* (1996), claimed that his misogynist movie is the *Exhale* for Black men. As an African-conscious film critic, I feel that Black women and men must be consistent in their critiques of how Hollywood films misrepresent both women and men.

Black actors, filmmakers, producers, and others involved in the film communication process should be held accountable for the part they play in furthering negative or positive Black images. There is a tendency for some artists and others to talk about Black people in terms of a community that should be supportive of us when we want something (i.e., an audience, respect, support, fans, etc.), but when we gain acceptance from the mainstream—those who do not see the humanity of Black people—we suddenly become individuals and forget where we came from, at least until our one minute of fame is over and we again want to return to some part of the Black community to be revitalized.

Black women come from civilizations with distinct spiritual, cultural, educational, social, scientific, and economic systems (Diop, 1955/1974, 1990; Van Sertima, 1989; Williams, 1976). By ignoring us and perpetuating images that defame our identity, mainstream film communicators perform violent acts of subjugation. For this reason, filmmakers who take a chance and challenge the negative formulas must be morally and financially supported. What if Julie Dash had to give up when she could not get one Hollywood company to distribute the completed version of *Daughters of The Dust* (Dash, 1992)? There are many stories yet to tell about Black women. There have been no films about Hatshepsut, the first warrior queen in African history, nor any about Queen Nzinga, who led her people in resisting the Portuguese forces that wanted to steal land and people in what is now called Angola (Van Sertima, 1989). No blockbusters have been made about Sojourner Truth, Zora Neale Hurston, Mary McCloud Bethune, Angela Davis, or Lenora Fulani or about the everyday dramas in the lives of African women around the world.

Regardless of what optimistic observers—encouraged by the momentary success of a few Black actresses or films—say about the improvement in Black women's representation in Hollywood movies, the real picture is not encouraging. In fact, it is business as usual. The Hollywood system is infected by the same racism and sexism present in other institutions in our society. Any affirmative steps taken to eliminate white supremacy and to address and solve the pervasive racism and sexism around the world should help better the content of movies so that they represent Maat.

Note

1. Throughout this chapter I use the labels *African* and *Black* to refer to people of African descent.

References

Akbar, N. (1984). *Chains and images of psychological slavery.* Jersey City, NJ: New Mind Productions.

Bobo, J. (1989). *Articulation and hegemony: Black women's response to the film* The Color Purple. Unpublished doctoral dissertation, University of Oregon.

Bogle, D. (1988). *Blacks in American films and television: An illustrated encyclopedia.* New York: Fireside.

Bogle, D. (1989). *Toms, coons, mulattoes, mammies and bucks: An interpretive history of Blacks in American film* (expanded ed.). New York: Continuum.

Bordwell, D., Staiger, J., & Thompson, K. (1985). *The classical Hollywood cinema: Film style and mode of production to 1960.* New York: Columbia University Press.

Chambers, V. (1993). Sisters are doin' it for themselves: Black actresses are better off than in Dandridge's day—but how much? *Premiere* [Special issue, "Women in Hollywood"], pp. 90-94.

Clark, R., & Clark, M. (1958). Racial identification and preferences in Negro children. In E. Maccoly, T. Newcomb, & E. Harley (Eds.), *Readings in social psychology* (pp. 602-611). New York: Holt.

Dash, J. (1992). Daughters Of The Dust: *The making of an African American woman's film.* New York: New Press.

Diop, C. A. (1974). *The African origin of civilization: Myth or reality* (M. Cook, Trans.). Westport, CT: Lawrence Hill. (Original work published 1955)

Diop, C. A. (1990). *The cultural unity of Black Africa.* Chicago: Third World Press.

Donalson, M. B. (1982). *The representation of Afro-American women in the Hollywood feature film, 1915-1949.* Unpublished doctoral dissertation, Brown University.

Hilliard, A. G. (1993, March 29). *Bringing ma'at, destroying isfet: The African and African diasporan presence in the study of ancient Kemet.* Carter Goodwin Woodson lecture presented at St. Mary's College of Maryland, St. Mary's City.

Hilliard-Nunn, M. P. E. (1993). *African consciousness and the responses of African American college students to* House Party, House Party 2, New Jack City, *and* Malcolm X. Unpublished doctoral dissertation, Florida State University, Tallahassee.

hooks, b. [Gloria Watkins]. (1981). *"Ain't I a woman?": Black women and feminism.* Boston: South End Press.

hooks, b. [Gloria Watkins]. (1989). *Talking back: Thinking feminist, thinking Black.* Boston: South End Press.

hooks, b. [Gloria Watkins]. (1992). *Black looks: Race and representation.* Boston: South End Press.

Horowitz, J. (1991, May 29). Black actresses are still waiting for starring roles. *New York Times,* pp. B1, B7.

Jarvie, I. C. (1978). *Movies as social criticism: Aspects of their social psychology.* Metuchen, NJ: Scarecrow Press.

Jones, J. (1991). The new ghetto aesthetic. *Wide Angle, 13*(3/4), 32-43.

Jowett, G., & Linton, J. M. (1989). *Movies as mass communication* (2nd ed.). Newbury Park, CA: Sage.

Kaplan, A. (1983). *Women and film: Both sides of the camera.* New York: Methuen.

Konigsberg, I. (1987). *The complete film dictionary.* New York: New American Library.

Kuhn, A. (1985). *The power of the image: Essays on representation and sexuality.* London: Routledge & Kegan Paul.

Larkin, A. S. (1988). Black women film-makers defining ourselves: Feminism in our own voice. In E. D. Pribram (Ed.), *The female spectators: Looking at film and television* (pp. 157-173). London: Verso.

Mulvey, L. (1989). *Visual and other pleasures.* Bloomington: Indiana University Press.

NAACP (National Association for the Advancement of Colored People). (1991). *Out of focus—Out of sync: A report on the film and television industries.* Baltimore: Author.

Null, G. (1975). *Black Hollywood.* Secaucus, NJ: Citadel Press.

Perkins, K. P. (1992). Arts and entertainment: Black actresses speak out. In *Blackbook: The African-American international reference guide* (Vol. 22, pp. 49-54).

Shaheen, J. G. (1984). *The TV Arab.* Bowling Green, OH: Bowling Green State University Popular Press.

Van Sertima, I. (Ed.). (1989). *Nile Valley civilizations* (3rd ed., Proceedings of the Nile Valley Conference). Atlanta, GA & New Brunswick, NJ: Journal of African Civilizations.

Wallace, M. (1992). Boyz N The Hood *and* Jungle Fever [films]. In G. Dent (Ed.), *Black popular culture* (pp. 123-131). Seattle: Bay Press.

Williams, C. (1976). *The destruction of Black civilization: Great issues of a race, 4500 B.C. to 2000 A.D.* Chicago: Third World Press.

African Americans in Television

12

An Afrocentric Analysis

Alice A. Tait
Robert L. Perry

> *You've taken my blues and gone—*
> *You sing 'em on Broadway*
> *And you sing 'em in Hollywood Bowl,*
> *And you mixed 'em up with symphonies*
> *And you fixed 'em*
> *So they don't sound like me.*
> *Yep, you done taken my blues and gone.*
>
> *You also took my spirituals and gone.*
> *You put me in Macbeth and Carmen Jones*
> *And all kinds of Swing Mikados*
> *And in everything but what's about me—*
> *But someday somebody'll*
> *Stand up and and talk about me.*
> *And write about me,*
> *And put on plays about me!*
> *I reckon it'll be*
> *Me myself!*
>
> *Yes, it'll be me.*
>
> —*"Note on Commercial Theater," from*
> Selected Poems of Langston Hughes

This chapter originally appeared as an article in *Western Journal of Black Studies* (Vol. 18, No. 4, 1994, pp. 195-200). Copyright © Washington State University Press. Reprinted with permission.

Presence and Absence: An Introduction

This chapter proposes that historically and contemporarily African-Americans were and are severely underrepresented in the Eurocentric press, are portrayed stereotypically, depicted in low-status occupational roles and denied news or public affairs programs to adequately serve their informational needs (Poindexter & Stroman, 1981; Gardner, 1983; Addessa, 1991; Entman, 1992). Specifically, the social forces identified by the Kerner Commission Report directly, and continuously affect the level of participation of African-Americans in television news media (Tait & Perry, 1987). Furthermore, where African-Americans were placed in programming policy-making positions, subsequent news content and coverage displayed an Afrocentric perspective.

The following theories discuss the potential impact of mass media on society and individuals and serve to underscore the media's traditional impact on them both. The *agenda-setting* function of the media is the close relationship between the relative emphasis the media gives to different issues and the relative importance the public places on them (Cohen, 1963; Shaw & McCombs, 1977). Lazarsfeld and Merton (1960) described *"status conferral"* as coverage by the press that enhances the status or perceived importance of the person or event covered. *Meaning theory* describes the mass media as an important part of the process of communication in modern society. The media plays a significant role in shaping and stabilizing the meanings experienced for the symbols of language. These meanings, in turn, shape behaviors towards those aspects of the social and physical order that are labeled by words. According to this theory, a medium like television can influence the public on how to interpret such labels as "women," "African-Americans" and "sexual attractiveness" (Ball-Rokeach & DeFleur, 1975).

Television presents African-Americans to the viewing public as deviant, threatening, and unintelligent subhumans. Based on the agenda-setting status conferral, and meaning theories, television news makes an indelible impression because of its visual impact and its tendency, by means of inertia, to shape and stabilize the meanings experienced from the symbols of language. The way to correct these negative stereotypical images would be to develop programming which examines from a "Black perspective" the African-American experience. In the media world this would require station owners, writers, producers and individuals who have the perspective to present the African-American experience. A paradigm for creating such foci of analyses that some African-American media scholars historically embraced, without the benefit of the label, is Afrocentrism. Afrocentricity involves a systematic exploration of relationships, social codes, cultural and commercial customs, mythoforms, oral traditions and proverbs of the peoples of Africa and the African Diaspora. Afrocentricity is the belief in the centrality of Africans in Postmodern history.

Nija: The Way is the Afrocentricity doctrine, that is, the collective expression of the Afrocentric worldview. Nija represents the inspired Afrocentric spirit found in the traditions of African-Americans. There are six parts to a Nija meeting. They are: (1) Libation to Ancestors (honors ancestors), (2) Poetry and Music Creativity (free expression of creativity), (3) Nommo: Generative Word Power (Afrocentric discussions of all the problems of the world occur), (4) Affirmation (reinforce victorious beliefs), (5) Teaching from Nija (Afrocentric ideology), and (6) Libation to Posterity.

Nommo is especially relevant to an analysis of Afrocentric television programming. Nommo is an opportunity for the discussion of problems and the place where facts are disseminated. Historical, cultural and political information can also be discussed during Nommo. An Afrocentric television program attempts to reflect all of these concepts in various forms. Afrocentric television programming is also a form of Nommo (Asante, 1989). *The Cosby Show,* although not explicating every avenue of African-American life, represents the prototype Afrocentric television program as the images produced in the show were consistently reflective of African-American culture. The direction of the programming was African-American influenced. Conversely, the *Amos and Andy* show was the antithesis of Afrocentrism. In this work Afrocentric theory is utilized to interpret how African-Americans are portrayed and should be portrayed in the influential mass media. The effects of the portrayal are inextricably intertwined to viewing habits, to the extent that viewing habits reify negative portrayals.

Research has indicated that television is significant in the lives of all African-Americans—with notable social class differences in the amount of significant effect—because they rely heavily on television as an important source of information about other African-Americans and the larger African-American community (Poindexter & Stroman, 1981). African-American children are also more likely to be influenced by television commercials and to adopt behavior patterns from televised models than non-African-

American children. Since African-American children are the heaviest prime-time television viewers, the problems associated with *agenda-setting, status-conferral* and *meaning* theories are thus magnified (Dates, 1980; Donohue & Donohue, 1977; Greenberg & Harneman, 1977; Heckel, Leichtman & Neeley, 1973; Heckel, McCarter & Nicholas; 1971: Thelen & Soltz, 1969).

Because the media sets an agenda, confers status and interprets meaning, one effect of all this television viewing is that it legitimizes deviant, threatening and unintelligent behavior. A self-fulfilling prophecy thus emerges; television creates the problem, and because of its power and appeal, perpetuates the problem by socializing African-American youth into believing that deviant behavior is acceptable and rewarding. Furthermore, non-African-American youth are provided with only the resultant negative stereotypes of African-American youth that continue to mar inter-ethnic relations.

From 1952 to 1969 a series of studies concluded that African-Americans: changed from low to high media usage for political news (McCombs, 1968), used television as a primary source of general and especially political information (Becker & Stroman, 1978), were devoted to news and minimally researched public affairs programs, viewed local newscasts and listened to radio news regularly, and, for older and more educated African-Americans as opposed to younger and less educated African-Americans, were more likely to be regular viewers of public affairs programs. These observations suggest African-Americans viewed television as a credible source of information concerning other African-Americans; again, the agenda-setting function of mass media. One explanation for this attitude lies in the increased visibility of African-Americans, which resulted in *status conferral,* as other media oriented African-Americans began to recognize their importance.

Given these trends as reported in the Eurocentric media, in order to further explicate this information in Afrocentric terms, it is necessary that the media directed at African-Americans embody both information and role modeling. While the ideal is seldom achieved historically, several other programs have attempted to report, record, and portray the African-American community from the perspective of its people. The most notable of these: *Profiles in Black* (Detroit, MI), a series about well-known African-Americans, *Black Journal* (Detroit, MI), *Tony Brown's Journal* (New York, NY), and *For My People* (Detroit, MI)—all representative series dealing with a variety of contemporary and historical African-American issues.

Eurocentric Window Dressing

In the early days of television, African-Americans were rarely seen on the screen. A 1962 study, for example, found that three African-American faces appeared once every five hours (Lowenstein, Plotkin & Pugh, 1964). The drama of the civil rights movement, however, captured media attention. African-Americans became more visible and instilled a new awareness in the American public that they had been denied equality under the law and that they were determined to achieve it.

Television's role in publicizing the civil rights movement raised an important issue: to what extent and in what ways had television played a role in perpetuating the inequality that non-African-Americans were just beginning to perceive had been suffered by African-Americans? The first major study of this issue, popularly known as The Kerner Commission Report, investigated a series of racial disorders in order to discover what happened, why it happened, and what could be done to prevent it from happening again (Werner, 1968). The Commission Report concluded, among other things, the news media failed to communicate to the American people "on race relations, and problems of the underclass. Further the commission found the news media routine portrayal of African-Americans as part of the society was law, and presented African-Americans as whites saw them. not as they saw themselves." The Kerner Commission was concerned about the effect—on whites as well as on African-Americans—of a television world that is "almost totally white in both appearance and attitude." Inherent in this statement, made by a culturally diverse commission, lies the importance of the Afrocentric idea being represented and needed in television programming.

This indictment of the media was directed toward its portrayal of African-Americans, and the ways in which African-Americans and whites perceived African-Americans, and at how media portrayal and presentation of African-Americans contribute to the hypothesized psycho-sociological effect of African-American negative self-esteem. The key to addressing the still unfulfilled Kerner Commission documented concern lies in the willingness and the media ability to project an Afrocentric perspective.

In support of the Commission, Roberts (1975) concluded "the most notable quality of the newscasts . . . is the relatively few appearances made by African-Americans and their low visibility in those appearances." Visibility alone does not address the concern of the Commission that was interested not only in appearance but in attitudes and values expressed by African-Americans. Contemporary programming, *Black Entertainment* and *The Bill Cosby Show,* tend to take on more Afrocentric perspectives, as outlined by definitions stated in this chapter, but this is not true of television news in general. Thus, the struggle for African-American identity and value perspective television programming remains elusive.

The Kerner Commission's conclusion that a Eurocentric mass media will ultimately fail in its attempts to communicate with an audience that includes African-Americans and other Americans is no less valid approaching the 21st century than when it was published 25 years ago. The continuance of this phenomenon served in part to encourage the Federal Communications Commission (FCC), the agency which regulates the broadcast industry, to adopt policies and procedures designed to assure equal employment opportunities in all television and radio stations.

Contemporary African-American News Programming

In 1968, however, the Kerner Commission suggested that the news media should perform another function—to condition viewers' expectations regarding what is "ordinary and normal" in society. The Commission found that African-Americans were not presented in the news as a matter of routine, nor were they presented within the context of the society. Primarily, they appeared in the context of disorder. This observation is still accurate today.

From 1973 to 1992 researchers found: that race relations as an issue was covered in a balanced manner during a typical week of news programming by the networks (Pride & Clark, 1973), during particular incidents in which tensions were high, that coverage of the race issue tended to exacerbate racial polarization (Warren, 1972). In stories covered during 1974, 1975 and 1977 by ABC, CBS and NBC, African-Americans, Hispanics, Asians and Native Americans rarely appeared in or reported the news; there was little news specifically devoted to the problems or achievements of these ethnic groups and women.

Harold Lasswell, a European mass media theorist, postulated in a serendipitous fashion some of the elements of Afrocentricity in his presentation of the unity, of mass media functions: that is, that environment, social heritage and entertainment are inextricably intertwined as mass media functions. In presenting this hypothesis. Lasswell embraced the essence of the African aesthetic. However, results from research presented above and elsewhere in the present document indicate television news was potentially dysfunctional for African-Americans. In terms of the theorized mass media functions, therefore, the medium probably did not fulfill Lasswell's serendipitous thesis nor the Afrocentric idea. Local newscasts were also stereotypically negative, conflict oriented (Gardner, 1983), sparsely covered African-American issues (Addessa, 1991), and promoted modern racism (Entman, 1992).

In order to more fully understand the extent of change since the Kerner Commission Report and the quality of that change, an analysis of African-American television management and ownership needs to be accomplished. Alter (1986) stated that African-Americans, Hispanics, Asians and Native Americans believe news coverage of their communities could be better served if there were minority representation in management, a belief which coincides with the Kerner Commission's call for better coverage of racial issues. Most of the few African-American news directors in television were either heading low-budget operations or at ethnic stations (Stone, 1987). Alter (1986) stated "the desire to manage is partly healthy ambition and partly a reflection of unhappiness over how white-dominated news organizations cover the news."

This section explores several Nommo examples of African-American produced and directed programs. These programs were and are unique because they all sought to offer a diverse balanced perspective of African-Americans and embodied Afrocentric programming. According to Asante (1988), "When the oppressor seeks to use language and images (added) for the manipulation of our reality; Nommo, for ourselves, and of ourselves, must continue the correct path of critical analysis. Such a path is not dictated necessarily by the oppressor's rhetoric but [by] Nija for the Afro-American intellectual. Objectivism, born of the history, culture, and materials of our existence must be at the base of our talk and our essaying." The goal of these programs was to document, explore and articulate African-American political, economic, cultural issues. The programs themselves served as training programs by providing internships to African-Americans so they might enter the broadcasting market. *Profiles in Black* and WPGR-TV represent two examples.

An analysis of the conception, creative format, audience feedback, and content analysis of *Profiles* demonstrated that *Profiles* portrayed African-Americans realistically in its broadcasts, reversing the trend of portraying

African-Americans as deviants (Tait, 1989). Gilbert Maddox, *Profiles* host and producer, made the following observations, published by *The Detroit News:*

> We black people are moving in the direction of establishing identities, of gaining political, economic and social control of the black community. We are not opposed to the white community, but we want to make our own community as viable as possible. . . . The series will show the full range of people comprising the black population—the professionals who have succeeded. ADC mothers with their problems and hopes, young students, conservative and militant clergymen. . . . (Maddox, 1978)

Maddox demonstrates in this published statement essential ideas of Afrocentric theory by showing the interrelatedness of all African-Americans transcending social status and class. Maddox thus enlarges the American universal discourse because he embodies the whole spectrum of Black culture and allows African-American voices to speak for themselves without imposing definitions.

A half-hour weekly television community service series, WWJ-TV (Detroit) filmed and broadcast *Profiles* initially during prime time (Saturday, 8:30 p.m.) from November 1969 through December 1979. Developed because of WWJ-TV's desire to operate more effectively in the public interest and, additionally, to employ increased numbers of African-Americans, *Profiles* became WWJ's response to the Kerner Commission Report.

Maddox portrayed the African-American community's hopes and frustrations as well as highlighted their accomplishments and achievements. One technique he employed was to interview guests in their homes with their families to display their degree of community involvement. Maddox presented African-American professionals, politically active persons such as retired Congressman George Crockett (a former Judge) and Mayor Coleman Young; significant events such as the NAACP Freedom Fund dinner, that organization's annual fund raiser, usually featuring some nationally renowned speaker; the historical contributions of Paul Robeson and Malcolm X; contributions of the working class; Detroit's African-American and African-American controlled institutions such as Homes for Black Children, and the community's dissident voices, including those of the Minister of the Nation of Islam. These stories appealed to youths, adults, Caucasians, African-Americans, female and male audiences, and also showed alternative role models available in the African-American community (Maddox, 1978).

Throughout its ten-year history, *Profiles* continued its presentation of public affairs programming for the Metropolitan Detroit viewer. According to Frank Angelo (1974): "Maddox . . . has done about as much as any one in America to destroy stereotypes that whites have of Blacks—and too often Blacks have of themselves." Prior to producing, hosting, and directing *Profiles*, Maddox was responsible for a number of other programs with similar objectives of those of *Profiles*, most notably: *Black and Unknown Bards, Negro History Series, Office of Economic Opportunity, Mayor's Development Team Report,* and *C.P.T. (Colored Peoples' Time) Television Program.* Maddox's work as chronicled in this discussion revealed that he was deeply grounded in the applied aspects of Afrocentricity, before *Profiles*, subsequent to, and concomitant to such scholars as M. Karenga (Kawaida theory) and M. Asante (Afrocentricity). *Profiles* reflected Afrocentric programming.

The relationship between Afrocentricity and ownership can best be understood by reviewing the work of Fife (1979). She found that: African-American ownership does impact images in the news, such images are influenced by philosophies of ownership and philosophies of ownership are in turn influenced by community characteristics.

WGPR-TV debuted September 1974, and holds the distinction of being the first black-owned and operated TV station in the U.S. It is owned and operated by the International F.M. and A.M. Modern Masons and Eastern Star, a fraternal organization founded by William V. Banks, the first President and General Manager of WGPR, Inc., who also owns Detroit radio station WGPR-FM since 1964.

WGPR's philosophy is that African-American Detroiters deserve a television station attuned to their community in the same way that the "mainstream" media are attuned to the white community. WGPR's stated purpose is to provide African-American Detroiters the opportunity to have experiences with the broadcast industry, so they stress training and community access, and they emphasize a Black perspective to the largest degree possible.

WGPR aired several hours daily of locally-produced programming including "Big City News," discontinued in 1992, a 30-minute, Monday through Friday newscast. Both the management and ownership see "Big City News" (BCN) as focusing on the African-American community, while complementing mainstream media with alternative aspects on current events. BCN uses the same newscast format as larger operations. Crews are sent out on assignment of general news events as well as specific events in the African-American community not covered by mainstream media. Management stresses that a BCN viewer could not watch other stations and still feel adequately informed on Detroit news, with the unique asset of getting that news from an African-American perspective. By "African-American perspective," management means that (1) the implications of issues for minorities are discussed, and (2) the participation of African-American leaders in area events is fairly and fully covered. BCN sees itself as "commitment coverage" to represent the African-American community.

To that end, WGPR monitors their syndicated news sources for stories about African-American issues to supplement local coverage. They sometimes contact syndication services to complain about the dearth of African-American issues to supplement their local coverage. They include as many visible minorities in stories as possible, including neighborhood leaders as much as city-wide or national leaders. They especially try to showcase "success stories" of African-Americans. Results from a content analysis of WGPR-TV programming showed that the programming reflects the station's philosophy.

Thus the essence of WGPR's television programming philosophy is Afrocentric because it places African ideals at the center of its programming philosophy and the ownership does not separate itself from the community, it is part of the community. It is also unique reporting in that it exemplifies the "caring or nurturing mythoform" that is part of the Afrocentric idea (Asante, 1987).

These two programs (*Profiles* and WGPR-TV) were directly successful in their attempts to address the issues raised by the 1968 Kerner Commission Report. Furthermore, it has been demonstrated that African-American producers and directors designed programs to present African-American family life and social issues as ordinary and normal subject matter. Such achievements were accomplished where African-Americans were in policy-making positions. However, even this sparse programming accomplishment could hardly have occurred without the Kerner Report's findings and its subsequent effect on FCC policy.

Research discussed in this chapter and conducted over a period of years documented the neglect of African-Americans in the news. Research designs of this study focused on African-Americans in the news and in the production of news programming. *Profiles in Black* and WGPR addressed issues raised by the Kerner Commission Report; to wit, that African-Americans were not being represented and were not, moreover, being presented in an Afrocentric context. The two programs surveyed present family and social issues from a patently African-American perspective.

One implication to be drawn from this initial study is that the strongest impact on the portrayal of African-Americans in the news appears to be achieved when African-Americans influence the conception and the news selection process. The studies indicate change is occurring, although from all accounts, such change appears to be painfully slow. We found that, although Afrocentricity had not been fully or faithfully articulated, these programs clearly operated within the spirit and context embraced by the philosophy.

References

Addessa, R. 1991. *Women, Minorities and AIDS: The Impact of Broadcast Deregulation on Public Discourse*, p. 3. Rita Addessa, Executive Director, Philadelphia Lesbian and Gay Task Force, 1501 Cherry Street, Philadelphia, PA 19103.

Alter, J. 1986. "No Room at the Top." *Newsweek* (December): 79-80.

Angelo, F. 1974. "Gilbert Maddox TV Host Profiles Breaks Black Stereotypes." *Detroit Free Press* (February 8): 7-8.

Asante, M. K. 1989. *Afrocentricity*. New Jersey: Africa World Press, Inc.

Ball-Rokeach, S. & DeFleur, M. 1975. *Theories of Mass Communication*. New York: David McKay Company, Inc., pp. 133-35.

Becker, B. & C. A. Stroman. 1978. "Racial Differences in Gratifications." *Journalism Quarterly* 55: 767-71.

Bourne, S. C. 1988. "Bright Moments." *The Independent* (May): 10-11.

Cohen, B. 1963. *The Press and Foreign Policy*. Princeton, N.J.: Princeton University Press.

Dates, J. 1980. "Race, Racial Attitudes and Adolescent Perceptions of Black Television Characters." *Journal of Broadcasting* 24: 549-60.

Donohue, W. A. & T. R. Donohue. 1977. "Black, White, White Gifted and Emotionally Disturbed Children's Perceptions of the Reality in Television Programming." *Human Relations* 30: 609-12.

Entman, R. M. 1992. "Blacks in the News: Television, Modern Racism and Cultural Change." *Journalism Quarterly* (Summer): 341-61.

Fife, M. D. 1979. "The Impact of Minority Ownership on Broadcast Program Content: A Case Study of WGPR-TV's Local News Content." *Report to the National Association of Broadcasting Office of Research and Planning* (September).

Gardner, T. 1983. "Cooperative Communication Strategies: Observations in a Black Community." *Journal of Black Studies* 14: 233.

Greenberg, B. S. & T. R. Harneman. 1977. "Racial Attitudes and the Impact of TV on Blacks." *Educational Broadcasting Review* 4: 27-34.

Heckel, R. V., H. M. Leichtman, & J. T. Neeley. 1973. "The Effect of Race Model and Response Consequences to the Model on Imitation in Children." *Journal of Social Psychology* 89: 225-31.

Heckel, R. V., R. E. McCarter, & K. B. Nicholas. 1971. "The Effects of Race and Sex on the Imitation of Television Models." *Journal of Social Psychology* 85: 315-16.

Judge, F. 1969. "Channel 4 to Launch *Black Profiles*." *The Detroit News* (November 27).

Karenga, M. 1982. *Introduction to Black Studies*. Los Angeles: University of Sankore Press.

Lasswell, H. D. 1948. "The Structure and Function of Society." *The Communication of Ideas*, pp. 37-51. Edited by Bryson, Lyman. New York: Harper & Bros.

Lazarsfeld, P. & R. Merton. 1960. "Mass Communication, Popular Taste and Organized Social Society." *Mass Media*. Edited by Schramm, Wilbur. Urbana: University of Illinois Press.

Liebert, R. M. & R. A. Maron. 1971. "Short-term Effects of Televised Aggression on Children's Aggressive Behavior." *Television and Social Behavior, Vol. II: Television and Social Learning*. Edited by J. P. Murray, E. A. Rubenstein, & G. A. Comstock. Washington, D.C.: U.S. Government Printing Office.

Lowenstein, R., L. Plotkin, & D. Pugh. 1964. "The Frequency of Appearance of Negroes on Television." *The Committee on Integration*. New York Society for Ethical Culture, 4.

Maddox, G. A. 1978. "An Overview of Profiles: Past and Future." *Report to WWJ-TV* (August).

McCombs, M. E. 1968. "Negro Use of Television and Newspapers for Political Information, 1952-1964." *Journal of Broadcasting* 12: 261-66.

Norment, L. 1985. "The Bill Cosby Show: The Real Life Drama Behind the TV Show About a Black Family." *Ebony Magazine* XL: 28.

Poindexter, P. M. & C. A. Stroman. 1981. "Blacks and Television: A Review of the Research Literature." *Journal of Broadcasting* 25: 103-21.

Pride, R. A. & D. H. Clark. 1973. "Race Relations in Television News: A Content Analysis of the Networks." *Journalism Quarterly* 50: 319.

Roberts, C. 1975. "The Presentation of Blacks on Television Network Newscasts." *Journalism Quarterly* 52: 50-55.

Shaw, D. L. & M. McCombs. 1977. *The Emergence of American Political Issues: The Agenda-Setting Function of the Press*. St. Paul, Minn.: West Publ.

Stone, V. A. 1987. "Minority Employment in Broadcast News, 1976-1986." Paper presented at the annual meeting of the Association for Education in Journalism and Mass Communication, San Antonio, Texas.

Tait, A. A. 1989. "Profiles Portrayal of African-Americans 1969-1979: Detroit's Direct Response to Negative Stereotypes." *Michigan Academician*, Vol. 21. No. 4, Summer.

Tait, A. A. & R. L. Perry. 1987. "The Sociological Implications of the Civil Rights Movement for Black Character Development and Generic Programming Within the Television Medium, 1955-1985." *The Negro Educational Review* 38: 224-37.

Thelen, M. H. & W. W. Soltz. 1969. "The Effect of Vicarious Reinforcement on Imitation in Two Social Racial Groups." *Child Development* 40: 879-87.

Warren, D. 1972. "Mass Media and Racial Crisis: A Study of the New Bethel Church Incident in Detroit." *Journal of Social Issues* 28: 111.

Werner, O. 1968. *Reports of the National Advisory Commission on Civil Disorders*. New York: Bantam Books.

"Window Dressing on the Set: Women and Minorities on Television." 1977. United States Commission on Civil Rights, 4.

PART IV

WHERE DO WE GO FROM HERE?
CHALLENGES AND IMPLICATIONS
OF THE AFROCENTRIC PERSPECTIVE

Part IV raises the question of where we go from here in three chapters that challenge the reader's thinking about African American studies, the Afrocentric perspective, and locating one's place in society and the world.

Victor Okafor (Chapter 13) offers some functional implications to the implementation of Afrocentricity in the African American community.

In Chapter 14, Peter Nwosu, Donald Taylor, and Cecil Blake discuss several conceptual and methodological issues that plague research and suggest elements to be included in any new African-based research.

Na'im Akbar argues in Chapter 15 that there is a challenge in implementing an Afrocentric perspective. Those coming from the Afrocentric perspective are to be the vanguard in developing a technology that is compatible with the Afrocentric concept of harmony and nature.

The Functional Implications of Afrocentrism

13

Victor O. Okafor

This chapter attempts to articulate the Present Moment—that is, the contemporary state of the African-American community in the United States. As some—if not most—people are aware, a disproportionate number of the present generation of African American families are headed by Black women. In fact, about sixty percent of the households in the African-American community are headed by women.[1] Those of them with children represent 30.7 percent of the national total at a time the overall population of African Americans constitutes roughly twelve percent of the U.S. national population.[2] This, as one can imagine, places an unduly harsh burden on the shoulders of African-American women; it also means that Black men may no longer participate significantly in the upbringing of their children. In the absence of appropriate male support, single mothers are left to bear alone the difficult burden of nurturing their sons and daughters. Worse still, the environment in which most of these sons and daughters are raised, more likely than not, hardly qualifies as a bed of roses or role models. Several scholarly works have been done on this issue, including Haki R.

Madhubuti's nerve-wracking book entitled *Black Men: Obsolete, Single and Dangerous?* One of the sad realities of the present moment is that the socialization of African young ones is, for the most part, no longer a balanced process—that is, a process that ought to be enriched with the inputs of the male and female leaders of the family.[3]

Although this state of affairs is attributable to a host of factors, Madhubuti, in his work, points the most serious accusing finger at the system of white supremacism as a debilitating influence on Black families and Black manhood. Among other things, he states, the system not only seeks to incapacitate Black men economically, it systematically rewards Black men and women who assist in the oppression of the Black community. In like manner, the system targets, labels and harasses Black men and women who dare to speak out on behalf of the community. Prime examples include Martin Luther King, Jr. and Malcolm X.[4] There are, of course, lesser examples.

The preceding picture ought not to be taken as the viewpoint of an individual scholar or even a minority of scholars. Take it or leave it, it represents a theme that runs through almost the entire spectrum of contemporary African-American sociopolitical thought. The scholars may differ in their choice of words, but their message remains basically the same. Thus, another scholar, one who is nationally known, Cornel West, frames the African situation this way:

> New World African modernity consists of degraded and exploited Africans in American circumstances using European languages and instruments to make sense of tragic predicaments—predicaments disproportionately shaped by white supremacist bombardments on black beauty, intelligence, moral character and creativity.[5]

In the face of these tragic predicaments, the following question becomes logical: is there not an urgent need for the community, like any other self-conscious group, to strengthen itself by conscientiously enhancing its *structural capacity,* including forging a sense of cohesion—a collective consciousness—necessary for an effective and creative response to the challenges of the day? The survival of a group of people, as well as its potential for self-fulfillment, has a great deal to do with that group's capacity to define, develop and defend its interests.

It has been suggested that, generally-speaking, African people do not believe in themselves and do not know who they are. As Molefi Kete Asante puts it, "many people of African descent are dislocated, and alienated from their own history, suffer amnesia, and believe in white supremacy.[6] Na'im Akbar, a noted psychologist, writes about sociopsychological forces that threaten Black life and development. He describes one of these as anti-self disorder, which manifests itself in "overt and covert hostility towards the groups of one's origin and thus one's self."[7] No doubt, this is not a pleasant state of human affairs, but it must be remembered that it is a product of history. During the time of enslavement, for instance, Africans were negatively reinforced for trying to be themselves. Over time, Africans, in the Americas in particular, developed an ambivalence about their Africanness. Vincent Bakpetu Thompson, a well-known and authoritative scholar of African Diasporic History, had the following to say about this phenomenon.

> The process of conditioning Africans to accept slave status began even as they were leaving the shores of Africa; it was intensified in the form of psychological warfare on the far side of the Atlantic in the Americas, with adverse consequences for the [enslaved] themselves.[8]

He continues by observing as follows:

> It is not difficult to imagine the havoc wrought on the enslaved Africans' psychology in this long period of acculturation to the New World environment. It is, therefore, easy to understand the many and conflicting tendencies exhibited by Africans and their descendants in the diaspora resulting from centuries of sustained conditioning, propaganda, badgering and brutalization.[9]

Even though times have changed measurably, contemporary society is still saddled with vestiges of the past, among which is the fact that, at this time, some of the actions that spew forth from the system tend to generate an impression that the system's psychological orientation and philosophical underpinning remain anti-African. Up till the present time, individuals are punished for their Blackness—not through overt lynching as was the case in the nineteenth and early twentieth centuries,[a] but through stealthy, *"high-tech lynching."* In a 1992 best seller entitled *Two Nations: Black and White, Separate, Hostile, Unequal,* Andrew Hacker spoke to this fact of contemporary life. He reports:

Many black men and women are concluding that they can best be described as African-Americans, considering how much their character and culture owe to their continent of origin. A pride in this heritage and history has helped them survive slavery and subsequent discrimination. . . . However, most white Americans interpret the African emphasis in another way. For them, it frequently leads to a more insidious application of racism.[10]

Hacker concludes with a climatic confession of sorts:

There persists the belief that members of the black race represent an inferior strain of the human species. In this view, Africans—and Americans who trace their origins to that continent—are seen as languishing at a lower evolutionary level than members of other races.[11]

Needless to say, the right to define oneself is a fundamental human right. Thus, a people cannot allow others to tell them who they are or who they should be. Alienation from self ought to be viewed not as a strength but as a weakness—a major weakness. How could this be solved? African students (diasporic and continental) need to be educated to understand and appreciate their cultural roots and to identify with, and thus, show respect for not only themselves, but also their communities. "Migrating Back to Africa" in a symbolic, philosophical sense has historically been espoused as a remedy to the anti-self orientation which this chapter mentioned earlier.

Historically, the "Back to Africa" concept has been espoused from two broad angles: one is literal; the other is symbolic. This chapter examines those contexts as well as other implications of a trend which, in some quarters, has been characterized as "migrating back to Africa." The first context—that is, the literal—is what this writer called the Marcus Garvey Movement. The second, symbolic context is labelled as the Malcolm X Movement.

In the early part of this century, Marcus Garvey had championed a movement for the creation of a United African Nation free from what he described as "the hands of alien exploiters.[12] Such a nation, he believed, would be "strong enough to lend protection to [Africans] scattered all over the world and to compel the respect of the nations and races of the earth."[13] Garvey wanted "talented" diasporic Africans to return to the continent in order to help build a strong African society. However, Garvey was not the first notable diasporian to call for the return of the Africans. It will be recalled that long before him, between 1817 and 1857, the American

Colonization Society resettled 13,000 African Americans in Liberia[14] although for different motives. In his time, Garvey advocated this cause with such vehemence that the theme of migrating back to Africa almost went down in history as a synonym for his name.[15]

Garvey lived in the United States during one of the ugliest chapters of America history—an ugliness whose odium was surpassed only by the Great Enslavement. It was a time of legally sanctioned racial segregation in America—otherwise known as Jim Crow. The only difference between Jim Crow and the Great Enslavement was that enslavement meant compulsory and unrequited labor. Jim Crow, just like the era of enslavement, retained the institutions and legal instruments of racism—the pillar of the ideology and practice of white supremacism. Also characteristic of Jim Crow were the Anti-African, academic doctrines promulgated and propagated by the masters of "objectivity." Those doctrines include Biological Determinism, social Darwinism, and Kindly Paternalism. Prominent names in academia (some of whom were located in so-called prestigious schools) churned out Anti-African ideas which helped to give the stamp of academic objectivism to the blatant racial oppression of the period. These dogmas were ingrained into the consciousness of private and official America through the help of the masters of objectivity. Thus, Anti-African ideas, over time, became a part of the bedrock of the system's definitional framework.

For Malcolm X, "back to Africa" had a different meaning from Garvey's—a symbolic meaning. For him, it did not mean the physical return of U.S. Africans to Africa. Malcolm's vision was that Africans in the United States should return to Africa culturally, philosophically and psychologically.[16] A reinvigorated spiritual bond with continental Africa, he argued, would strengthen the position of Africans in America. In essence, Malcolm advocated Afrocentric consciousness for African Americans. He believed that Afrocentric consciousness would make U.S. Africans stronger American citizens. Afrocentric education would give African Americans the cultural and historical "centeredness" which had been severely impaired by the systematic brain-washing that has, more or less, been the lot of the African. The educational and mass communication order appears, for the most part, to be characterized by a psychological orientation and philosophical underpinning which inevitably yield anti-African consciousness. Carter G. Woodson, in his classic work, *The Miseducation of the Negro,* articulated a sombering viewpoint. Lamenting the consequences of miseducation, he declared that many an African lacks "both a clear understanding of [the] present state and sufficient foresight to prepare for the future."[17] That's a profound thought which calls for sober reflection on the part of African Americans.

This writer concurs with Malcolm X's perspective on the question of symbolically migrating back to Africa, but it must be pointed out that a spiritual bond has always existed between Diasporic and Continental Africans. This bond was not broken by the Great Enslavement. Indeed, it lives on and can only be strengthened. Ironically, the anguish, the injustices, the institutional and subtle racism which have been inflicted upon Africans in the diaspora have had the effect of keeping Africa alive in the memories of succeeding generations. This view is amply supported by Dona Marimba Richards, a leading African Americanist, in her articulation of the markings and vitalism of African spirituality in the Americas as a whole. She, like several other scholars who have written on this subject, observes that besides the skin pigment, African spirituality remains one of the enduring threads that bind the African Diaspora with the Continentals. In fact, the African world-view, she writes, is distinguished by unity, harmony, spirituality, and organic interrelationships.[18] Richards observes that African spirituality accounts for the resilience of the Diasporic African and was the major factor that enabled enslaved Africans to survive the brutality of their bondage.[19] Richards explains:

> Faced with the realities of slave existence we had to find ways of expressing, energizing and revitalizing the spiritual being we had salvaged from the wreckage of the holocaust. . . . Out of the chaos and trauma of slavery, the spirit of Africa was reborn in the form of the African American ethos.[20]

Ethos refers to the emotional flavor of a cultural group; Richards characterizes the African-Diasporic ethos as "our unique spirit and spiritual being. It is a result of our shared cultural history and is derived from Africa."[21] This ethos is reflected in the African-American music, language, dance, thought patterns, laughter, and walk.[22] Expounding on this theme, Richards adds:

> They took from us everything they could, but there was something left inside that slavery couldn't touch. That something was the fragmented pieces of a shattered world-view, so different from that of the Europeans, that in time it repudiated the materialism that they [had] assumed. The

African world-view stresses the strength of the human spirit. It places paramount value on human vitality as the ground of spiritual immortality.[23]

An expression of this vitality takes the form of a phenomenon which has been described as the African-Diasporic Soul-Force. Leonard Barrett describes it:

> Soul-Force is that power of the Black man that turns sorrow into joy, crying into laughter, defeat into victory. It is patience while suffering, determination while frustrated and hope while in despair. It derives its impetus from the ancestral heritage of Africa, its refinement from the bondage of slavery, and its continuing vitality ·from the conflict of the present.[24]

But there are concrete forms of African retentions in the Diaspora. These include the African-Brazilian musical tradition known as the Candomble, the Caribbean Calypso, the use of proverbs as pedagogical tools in the Caribbean, and such religious systems as the Haitian Vodun. The continued practice of African historical medicine in the Caribbean represents another manifestation, among others, of African imprints on the diasporic landscape.[25]

Besides Malcolm X, Martin Luther King, Jr. and W. E. B. Du Bois, as well as others, had, in various ways, also wrestled with the issue of how to strengthen the African capacity for full-fledged citizenship. In discussing this subject, these heroic activists pointed to an undeniable reality of America: Africans have made mighty contributions to the economic, technological and sociopolitical development of this country, including two hundred and fifty years of unrequited labor. In addition, they have fought side by side with other Americans in the battles that this country has fought to preserve and advance itself. In *The Souls of Black Folk,* Du Bois called for an America which would respect the pluralistic character of its cultural landscape—an America which would not place overt and covert obstacles to the full-fledged citizenship of Africans in America. As part of what could be described as a philosophy of live and let live, Du Bois stated:

> the [African American] simply wishes to make it possible for a man to be both [an African] and an American without being cursed and spat upon by his fellows, without having the doors of Opportunity closed roughly in his face.[26]

Reflecting similar concerns in *The Miseducation of the Negro,* Woodson pin-pointed the significance of educating African children in a manner that would infuse them with correct historical and cultural consciousness. He criticized the educational order for being exclusive of the historical and cultural experiences of a major segment of the American population. He also criticized the Black Church for being mired in Eurocentric theology and for being more imitative than creative.[27] Woodson emphatically stated that the education of Africans in the United States must include African and African-American history, African literature, African religion and the African philosophy of human existence. Even though Woodson had obtained his doctoral education from none other than Harvard University, he came to a realization, later in his life, that centered education was indispensable to the attainment of intellectual maturity—was vital to cultivating the capacity for critical reasoning.[28]

Eighteenth, nineteenth and early twentieth century scholars of the African experience had also called for the scientific study and promotion of the African cultural heritage at a time the African was systematically denigrated as a biologically inferior being through a string of racist dogmas. Such African scholars/writers include Olaudah Equino, Alexander Crummell, James Africanus Beale Horton, David Walker, Edward Wilmot Blyden and J. E. Casely Hayford.

These scholar-activists had boldly challenged racist doctrines about Africa. Horton in particular contended that in human history, civilizations had risen and fallen and that Africa, like other human centers, had had a glorious past as exemplified by the magnificence of ancient Egypt. This line of argument was reinforced by Blyden's "African personality" concept which stated, among other things, that human races are equal and complementary.[29]

Horton called for the establishment of a West African University which, he believed, would serve to cleanse the minds of Africans of the poison of negative self-consciousness and also help the continent to take advantage of its huge mineral and human resources. It is pertinent to note that Horton called for not just a business-as-usual university, but one which would be African-centered in its epistemological frame of reference.[30]

The idea of a West African university makes sense for a number of reasons: one, such a university would strengthen the process of economic and political cooperation and coordination across the Atlantic by serving as a major intellectual power house and center of research; two, the university would experience greater academic freedom than national universities, which in Africa tend to operate under the suffocating influence of state authorities; three, given its greater academic freedom, a West African university would be more effective in pursuing African-centered epistemology; and lastly, given the preceding reasons, the university would be in a better position to pull diasporic and continental intellectuals—the combination of which would give the African world an unfettered and much-needed academic prop.

Although the African intellectual ancestors mentioned in the preceding passage did not employ the terminology of *Afrocentrism,* they had a clear understanding of the necessity for correct historical and cultural training for African children. In the current era, Molefi K. Asante has advanced a theoretical framework for "centeredness" in the education of Africans through his Afrocentric Idea. In three seminal works, *The Afrocentric Idea* (1987), *Afrocentricity* (1988) and *Kemet, Afrocentricity and Knowledge* (1990), Asante articulates the straight-forward idea that Africans should be studied as the subjects of their own history rather than as appendages of someone else's history and culture. Afrocentric research, therefore, "seeks to uncover and use codes, paradigms, symbols, motifs, myths, and circles of discussion that reinforce the centrality of African ideals and values as a valid frame of reference for acquiring and examining data."[31] Other scholars who have contributed profoundly to the promotion of African-centered scholarship include Cheikh Anta Diop, Chancellor Williams, John G. Jackson, Theophile Obenga, Ivan Van Sertima, C. Tsehloane Keto, Maulana Karenga, Dona Marimba Ani, Abu Abbary, Abdias Dos Nascimento, Na'im Akbar, Linda James Myers, Asa Hilliard, and Wade Nobles. There are several others who could not be listed here for lack of space.

To some individuals, all this talk about culture may sound like much ado about nothing. But this writer hastens to suggest that they're mistaken. The centrality of culture to a people's life was brilliantly articulated by Ngugi Wa Thiong'O in his new and riveting work, *Moving the Centre:*

> Culture carries the values, ethical, moral and aesthetic by which people conceptualize or see themselves and their place in history and the universe. These values are the basis of a society's consciousness and outlook, the whole area of a society's make-up, its identity. A sense of belonging, a sense of identity is part of our psychological survival. Colonialism [and enslavement] through racism tried to turn us into societies without heads. Racism, whose highest institutionalized form is apartheid, is not an accident. . . . Thus psychological survival is necessary. We need values that do not distort

our identity, or conception of our rightful place in history, in the universe of the natural and human order.[32]

Wa Thiong'O's thought-provoking paragraph comes at a time of cultural aggression—a time when there exists a greater need than ever before to protect African culture from "decadent" influences—particularly those mass media images and messages which are tailored after the least common denominator. In effect, Wa Thiong'O's position represents a challenge to scholars and writers who have committed their lives to the systematic study of diasporic and continental African cultural experiences.

This writer believes that a human being is both a biological and a cultural organism. Therefore, to exclude the cultural and historical experiences of a group from the curriculum of education is to negate the other half of its humanity. It is another way of saying: "you are not human enough." As a concept which is rooted in history and culture, Afrocentricity belongs to the pluralist perspective, and pluralism constitutes one of the core elements of American democratic ideals. Afrocentricity incorporates Malcolm's vision of a cultural and philosophical return to Africa. Afrocentricity, this writer contends, does not represent the Black version of Hegemonic Eurocentrism, which, as empirical experience has shown, can operate as an ideology and practice of exclusion and objectification of the cultural other.[b] Asa G. Hilliard III captures this fact rather succinctly when he recalls as follows:

> At the turn of the century, theologians in seminaries were debating whether African people had souls, psychologists were debating whether Africans were genetically inferior mentally, anthropologists were labeling Africans 'primitive,' historians were saying that Africans had no history, biologists were even debating the fundamental humanity of Africans.[33]

Such bombardments of the human mind against the African apparently laid the foundation for the mind-set (the persistence of a belief in African inferiority in the current era) which Hacker addressed earlier in this article.

Afrocentric scholars and students conceptualize America as a mosaic of cultures[34] where Africans should co-exist alongside others—not below or above anyone else.[35] The African American community's consciousness of its collective historical and cultural heritage that goes back to Africa with its thousand-year history is important for the collective survival and self-fulfillment of the community. It is true, by and large, that the American model of the free market economy hinges on individual initiative, but it is also true, as realists would argue, that a person's life chances as an American do not depend solely on his/her personal efforts. Harold Cruse articulates this point succinctly in *The Crisis of the Black Intellectual.* In it, Cruse points out the significance of "ethnic group democracy" in America. He states that American ethnic group democracy manifests itself through the self-conscious activities of such segments of the population as the White Anglo Saxon Protestants (WASP), White Catholics, White Jews, and Asian-Americans.[36] Apparently, it was the Rev. Jesse Jackson's realization of this thinly-veiled truth of American multicultural life which compelled him to declare in 1989 that "African Americans" should become the official name for Africans in the U.S.[37] In making this declaration, Jackson stated that the term "African America" had cultural integrity. Jackson could not be more correct. Africans are not known to cry wolf when others assert their Irishness or Jewishness. In fact, Chinatowns abound in America. No one complains about this fact; and, in fact, no one should. These groups assert their self-consciousness because it strengthens them; it makes them stronger Americans. Why then, one may ask rhetorically, does the body politic respond with hysteria to the African's quest for self-definition? Why is that which is a sweetener for others, a sour pill for the African?

It can be said with confidence that the Second African Revolution of the 1960s, which is popularly referred to as the 1960s Protest Movement, owed much to ethnic group democracy. Thus, Affirmative Action, as well as other offshoots of that revolution, including the 1964 Civil Rights Act and the 1965 Voting Rights Act,[c] was designed to open doors that had hitherto been closed to the Africans although as a policy instrument, Affirmative Action is intended to promote equality of access but not equality of results.

For Africans in general, migrating back to Africa philosophically implies, among other things, a reconnection with or strengthening of African *humanistic* heritage. The ancient Egyptians were the first in the world to place on record a philosophy of *humanism* under a system which they called *Maat. Maat* was the name the African ancestors in ancient Egypt gave to the set of principles which governed the Code of Conduct of a humanistic society. *Maat* means order, harmony, balance, righteousness, and truth.[38] Those principles determined what the Egyptians and in fact other historical African societies considered to be correct human conduct, correct societal norms and values. *Maat* was central to the Egyptian philosophy of life. *Maat* conceives life as an orderly system. Maulana

Karenga, an African Americanist who has done impressive work in the area of Egyptology, interprets *Maat* as "the foundation of both nature and righteousness in human society."[39] Karenga observes that *Maat* was the Kemites' "spirit and method of organizing and conducting the relations of human society."[40]

Dona Richards, who was cited earlier, notes that "the [African] culture from which the diasporians had been taken was humanly oriented and organized on the basis of the recognition of the human need for love, warmth, and interrelationship."[41] That is indeed true, and, at this point, this writer would like to state the question which students raise when *Maat* is discussed in class. They ask, "is it pragmatic to practice *Maat* in a hedonistic and ravenous society where the kind of values enshrined in *Maat* appear to be taking a back-stage?" This writer's response has always been as follows: the real question should be about how the African community, riven by internal disharmony, as well as Black-on-Black spiritual and physical killings, can put its divided and troubled house in order; as the saying goes, a house divided against itself cannot stand. Furthermore, *Maat* does not dilute the imperative for *intellectual vigilance* on the part of the community, and for taking all ethical and morally-defensible measures necessary for the defense and protection of its vital and legitimate interests. It has been well-stated that as a victimized people "fighting for survival and development, African Americans must see our children as future 'warriors' in [the] struggle for liberation."[42]

Maat embodies the concept of an ideal human being. The ancients viewed the ideal human being as a silent, moderate, and sensible person who lives up to society's norms and values. The ideal person, who is also known as the "silent one," manifests self-control, modesty, kindness, generosity, discretion, truthfulness, and serenity. The contrast to the ideal person is an individual whom the ancients described as the fool or the hothead—a person who is controlled by "his emotions and instincts which lead to a behavior disapproved by society."[43] The hothead is given to gluttony, greed, arrogance, bad temper, and vindictiveness.

In effect, to return to the motherland philosophically would mean ordering one's life in accordance with the teachings of *Maat*. A cultural return to Africa would mean much more than the adornment of African motif—attires, home decorations and what have you—even though they serve a useful purpose of nourishing aesthetic sensibilities. It could also mean much more than the acquisition of knowledge of African history.

After all, without the ability or will to apply whatever knowledge a person has acquired to his/her daily life, knowledge becomes wasted information. Returning to Africa also means a conscious attempt to lead a life of honesty, self-control, self-respect and a respect for fellow human beings, refinement in spoken and written language, hard work, and excellence. In fact, *Maat* enjoins its adherents to strive for excellence in all endeavors "so that no fault can be found in [our] character."[44] *Maat* also calls for a temperament of deferred gratification and a consciousness that "I exist because we exist." Migrating back to Africa would mean respect for elders and a keen sense of family. It means a willingness to serve as one's brother's or sister's keeper.

This writer contends that the ultimate test of Afrocentric consciousness would be the extent to which the mind has been freed of the bondage of "slave" or "colonial" mentality. Killing each other, physically and spiritually, does not reflect Afrocentric consciousness on the part of the killer. Rather, Afrocentricity enjoins its adherents to inspire and uplift each other. What is expected is creative courage, as opposed to destructive courage. While Afrocentric consciousness allows for healthy competition amongst the people, it, however, simultaneously stresses cooperative endeavors. For instance, if Africans do not patronize the businesses in their neighborhoods, who would?

Furthermore, it is not enough for individuals or groups to lament (as should be done from time to time) African community's lack of control over its economic sector—a situation which is, in part, a legacy of slavery, Jim Crow and dashed promises like the unfulfilled promise of forty acres and a mule; it is important that Africans initiate personal business enterprises and try to strengthen them through cooperative ventures, among other measures. It is necessary that the inhabitants of a given neighborhood work together to keep that neighborhood safe and to dissuade juvenile children from defacing the structures that individuals labored hard to put up in such communities. Through collective vigilance over the neighborhoods, the inhabitants can deter those who live by infesting the environment with drugs, and neighborhood vigilantes can also deter those who threaten lives and property.

The history of African institution-building teaches an important lesson: there is a splendid record of building institutions, but often a poor job is done of sustaining them. This writer postulates that the causal factors stem from within and without. The internal factors appear to be failure to groom successors, in-fighting, poor planning and poor management. Yes, the community is confronted with a clear and present threat from with-out—that evil known as racism that ever looms large! African women face the double jeopardy of racism and sexism. It is a world where whiteness per se gives an individual an advantage in the struggle of life. This psychological malady prompted W. E. B. Du Bois to declare in 1900, at the 2nd Pan-African Congress[45] in London, that the major problem which confronts the twentieth century is the problem of the color line. Ninety-four years later, that profound statement remains, by and large, a valid truth. As happens from time to time, the questions and innuendos which preceded the collegial basketball championship of April 4, 1994, brought the problem of the twentieth century to the fore.

Be that as it may, migrating back to Africa philosophically would help rebuild collective African consciousness which had been shattered by the major interventions in African history. Global African consciousness would augur well for the recovery process that is going on now in the African world, for it is this writer's informed conviction that the African world, like a convalescing patient, is still at the stage of recovering from the devastating consequences of the Great Enslavement and colonial exploitation and brainwashing. Global African consciousness would facilitate educational, political and socioeconomic linkages between diasporic and continental Africa—linkages which are necessary if the African world is to become a real actor on the world stage. In the last five hundred years, the African world has found itself at the receiving end of history. This hope for a global African consciousness need not be viewed with alarm by non-Africans; for to seek to promote the African interest is not to stand against anyone's interest. The world is large enough to accommodate everyone. Rather, non-Africans should understand that to seek to promote the African interest is to promote the interest of humanity as a whole through one of its branches. This is not a doctrine for how others could be dominated or exploited; this is a quest for universal racial justice, for the improvement of the lot of the long-suffering African.

In the wake of the disintegration of the Eastern Bloc's ideological camp and the consequent demise of the Cold War, scholars of international geopolitics and even politicians have been discussing the contours of an emerging world order. In order to become a force to be reckoned within the emerging world order, Diasporic and Continental Africans must build more linkages and strengthen existing ones.

Apart from bringing direct pressures to bear on the U.S. foreign policy formulation process, African American organizations and intellectuals should expand and create Pan-African linkages. Without Pan-African linkages, the African world cannot exert a significant influence on the emerging world order, let alone define and direct it in its own interest.

International politics is power politics. The greater the leverage at the disposal of the strategically placed individual, the more likely that he/she can make the system work in the desired direction. Walter Rodney, the late distinguished African-American historian, left behind an eloquent truth about the centrality of power to human life. As he put it,

> Power is the ultimate determinant in human society, being basic to the relations within any group and between groups. It implies the ability to defend one's will by any means available. In relations between peoples, the question of power determines maneuverability in bargaining, the extent to which one people respect the interests of another, and eventually the extent to which a people survive as a physical and cultural entity.[46]

Pan-African linkages would increase the leverage open to the institutions and individuals who shape the place of the African world in the global scheme of things. Examples abound of successes achieved through Pan-African cooperation. African Americans rose to the occasion when Italy invaded Ethiopia in 1935, despite the fact that this was a time when the diasporic Africans themselves were reeling under the weight of virulent white racism[d] in America. Historians John Hope Franklin and Alfred A. Moss, Jr. recall a memorable display of diasporic solidarity with the Ethiopians.

> Almost overnight even the most provincial among Negro Americans became international-minded. Ethiopia was a black nation, and its destruction would symbolize the final victory of white over blacks. In many communities funds were raised for the defense of the African Kingdom, while in larger cities elaborate organizations were set up.[47]

The general Decolonization effort in Africa stands out as another example. Among others, W. E. B. Du Bois's Pan-African Congresses and literary campaigns not only helped to inspire a generation of African nationalist leaders, but also brought the plight of colonized Africa to the attention of world opinion. Champions of African independence like the late Kwame Nkrumah and Dr. Nnamdi Azikiwe, the Owelle of Onitsha, had been inspired by the works of Du Bois. In turn, the decolonization process in

Africa doubled as a psychological boost for oppressed and abused African men and women across the Atlantic, resulting in the just struggle known as the Civil Rights Movement. Franklin and Moss, Jr. recall, with relish, that august moment in the history of the African world.

> The emergence into independence of the [African] nations enormously changed the worldwide significance of the American race problem and provided a considerable stimulus to the movement for racial equality in the United States. . . . It seemed that black men from the Old World had arrived just in time to help redress the racial balance in the New.[48]

Pan-African interaction has thus been a symbiotic process. There are examples from contemporary times. Without the activism of Trans Africa, African American/African Student Unions across American college campuses, and the Congressional Black Caucus, the sanctions and divestments achieved against South Africa, when it was under an apartheid regime,ᵉ would not have been possible. The same argument can be made about Namibian independence in 1990.

Economic, educational and technological progress in the African world would profit from Pan-African linkages. African American Studies Departments and African American businesses are the appropriate channels for Pan-African economic, educational and technological linkages. In 1991, a Pennsylvania African-American business mission visited Nigeria and other African countries where it explored investment opportunities. This was a step in the right direction, and there should be more of such business missions to Africa. The Congressional Black Caucus should initiate talks with the Organization of African Unity (OAU), the Economic Community of West African States (ECOWAS) and the South African Development Coordinating Council (SADCC) for special economic investment terms for African Americans, including land acquisition.

Communications technology represents a major lever of power. Whoever controls the apparatus for global communications exercises immeasurable influence on the flow and ideological slant of information and thus helps to determine how people view the world and also themselves. To a large degree, the international media decide what and who get priority attention on the agenda of world affairs. Needless to say, communications technology and manpower deserve priority attention from Pan-African strategists.

As this chapter discussed at length in the preceding pages, the cultural vitality of Afrocentricity and the African diaspora will profit from Pan-African linkages. Beside rejuvenating the cultural life of the African diaspora, Pan-African linkages would bear collateral economic fruits. Diasporic cultural groups and think tanks are the appropriate channels for such linkages. Visible action is already being taken in this direction as more and more U.S. Africans have demonstrated practical interest in tourism to Africa.

Text Notes

a. Readers are referred to Ralph Ginburg's *100 Years of Lynchings* (Baltimore: Black CP, 1962), for insights into the magnitude and odium of racial prejudice and the attendant violence. I imagine that readers would be intrigued by a December 30, 1900 report, in this hair-raising and chilling book, which quoted one Professor Albert Bushnell Hart of Harvard College as suggesting, before a convention of the American Historical Convention, that "if the people of certain States are determined to burn colored men at the stake, those States would better legalize the practice." Ginzburg, Ralph. *100 Years of Lynchings*. Baltimore: Black CP, 1962: 36.

b. Dona Marimba Ani's latest explosive and highly documented book, *Yurugu: An African-Centered Critique of European Cultural Thought and Behavior.* Trenton: Africa WP, 1994, represents a rich resource for readers who may want to explore the historical, ideological and even religious roots of Hegemonic Eurocentrism.

c. It is pertinent to recall that the passing of the Civil Rights and Voting Rights Acts in the '60s was a re-invention of the wheel. During the Great Reconstruction (1865-1877), Congress enacted Civil Rights Acts in 1866 and 1875. (It was the Supreme Court of the United States which outlawed the 1875 Civil Rights Act in 1883.) Franklin, John Hope & Alfred A. Moss, Jr., *From Slavery to Freedom: A History of Negro Americans*. New York: McGraw-Hill, 1988: 238.

d. I hope the reader would not interpret this statement to imply that racism is a phenomenon of the past.

e. South Africa has now come under a black majority rule. Nelson Mandela, easily the foremost leader of what was a world-wide movement against apartheid in South Africa, took office on May 13, 1994 as the first president of a free South Africa. He had paid a heavy price for his dogged struggle, including spending twenty-seven years of his youthful life behind bars.

Notes

1. Haki R. Madhubuti, *Black Men: Obsolete, Single, and Dangerous?* Chicago: Africa WP, 1990: 72.

2. *U.S. Bureau of the Census, Statistical Abstract of the United States: 1992* (12th edition). Washington, D.C., 1992: 39.

3. Haki R. Madhubuti, *Black Men: Obsolete, Single, and Dangerous?* Chicago: Africa WP, 1990: 72-73.

4. Madhubuti 73.

5. Cornel West, *Keeping Faith: Philosophy and Race in America.* New York: Routledge, 1993: xii.

6. Molefi Kete Asante, *Open Letter to Dr. Henry Louis Gates, Jr.* 25 July, 1992.

7. Na'im Akbar, quoted in Maulana Karenga, *Introduction to Black Studies.* 1982. Los Angeles: University of SP, 1993: 444.

8. Vincent Bakpetu Thompson. *The Making of the African Diaspora in the Americas, 1441-1900.* New York: Longman, 1987: 119.

9. Thompson 153.

10. Andrew Hacker, *Two Nations: Black and White, Separate, Hostile, Unequal.* New York: Ballantine, 1992: 23.

11. Hacker 23.

12. Tony Martin, *Race First: The Ideological and Organizational Struggles of Marcus Garvey and the Universal Negro Improvement Association.* Dover: the Majority P, 1976: 41.

13. Martin 41.

14. Olisanwuche P. Esedebe, *Pan-Africanism: The Ideas and Movement, 1776-1963.* Washington, D.C.: Howard UP, 1982: 10.

15. Martin 136-137.

16. George Breitman, *The Last Year of Malcolm X: The Evolution of a Revolutionary.* New York: Pathfinder, 1967: 63.

17. Carter G. Woodson, *The Miseducation of the Negro.* 1933. New York: AMS P, 1977: 96.

18. Marimba Dona Richards, *Let the Circle Be Unbroken: The Implications of African Spirituality in the Diaspora.* New York: Djifa, 1980: 51-53.

19. Richards 51-53.

20. Richards 23-24.

21. Richards 3.

22. Richards 14.

23. Richards 14.

24. Leonard Barrett, quoted in Marimba Dona Richards, *Let the Circle Be Unbroken: The Implications of African Spirituality in the Diaspora.* New York: Djifa, 1980: 34.

25. Richards 14-15, 17, 19 & 20.

26. W. E. B. Du Bois, *The Souls of Black Folk.* New York: Penguin Books, 1969: 46.

27. Woodson 61.

28. Woodson 150.

29. Esedebe 33-37.

30. Esedebe 28.

31. Molefi K. Asante, *Kemet, Afrocentricity and Knowledge.* Trenton: Africa WP, 1990: 6.

32. Ngugi Wa Thiong'O, *Moving the Centre: The Struggle for Cultural Freedoms.* Portsmouth: Heinemann, 1993: 77.

33. Asa G. Hilliard III, "Afrocentrism in a Multicultural Society," *American Visions,* August, 1991: 23.

34. Ella Forbes, "The African American View of America," a Presentation at a Debate on Multicultural Education. Mount Pocono, PA: East Strausbourg University, Sept. 25, 1992.

35. Molefi Kete Asante, "Multi-Culturalism: An Exchange," *The American Scholar,* Spring, 1991: 268.

36. Harold Cruse, *The Crisis of the Negro Intellectual.* New York: Bazel E. Allen and Ernest J. Wilson, 1984: 317.

37. " 'African-American' Favored by Many of America's Blacks," *New York Times,* January 31, 1989: Sec. A. (1).

38. Rnjhild Bjerre Finnestad, *The Religion of the Ancient Egyptians: Cognitive Structures and Popular Expressions (Proceedings of Symposia in Uppsala and Bergen 1987 and 1988).* Stockholm, Sweden: Tryckeri Balker AB, 1989: 23.

39. Maulana Karenga, *Selections from the Husia.* 1984. Los Angeles: The University of Sankore P, 1989: 29.

40. Karenga (1989) 30.

41. Richards 13.

42. Madhubuti 192.

43. Finnestad 81.

44. Maulana Karenga, "Towards a Sociology of Maatian Ethics: Literature and Context," *Egypt Revisited.* Ed. Ivan Van Sertima. New Brunswick: Transaction Books, 1993: 373.

45. Olisanwuche P. Esedebe, *Pan-Africanism: The Ideas and Movement, 1776-1963.* Washington, D.C.: Howard UP, 1982: 37.

46. Walter Rodney, *How Europe Underdeveloped Africa.* 1972. Washington, D.C.: Howard UP, 1972-224.

47. John Hope Franklin. *From Slavery to Freedom: A History of Negro Americans.* New York: McGraw-Hill, 1988: 385.

48. Franklin & Moss, Jr. 438.

49. "Dual Nationality at Last," *West Africa,* November 2-8, 1992: 1867.

REFERENCES

" 'African-American' Favored by Many of America's Blacks." *New York Times,* January 31, 1989: Sec. A(1).

ANI, MARIMBA. 1994. *Yurugu: An African-Centered Critique of European Cultural Thought and Behavior.* Trenton: Africa WP.

ASANTE, MOLEFI. 1988. *Afrocentricity.* Trenton: Africa WP.

_____. 1987. *The Afrocentric Idea.* Philadelphia: Temple UP.

_____. 1990. *Kemet, Afrocentricity and Knowledge.* Trenton, N.J.: Africa WP.

_____. Spring, 1991. "Multi-Culturalism: An Exchange." *The American Scholar.*

_____. July 25, 1992. *Open Letter to Dr. Henry Louis Gates, Jr.*

BREITMAN, GEORGE. 1967. *The Last Year of Malcolm X: The Evolution of a Revolutionary.* New York: Pathfinder.

"Dual Nationality at Last." 1992 (1867). *West Africa.* November 2-8.

DU BOIS, W. E. B. 1969 (1903). *The Souls of Black Folk.* New York: Penguin Books, 1969.

ESEDEBE, OLISANWUCHE P. 1982. *Pan-Africanism: The Ideas and Movement, 1776-1963.* Washington, D.C.: Howard UP.

FINNESTAD, BJERRE RJNHILD. 1989. *The Religion of the Ancient Egyptians: Cognitive Structures and Popular Expressions (Proceedings of Symposia in Uppsala and Bergen 1987 and 1988).* Stockholm, Sweden: Tryckeri Balder AB.

FORBES, ELLA. Sept. 25, 1991. "The African American View of America." A Presentation at a Debate on Multicultural Education. Mount Pocono, PA: East Strausbourg University.

FRANKLIN, JOHN HOPE & ALFRED A. MOSS, JR. 1988. *From Slavery to Freedom: A History of Negro Americans.* New York: McGraw-Hill.

GINZBURG, RALPH. 1962. *100 Years of Lynchings.* Baltimore: Black CP.

HACKER, ANDREW. 1992. *Two Nations: Black and White, Separate, Hostile, Unequal.* New York: Ballentine.

HILLIARD III & G. ASA. 1991. "Afrocentrism in a Multicultural Democracy." *American Visions,* August: 23.

KARENGA, MAULANA. 1989. *Selections from the Husia.* 1984. Los Angeles: The University of Sankore P.

_____. 1993. "Towards a Sociology of Maatian Ethics: Literature and Context," *Egypt Revisited.* Ed. Ivan Van Sertima. New Brunswick: Transaction Books.

_____. 1993. *Introduction to Black Studies.* 1982. Los Angeles: University of SP.

MADHUBUTI, HAKI R. 1990. *Black Men: Obsolete, Single, and Dangerous?* Chicago: Africa WP.

MARTIN, TONY. 1976. *Race First: The Ideological and Organizational Struggles of Marcus Garvey and the Universal Negro Improvement Association.* Dover: the Majority P.

RICHARDS, MARIMBA DONA. 1980. *Let the Circle Be Unbroken: The Implications of African Spirituality in the Diaspora.* New York: Djifa, 1980.

THIONG'O, NGUGI WA. 1993. *Moving the Centre: The Struggle for Cultural Freedoms.* Portsmouth: Heinemann.

RODNEY, WALTER. 1972. *How Europe Underdeveloped Africa..* Washington, D.C.: Howard UP, 1972-224.

THOMPSON, VINCENT BAKPETU. *The Making of the African Diaspora in the Americas, 1441-1900.* New York: Longman, 1987: 119.

WEST, CORNEL. *Keeping Faith: Philosophy and Race in America.* New York: Routledge, 1993:

WOODSON, CARTER G. *The Miseducation of the Negro.* 1933. New York: AMS P, 1977: 96.

Communication and Development

14

Imperatives for an Afrocentric Methodology

Peter O. Nwosu
Donald S. Taylor
Cecil A. Blake

The Afrocentric tradition is essentially grounded in the use of core African perspectives as tools to understand African phenomena (Asante, 1980). The need to utilize such an approach in the study of communication and development in Africa has become increasingly apparent with the call for culture-sensitive research methodologies that are not encapsulated by dominant Western perspectives.

For a long time, communication and development scholars have taken Western concepts and measurement tools and applied them to African research problems in ways that have produced major gaps in what we know about communication processes in Africa. Blake (1993a) revisited extant research and scholarship on development communication and observed that the end of Eurocentric visions in this area is imminent. When we review the literature upon which development communication is grounded, it is all but clear that a thorough overhaul is required.

Our knowledge of how Africans communicate, and how communication messages impact them in purely African settings is fragmentary, unsystematic and Eurocentric in orientation. Although such gaps have been recognized by some communication scholars, no sustained attempt has been made to explore both conceptually and empirically the viability of a uniquely integrated Afrocentric approach to study communication and development in Africa.

Some African scholars (Blake, 1979b, 1981; Boafo & George, 1992; Nwosu, 1990; Obeng-Quaidoo, 1985, 1986; Okigbo, 1985; Taylor, 1991; Ugboajah, 1985) have emphasized the importance of adopting appropriate or culture-sensitive research methods to study development communication in Africa. The recurring view of these scholars is that existing Western-derived research methods do not provide us with a sufficient basis to understand individual and collective needs of African audiences. For instance, Obeng-Quaidoo (1985) notes that Western research methods focus on the individual as a primary source and receiver of information and that even when the research goal is to investigate a group or an organization, the divergent views of a sample of individuals are merely or simplistically aggregated to represent the group or the organization. The accuracy of such reification of information is questionable in an African context where the community and community values are central to communication interactions and the decision-making process. An aggregation of individual views, for example, cannot be synonymous with consensual or mandated community views just as heterogeneity of group views cannot be regarded as the same as a homogeneous group view.

These and other observations attest to the urgent need either to recognize potential pitfalls with existing applications or to fashion out uniquely African investigatory tools (i.e., Afrocentric) that help advance knowledge of development communication processes in African societies. It must be pointed out at this juncture that what is being articulated here emerges from a fundamental premise: Communication as a discipline has stock issues that constitute its ethos but require frequent visits as non-Western societies in the process of social change seek to utilize appropriate communication strategies to carry out innovations. This chapter has emerged out of that ethos. Hence, its purpose is to present a discussion of the several conceptual and methodological issues that plague research and to suggest elements to be included in any new African-based direction. The discussion centers around the following: communication process and patterns in Africa, and an overview of current research methods (problems and challenges).

Process and Patterns of
Communication in Africa

There are two important conceptual questions that development communication scholars must address as a necessary first step to understanding
the challenges of conducting development communication research in
Africa. First, is the *communication process in Africa* so different from the
communication process in the West or elsewhere as to require special
attention and methodology? Second, are *communication patterns in Africa*
so different from those in the West or elsewhere as to require special
attention and methodology, or uniquely African investigatory tools?

The Communication Process

We mentioned earlier that this chapter has emerged from stock issues
that constitute the ethos of communication. Our position, therefore, is that
fundamental elements in the communication process are universal—
source, message, channel, receiver, feedback, and aspects of noise—and
that the basic rhetorical modes of proof—ethical, logical, and pathetic—are
found in all societies. For communication scholars conducting development research in Africa, there are at least three important points to note.
First, the universality of the communication process, as we have argued
here, does not presuppose a universalization of research foci. Development
research agenda must be governed by the unique needs and particular
circumstances of each region. A second point to note is that the universality
of the communication process does not presuppose that development
communication research must be conducted only with reference to Western
types of media (Chu, cited in Blake, 1993a). A third and final issue to
consider is that the universality of the communication process does not
presuppose a universalization of research methods for investigating the
various elements of such a process. Ugboajah (1985) observed the tendency
on the part of communication researchers to take little account of the
specific circumstances of the society under study in our use of a Western
research culture. A related concern hinges on what issues are being
investigated. The focus of communication research in the West has been
on media effects (Jayaweera, 1991).

As noted by Nwosu, Taylor, and Onwumechili (1995), a universal communication process merely indicates that the basic elements of the communication process are similar, but because these elements may mean or embody differences influenced by sociocultural contexts, the appropriate research methods should be those that successfully mesh with or match both the process elements and their contexts to achieve the following criteria for successful research:

- A valid outcome of the investigation (i.e., an outcome that accurately reflects the peculiarities of the development communication context)
- A measure that accurately upholds the context of the development communication process (i.e., a measure that not only respects and accepts possibilities of contextual differences but does not unduly pass value judgments on these differences).

Communication Patterns

Patterns represent shared symbols or ingredients that are present in a given communication environment and at the same time provide meaning to the interaction that takes place in that environment (Nwosu et al., 1995). Storytelling as a communication pattern in Africa entails shared norms about characters, roles, rules, rituals, beliefs, and values (Blake, 1979a, 1979b). These symbols enable the interaction that takes place in that environment to signify something, and their meanings are, of course, dictated by a society's culture and history. Communication patterns are therefore derived from a society's cultural patterns.

Thus, the *patterns* of communication in Africa are fundamentally different from the patterns of communication in the West because both societies have fundamentally different cultural patterns. Indeed, at an emergency meeting of African communication researchers held in Yaounde, Cameroon in 1981, participants concluded that the interplay between communication processes and the forces of Africa's culture and history give communication patterns in Africa a different profile from that in other regions of the world (Ugboajah, 1985, p. 325).

What, then, are the communication patterns in Africa, and what core values or cultural patterns govern the African communication environment? Answers to these questions are extremely vital in order to reach an understanding of the interplay between communication and culture in Africa, which communication researchers must then employ to focus attention on different sets of problems and research priorities and to fashion uniquely African investigatory tools for development communication inquiry, different from those that might interest their colleagues elsewhere.

Awa (1988) has identified three patterns of communication in Africa as a basis for understanding Africa's core values. These are verbal communication, nonverbal communication, and traditional media. Although he states that the line between verbal and nonverbal communication is fuzzy, Awa warns scholars to recognize the importance of nonverbal communication because cultural differences "can result in mutual perception of meaning between development experts (who are usually Western or Western-trained technicians) and their clients (who are mostly farmers in rural communities)" (p. 133).

Clearly, the first two patterns of communication identified by Awa are primarily interpersonal modes of communication and they fall within what Ugboajah (1985) calls *oramedia*. Oramedia, or folk media, are largely maintained through the symbolizing codes of oral tradition as Africa is predominantly an oral-aural society. These symbolizing codes

> include mythology, oral literature (poetry, storytelling, proverbs), masquerades, rites of passage and other rituals expressed through oracy, music, dance, drama, use of costumes, social interplay and material symbols which accompany people from womb to tomb and much beyond. (p. 166)

Traditional media, the third pattern of communication in Africa, are clearly subsumed in Ugboajah's concept because we find in them both symbolizing codes, such as oral literature and folk drama that Fiofori (1975), Blake (1979a), Ugboajah (1985), Nwosu (1986), and Awa (1995), among other scholars, adequately discuss, and indigenous *technologies* of communication, such as talking drums and gongs, which have been well documented by Doob (1961) and Asante and Appiah (1979). The above communication patterns represent, in a very clear sense, media forms unlike any found in Western societies.

An interesting concept often omitted in discussions about Africa's traditional media is the word *mass*. Because communication patterns in Africa generally do not go beyond the immediate rural setting, it is easy to assume that they are not forms of *mass communication*. Such concepts, it is argued, can only be reserved for Western forms of mass communication, for subsumed in those forms are other concepts such as *industrialization,* *mass society,* or *mass audience.* Broom and Selznick (1958) contend that

> the weakening of traditional bonds, the growth of rationality, and the division of labor, have created societies made up of individuals who are only loosely bound together. In this sense the word "mass" suggests something closer to an aggregate than to a tightly knit social group. (p. 38)

Several scholars have argued that it is only "mass communication if the production and distribution of messages are technologically and institutionally based" (see Dance, 1967). Other scholars who have engaged in this debate also argue that (a) in *mass* communication interpersonal communication is not possible and (b) the message is sent *indirectly* to receivers through some form of mechanical device, such as radio, television, or newspapers. It is this device that permits the mass reproduction and mass distribution of the message to audiences at the same time. Desmond Wilson, an African scholar, has offered a different explanation for the concept of *mass* communication in African settings, arguing that traditional modes of communication in Africa can also be described as *mass* forms of communication because of their function and context (Wilson, cited in Ugboajah, 1985).

Awa (1988) also has argued that

> unlike the Western media—radio, television, newspapers, magazines, and related technologies—which carry messages to hundreds of thousands of anonymous and culturally *heterogeneous* receivers, African traditional media—talking drums, gongs, folk drama, and oral literature—carry mass-communicated messages to groups that are relatively *homogeneous* in face-to-face settings. (p. 133).

Evidence from Nigeria, Ghana, Uganda, and other places in Africa provides numerous examples of the applications of traditional media in African social development (Awa, 1988; Fiofori, 1975; Nwosu, 1986), yet little research has focused on the challenges and opportunities inherent in these kinds of media. Rather, the emphases among communication researchers have been on Western types of media—radio, television, newspapers, and other related technologies—which can be classified here as the fourth in the line of contemporary communication patterns in Africa. The focus of most development communication research in Africa has been on these types of media.

Determining what core values or cultural patterns govern the African communication environment may enable us to begin to recognize why existing Western-derived methods do not provide sufficient tools to African communication scholars for understanding individual and collective needs of African audiences. Even though we are discussing "core" African values, there are notable cultural differences and value orientations from region to region. We are making a projection here of what constitutes some basic core values. A number of African scholars have written about African cultural patterns (Mbiti, 1975; Obeng-Quaidoo, 1986; Onwubiko, 1991; Sofola, 1982). Obeng-Quaidoo (1986), for example, identifies four of these patterns, which he calls *core value boundaries* of African culture. These are (a) the relationship of Africans to a supreme God/Allah and lesser gods, (b) concepts of time and reincarnation, (c) the concept of work, and (d) the concept of nonindividuality. Obeng-Quaidoo notes that the African's worldview evolves around one Supreme Deity (called different names in different parts of the continent) and lesser gods. The lesser deities, it is believed, have a supernatural connection with the Supreme Deity. Because the Supreme Deity is held so high but seems so far away, it is very common for Africans to consult the representatives (priests) of lesser deities to seek solutions to the challenges they face in their daily affairs.

The second core value that governs behavior in some African societies is the attitude toward time and reincarnation. First, the African concept of time is fundamentally different from the way time is structured and perceived in Western societies. Whereas time is central to all activities, both business and social, in Western societies, it is not central to life in Africa. Awa (1988) notes that

African concepts, structure, perceptions of time are dictated by nature. People wake up to the crowing of the cock, which happens at the crack of dawn. Dawn may be anytime from 5:30 to 6:00 a.m. If a paramount chief summons the cabinet, through a messenger, to convene at daybreak and some arrive at 5:30 a.m. and others at 6:00 a.m., none of them will be perceived as late. Decisions by "chiefs-in-council" require full representation and participation of all section heads, and such decisions are generally preceded by a social event—the ritual breaking of kola nut, a prolonged libation ceremony—deliberately calculated to allow time for a quorum to be attained. (p. 139)

Obeng-Quaidoo (1986) notes that subsumed in the concept of time (in some African societies) is the concept of reincarnation:

> Death, for the African, means the death of the physical body, but the real essence of the human being lives on and would be born again into the same family or clan. Added to this is the view that the African never accepts death as a natural phenomenon. There is always a reason for death; whether it comes to the youth or to the aged, and this explains our preoccupation with necromancy and visits to the priests and shrines to find out why someone is dead. (p. 93)

Furthermore, physical death does not mean spiritual death. It is believed that when an elderly person dies the spirit of that person lives on to join with other departed ancestors of the land in offering continued protection to the extended family or the clan. This explains why Africans first call upon the spirits of the departed ancestors to guide and protect them, in addition to the Supreme Deity and other lesser gods, whenever they offer supplications during different occasions.

Blake (1993b) notes that

> African societies share certain fundamental values that guide the day to day life of inhabitants in traditional African settings. . . . There are, for example, certain "rules" that guide discourse in the deliberative, forensic and epidiectic genres. The "rules" are grounded in values such as respect for elders; acceptance of the supremacy of hierarchical structures; performance of certain rituals in respect for ancestors; performance of rituals for various occasions ranging from farming to death and burial ceremonies; sibling relationships, etc. . . . The values, some of which are mentioned above, are critical in our efforts to understand communication philosophies, ethics, processes, structures and genres in traditional African settings. (p. 3)

A third core value that shapes African communication patterns is the African concept of work. There is a popular saying in some parts of Africa that when a white man is laid off from work, he may take a gun and shoot himself, but when an African is laid off, he takes his hoe and returns to the farm! This saying typifies the Westerner's concept of work—work is seen as an end in itself, a duty central to one's existence because it has some eternal reward, and that a loss of that work makes life meaningless and less worth living for. For the African, however, work is seen not as a duty that has some eternal reward but as means to an end, a necessity for survival, especially at the levels of subsistence. Although the African concept of work and activity has been tainted by European influence in urban Africa, the concept remains valid to explanations of life in rural Africa (Nwosu et al., 1995).

We see the above concept equally present in the final core boundary of African culture—the concept of communalism, which Awa (1988) calls the "core of social life" in Africa. Just as the concept of individualism has been elevated to the status of a national religion in the West (Stewart & Bennett, 1991), the same can be said of the concept of communalism in Africa. Whereas individualism represents commitment to independence, privacy, self, and the idea of "I," communalism represents commitment to interdependence, community affiliation, others, and the idea of "we." Communalism is the soul and fiber of work, activity, and social life in Africa. It is a testament to the nonindividuality of the African, "a vital part of the African cultural ethos . . . [providing] social security for the less fortunate members of a community. It is, in a sense, an outward expression of the empathy of the African—the impulse to show concern for others" (Awa, 1988, p. 136). Communalism is manifested, for example, through the extended family system, which has been well documented (see Awa, 1988; Karp & Bird, 1980; Mbiti, 1975).

Clearly, the African communication profile includes communication patterns that demonstrate the core boundaries of African culture. The core value boundaries provide a basis for understanding communication patterns in Africa and the implications of Western-derived methodologies for studying communication phenomena in African contexts. Furthermore, such understanding helps communication scholars begin to recognize more seriously the potential pitfalls of Western-derived research methods and begin to incorporate some new elements as part of the investigatory tools for development communication research in African settings. Let us now examine trends in current empirical research methods being used in Africa to study communication and development.

Current Research Methods: Problems and Challenges

Observation (Data Collection)

One major element in the empirical research process is observation. An important assumption is that the individual is the unit of analysis. Thus, the most widely used observation tool both in Western industrialized nations and in Africa has been survey research employing interview schedules. As Obeng-Quaidoo (1986) argued, most communication studies done in Africa have involved surveys. In these studies, there is a tendency to interview individuals and then aggregate their responses to achieve a composite score. In African settings, however, this approach has serious limitations because of the nonindividuality of the African (especially in the rural areas) regarding where, when, and how communication is received and processed.

Critical for the researchers is the expectation in an interview situation that the respondent will express opinions (i.e., responses) that accurately (i.e., reliability) reflect the phenomenon being studied (i.e., validity). But in Africa, expressing personal opinion is not a common feature of communication behavior. Opinion is often influenced by such factors as age, status, and gender of the interactants; group norms (e.g., resistance to self-disclosure in collectivist, high-context cultures); the political situation in the country; whether or not the questioner is from within or outside the group being interviewed; and the willingness of other members of the household to permit one member to be interviewed separately. Obeng-Quaidoo (1986) provides a vivid illustration of a typical interview setting. Specifically,

> we find that a whole troop of youngsters and even other adults would like to listen to the kinds of questions the interviewer is going to ask one member of the family. Persistent persuasion that the interview is for only one member of the family sometimes falls on deaf ears, and the interviewer is quite helpless to drive away the unwelcome crowd. This situation is especially common in compound houses in the village. (p. 94)

From this description, it seems clear that any responses obtained in such situations would be greatly contaminated by the research context in addition to some of the other variables that could confound accurate personal responses. Indeed, individuals are more likely to express a consensus view of the village, compound, or household. Thus, the assumption that the individual is the unit of analysis is at best erroneous and invalid when applied to African settings and problems.

A second problem closely tied to the interviewing quagmire is that of translation. In most cases, interview schedules and questionnaires are constructed in English, French, or some other major international language used as the official language of the country. This requires that interviewers must first be efficiently trained in the language of the questionnaire and then make appropriate translation into the language of the interview (an ethnic-based language). Both Gwebu (1977) and Taylor (1991) have argued that this process opens up major opportunities for misinterpretation and mistranslation due to lack of equivalencies, interviewer fatigue, and the quantity of interviewers used to complete these assignments. At the crux of this problem is the high rate of illiteracy in the major international languages. Researchers are invariably compelled to select interviewing as opposed to self-administered questionnaires that could limit the range and amount of interviewer errors.

A third problem with interviewing is that sensitive and taboo questions cannot be easily asked or answered. Custom, tradition, and moral codes differ from country to country, but in the main there is still an aversion in many African settings (e.g., rural areas) to discussions about sex, income, age, and other personal characteristics and traits (e.g., praising oneself for accomplishments).

Another problem associated with data collection is the lack of available data sources from which either probability or nonprobability samples may be drawn. A central tenet of survey research is that the sample frame should represent a constellation of the individuals in the group that is to be studied so that the sample drawn is representative. In advanced Western societies, phone directories and listings, census tracts, and other published data sources are readily available to aid selection of samples. In many African countries, however, government restriction of access to such data and the frequent political challenges to the accuracy of census data make them either unavailable or questionable.

Taylor (1991), for instance, found that the 1985 census data in Sierra Leone had been rejected by the Central Statistics Office in Freetown (the agency responsible at that time for compiling census data). By this action, the only remaining "reliable" benchmark was the 1963 census, which is clearly outmoded and outdated. Besides problems with census data, caution should also be exercised in the use of alternative data sources provided by international institutions such as the World Bank and UNESCO, among others. Data from these sources are often compiled with specific objectives and institutional dictates. This makes it difficult for researchers to draw random samples because actual numbers of demographic groups or spatial features are seldom accurate.

Cartwright (1978), for instance, noted that the sample for his study of political leadership in Sierra Leone was "shaky" due to the need to abandon scientific safeguards of randomness. In some cases, interviewers in the field resorted to the purposive selection of quota samples through acquaintances and influential persons, thereby abandoning randomness and introducing serious possibilities for sampling error. To ignore these issues in communication research in Africa is to conduct pretentious research.

Finally, there is a lack of tradition in African societies to participate or engage in the nuances of survey research as a problem-solving technique. More realistic are councils of elders and other consensus-building strategies. So, in essence, rural Africans in particular see surveys as an intrusion and an unwelcome agent of modern society. Ironically, as communication and development researchers try to investigate ways of bringing rural Africans into the mainstream of development, they may be using tools of inquiry that are part of the development environment that they themselves need to be diffused and adopted as a staple practice and feature of these societies.

In the rhetorical domain, an Afrocentric methodological concern with regard to research on rhetoric in Africa indeed is the process of observation, data collection, and codification. Blake (1993b) presents a research tool that should assist researchers who wish to use an Afrocentric methodology in researching the "speech act" in Africa. Again, the essential postulate of Afrocentricism is the centrality of African interests. In our case, we wish to focus on the centrality of peculiar African communication factors that guide African discourse. Blake's tool, called the Checklist/Inventory on Rhetorical Transactions, contains a framework that seeks to identify and codify items such as the following: philosophical assumptions about the nature of discourse; taboos and permissibles; types of discourses; modes of establishing proof and credibility; essential amplification devices and patterns of organization; essential stylistic devices; essential sources of topics; speech time and relationships; communication and ritual settings; nonverbal means; and institutional communication setups. The tool is advanced as a methodological means of researching African rhetorics—particularly a folk system of African rhetorics.

▥ Conceptualization

Another major element in the empirical research process is conceptualization. Babbie (1992) has established that concepts are mental creations that describe our real-world experiences. Therefore, a fundamental pillar of the research process must be the assumption that the terms (or concepts) we create have real meaning such that those real meanings provide a genuine measure of our experiences. The main conceptual problem then is to determine if variables operationalized from Western concepts adequately represent attributes of the specific country. Drake (1973) had long warned that variables derived from observation in Western nations may not correspond closely with important dimensions of real-world phenomena of the research situation in Africa. For instance, Taylor (1991), in his study of media use in Sierra Leone, operationalized self-reliance from established Western modes of thought—specifically, that a self-reliant person is one who "can usually find a way to get around" and is less likely to rely on other people to get things done. The obtained results were skewed toward men, suggesting that men more than women were most likely to be self-reliant, a very unlikely situation. Taylor (1991) reported this as a limitation of the study, suggesting that the Western interpretation of the concept emphasized individual efforts, whereas in Sierra Leone, collective effort is typical and greatly valued.

Other African researchers have also warned against the use of concepts that do not adequately reflect African worldviews (Obeng-Quaidoo, 1985; Ugboajah, 1985). This problem is inextricably linked to the problem of translation. Interviewers have often reported that it was difficult to identify equivalent translation for conceptually different but similar terms (e.g., excitement vs. enjoyment, compassionate vs. sentimental, and violence vs. abuse). Clearly, Ugboajah (1985) was correct to suggest that African communication scholars should begin to conceptualize research problems from the African worldview in ways that capture aspects of behavior and attitudes that are relevant to the setting. Gwebu (1977) noted that many African researchers have often had to discard questionnaires in the field because of major reliability problems trying to fit Western concepts to African settings.

A related problem for African researchers is the link that exists between conceptualization and theory. As African scholars try to test theories postulated in the West, they must invariably use concepts that inhere in those theories. The early Western pioneers of communication and development, for example, theorized the process of modernity as becoming more "civilized." In essence, they had ascribed all preexisting practices and institutions in Africa as "primitive." Of course, the resultant naiveté of this type of theorizing has been borne out by the subsequent dethronement of that paradigm. But it took researchers more than 20 years to come to terms with the inappropriateness of that model. Even today, scholars continue to use theories developed from Western observations of real-world phenomena to explain African processes, patterns, and effects. For instance, some communication and development scholars are still preoccupied with studying how best to use the mass media to bring about change in individuals' attitudes and behaviors. This clearly reflects a stubborn adherence to the media effects model that presumes direct causal relationships between media exposure and outcomes. The use of these and other theories (e.g., agenda setting, cultivation, uses and gratifications, diffusion of innovations, and knowledge gap) are essential barometers in the selection of concepts to be examined in the study.

In essence, when one uses a theory, one becomes tied to its concepts and its methodology. Uses and gratifications studies, for example, explore motives that are related to individual needs and expectations. Such a perspective would therefore dictate that the study employ individual observation mechanisms and use concepts that test individual attitudes and behaviors. The challenge for the researcher in Africa is to determine basically two things. First, is the theory that one intends to use relevant for the real-world environment? Second, if it is, how can one begin to Africanize it—in other words, to rid it of concepts that are inaccurate while retaining the underlying structure of the theory? It would, of course, require familiarity with the core values of indigenous communication processes and patterns in their relevant settings.

▧ *Measurement*

A third major element in the empirical research process is measurement. Once the researcher has determined data collection procedures and identified appropriate concepts, the task is to decide on the relevant range of variation between extremes on the variable so as to obtain precise dimensions of the variable. Here again, some researchers tend to borrow measures developed in Western societies to study African processes and patterns. This practice may be non sequitur and of little value to capturing precise and true indicators.

The use of survey research has often been accompanied by standard measures on nominal, ordinal, interval, and ratio scales. Also, different variables require different levels of measurement, depending on the research problem. But as Cartwright (1978) indicated for Sierra Leone, it is difficult in African settings to assess various response levels to represent dimensions of Western scales. People in some cultures may think in dichotomous terms (e.g., agree vs. disagree). When we use forced-choice items, we are imposing unusual parameters on respondents. Taylor (1991), for instance, found a need to collapse 5-point Likert-type ordinal scales to a 3-point scale in order to improve reliabilities on some of his measures for radio motives and individual resourcefulness. Such post hoc manipulation of data is less preferable to using more culturally appropriate parameters. As Gwebu (1977) has documented, providing ordinal or interval measures in African settings poses serious problems both for translation and for obtaining valid dimensions of a person's attributes on a specified variable. People in rural areas may not be able to think in terms of strongly agree, agree, neutral, disagree, or strongly disagree and so forth. Moreover, the researcher needs to be aware of the standard local dimensions of variables such as time, work, or age. For instance, age may be understood in terms of an event that occurred at the time of one's birth or the position of the farming cycle for that town several cycles ago. Thus the quest for a true age measure may be futile and unproductive.

To sum up, the time is ripe for communication and development scholars in Africa to move beyond reporting dissatisfaction with the narrowness and repetitiveness of standard Western modes of observation, conceptualization, and measurement. The task is to recognize that audience responses must be extrapolated from aspects of the society. Fear that abandoning ordinal or interval scales would lead to an unscientific image is to accept the continued futility of conducting research as we have done for half a century. Clearly, existing inadequacies have led to the unsuitability of measurement tools while limiting the ability of researchers to propose culture-sensitive theories and models.

In conclusion, discourses on an Afrocentric methodology are required to set the parameters necessary to address theory building, methodological constructions, and evaluation tools. It is more taxing on African scholars trained in "empirical" studies to come out with a comprehensive position on an Afrocentric empirical method. What this chapter has done is to set the context for further development of Afrocentric empirical methodology by pointing out the core set of issues that should inform the construction of such a methodology. A crucial first step, then, is to set up a "pilot" Afrocentric empirical study. As was mentioned earlier, the rhetorical domain has been provided with such a pilot instrument. The tasks are indeed daunting—but doable.

References

Asante, M. (1980). *Afrocentricity: The theory of social change.* Trenton, NJ: Africa World Press.

Asante, M., & Appiah, M. (1979). The rhetoric of the Akan drum. *Western Journal of Black Studies, 2,* 8-13.

Awa, N. (1988). Communication in Africa: Implications for development planning. *Howard Journal of Communications, 1*(3), 131-144.

Awa, N. (1995). The role of indigenous media in African social development. In P. Nwosu, C. Onwumechili, & R. M'Bayo (Eds.), *Communication and the transformation of society: A developing region's perspective* (pp. 237-251). Lanham, MD: University Press of America.

Babbie, E. (1992). *The practice of social research.* Belmont, CA: Wadsworth.

Berlo, D. (1960). *The process of communication.* New York: Holt, Rinehart & Winston.

Blake, C. (1979a). Communication research and African national development. *Journal of Black Studies, 10*(2), 218-230.

Blake, C. (1979b). Rhetoric and intercultural communication. In M. Asante, E. Newmark, & C. A. Blake (Eds.), *Handbook of intercultural communication* (pp. 85-94). Beverly Hills, CA: Sage.

Blake, C. (1981). Understanding African national development: Some challenges to communication specialists. *Journal of Black Studies, 12*(2), 201-217.

Blake, C. (1993a). Development communication revisited: An end to Eurocentric visions. *Development,* No. 3, pp. 8-11.

Blake, C. (1993b). Traditional African values and the right to communicate. *Africa Media Review, 7*(3), 201-216.

Boafo, S., & George, N. (Eds.). (1992). *Communication research in Africa: Issues and perspectives.* Nairobi: African Council on Communication Education.

Broom, L., & Selznick, P. (1958). *Sociology* (2nd ed.). Evanston, IL: Row, Peterson.

Cartwright, J. (1978). *Political leadership in Sierra Leone.* Toronto: University of Toronto Press.

Dance, F. E. X. (Ed.). (1967). *Human communication theory.* New York: Holt, Rinehart & Winston.

Doob, L. (1961). *Communication in Africa: A search for boundaries.* New Haven, CT: Yale University Press.

Drake, H. (1973). Research method or culture bound technique? Pitfalls of survey research in Africa. In W. O'Barr, D. Spain, & M. Tessler (Eds.), *Survey research in Africa: Its applications and limits* (pp. 58-69). Evanston, IL: Northwestern University Press.

Fiofori, F. (1975). Traditional media, modern messages: A Nigerian case study. *Rural Africana,* 27.

Gwebu, T. (1977). *Migration and the dynamics of a space economy: An investigation of spatial development in Sierra Leone.* Unpublished doctoral dissertation, Kent State University, Kent, OH.

Jayaweera, N. (1991). *Folk media and development communication.* Manila & New Delhi: Asian Social Institute & Indian Society for Promoting Christian Knowledge.

Karp, I., & Bird, C. S. (Eds.). (1980). *Explorations in African systems of thought*. Bloomington: Indiana University Press.

Mbiti, J. (1975). *African religion and philosophy*. London: Heinemann.

Nwosu, P. (1986). *The dominant paradigm and social change: Toward a new model of communication for national development in Black Africa*. Unpublished master's thesis, Towson State University, Baltimore.

Nwosu, P. (1990). *Communication and agricultural development in Swaziland: Toward a need-based integrative model*. Unpublished doctoral dissertation, Howard University, Washington, DC.

Nwosu, P., Taylor, D., & Onwumechili, C. (1995). Search for appropriate research methods. In P. Nwosu, C. Onwumechili, & R. M'Bayo (Eds.), *Communication and the transformation of society: A developing region's perspective* (pp. 397-426). Lanham, MD: University Press of America.

Obeng-Quaidoo, I. (1985). "Culture and communication research methodologies in Africa: A proposal for change. *Gazette, 36,* 109-120.

Obeng-Quaidoo, I. (1986). A proposal for new communication research methodologies in Africa. *Africa Media Review, 7*(1), 89-98.

Okigbo, C. (1985). Is development communication a dead issue? *Media Development, 4,* 23-25.

Onwubiko, O. (1991). *African thought, religion, and culture*. Enugu, Nigeria: Snaap Press.

Sofola, J. (1982). *African culture and the African personality*. Ibadan, Nigeria: University of Ibadan Press.

Stewart E., & Bennett, M. (1991). *American cultural patterns*. Yarmouth, ME: Intercultural Press.

Taylor, D. S. (1991). *Application of the uses and dependency model of mass communication to development communication in the Western Area of Sierra Leone*. Unpublished doctoral dissertation, Kent State University, Kent, OH.

Ugboajah, F. O. (1985). "Oramedia" in Africa. In F. O. Ugboajah (Ed.), *Mass communication, culture and society in West Africa* (pp. 165-186). London: Hans Zell.

Afrocentricity: The Challenge of Implementation

15

Na'im Akbar

The African-American students and scholars who will usher us into the dawn of the 21st century will be greeted by many of the paradoxes which have confronted African people since our entrance of bondage into North America. These paradoxes will be no less problematic than before, and the challenges facing our people over the next century will continue to be of the incredible magnitude that we, as a community of Africans in America, have come to know. As has been the case with each previous generation, this new generation will be called upon to reap the harvest of those who have sown before them and to carry on the process of plowing the fields of time for those yet unborn.

The last 20 years in America have generated a remarkable new crop in the intellectual fields of African-American life. The new crop has been described in the popular language of "Afrocentricity," which has unfortunately come to mean a wide variety of things from the wearing of Kente cloth shawls to a radical reinterpretation of world history. In any event, the new concept has heralded a massively important paradigm shift in African thought specifically and American scholarship in general. As the previous generation of African-American freedom fighters ignited the redefinition of freedom for all Americans (e.g., women's rights, handicapped rights,

This chapter originally appeared as an article in *Black Collegian,* September/October, 1991, and is used with permission.

etc.) this new conceptual analysis identified as Afrocentrism will no doubt usher in a universal reanalysis of Western scholarship in which people will boldly bring the particular perspective of their diversity to the table of human commonality.

Contrary to the claim of its critics, Afrocentricity is no more than the description of a perspective for the purpose of analysis. The so-called "scientific method" (which is in fact only a method of science) is a perspective which takes objectivity as its stance for analysis. This method suspends the reality of subjective factors only in creating an objective illusion. This is a valid suspension of belief not unlike that of the fiction writer who suspends disbelief to create a fantasy. It is a valid perspective for the purpose of a particular type of analysis.

The Afrocentric scholar claims that the perspectives of other experiences have been willfully suspended in the Eurocentric analysis of reality. This suspension has tremendously benefitted the ascension of European people and those capable of identifying with their experiences. This same suspension has massively handicapped people who have negated their own reality and sought to identify with a reality and an experience that was not their own.

No one can legitimately claim that the Eurocentric reality is not correct for Europeans in the same way that one cannot argue that the conditions of a genuine vacuum are not correct if we were capable of producing such an objective reality. We do argue that each people must enter the world of scientific and scholarly analysis from the path of their historically and culturally developed perspectives. These perspectives are not counter to universal reality and truth, but simply access the universal through the window of one's particular world view. Such a perspective can only enhance human understanding in general.

The real challenge for our young thinkers here at the dawn of the 21st century is how to execute the next step in the progression of this paradigm shift. Thanks to Diop, Van Sertima, John Henrik Clarke and others, we now know that history is not only what we have been taught from the Eurocentric perspective. Thanks to Nobles, Welsing, King, and others, we now know that psychology is not only what the European behavioral scientists have taught. We have a new grasp on the concept that Africans view the world differently, thanks to the work of Asante, Karenga, Carruthers, Jeffries, and others. We now need a new implementation, both in social construction and in technology.

Those coming from the Afrocentric perspective are to be the vanguard in developing a technology that is compatible with the Afrocentric concept of harmony with nature. They are obligated to develop systems of technology which are respectful of a much abused environment which Africans, from their perspective, view as a divinely given gift which requires humans to interact with it harmoniously. We need Afrocentric architects who construct buildings that are not only efficient, but also maintain human ties and facilitate human interaction. We need Afrocentric organization developers who build organizations sensitive to the human ties and the spiritual aspirations that the Afrocentric orientation teaches us. We must have educators who structure learning systems in such a way that children learn to respect who they are and see themselves as allies with the environment rather than oppressive conquerors. We must have social organizers who develop social systems that respect gender differences while facilitating the expressions and genius of all people.

The values and philosophical basis for the development of such systems are implicit in the Afrocentric system. The prophetic thinkers who have helped to reveal this system are neither capable nor have the longevity to implement the structures which must stand on the foundation that they have built. Those who opened the doors to greater civic freedoms could not simultaneously become the political brokers who developed a Harold Washington or empowered a Maynard Jackson.

In the same vein, it is overly messianic for us to expect that those who have revolutionized our thinking about ourselves can also implement the new techniques, structures, and systems which that new thinking will necessarily produce. Already, many of our young students are growing impatient with what they describe as too much "theory" and "rhetoric." They don't realize that this theory and rhetoric account for the re-energizing of themselves with a kind of vision and motivation for the rebuilding of African reality such as we have not seen since the Civil Rights Movement and the Harlem Renaissance. They must understand that they are having the baton passed to them and they must now implement the structures that demonstrate this great power of the African genius which the Afrocentric paradigm shift has revealed to us.

We now know what we have done and what we can do. The challenge for the carriers at the dawn of the 21st century is to demonstrate to the world that not only have we done the impossible in charting the course for all of humanity, repeatedly in the past, but also we are now taking it as our imperative for the people of Africa to once again bring a renaissance to all of humanity.

Epilogue

The Afrocentric theme must be struck in every quarter. Despite the bitter antagonisms against the culture of our ancestors, varied and uneven as that culture has been, we must seek to interpret contemporary development in every section and in every field in light of our own best terms. If we fail to do so, we will enter the 21st century still a people without a strong sense of collective conscious, which is necessary to recover our dignity and our economic and political place.

—Molefi Kete Asante
Malcolm X as Cultural Hero and
Other Afrocentric Essays, 1993, p. 47

Index

Abbary, Abu, 217
"An Address to Phillis Wheatley" (Hammon),
  124
Affirmative action, 29-30, 219
"Afraid" (Hughes), 135-136
Africa:
  communication in. *See* Communication
  culture, 3-4, 37, 91-92, 146-149, 170,
    215, 235-237
  decolonization, 223-224
  investment in, 224
  linkages with diaspora, 222-225
  movement to return to. *See* "Back to
    Africa" concept
  study of culture, 216
  tourism, 225
  values, 230, 235-237
  West African university proposed, 216-217
  See also Egypt; Yoruba culture
African American studies, 28
  Afrocentric framework for, 28-29, 30-31,
    33, 35, 43

subject matter, 35, 42
African Americans:
  class differences, 33-34, 63-64, 65-66,
    66-67, 77
  color consciousness, 183, 185
  desire for freedom and literacy, 16-18
  film directors, 188-191
  in Eurocentric culture, 3, 16
  male-female relationships. *See*
    Male-female relationships
  mental disorders, 10-11, 211
  popular stereotypes of, 51, 161-162, 164,
    171, 198
  responses to movies, 191-192
  socialization of, 16, 22
  use of term, 32-33, 219
  Whites' attitudes toward, 17, 165
  women. *See* Women
African consciousness, in film criticism,
  176-177
African Self-Consciousness (ASC) Scale, 57
Africanity theory, 36-37

253

About the Contributors

Abu Abarry is Associate Chair and Professor of African American Studies at Temple University. He has authored several books, including *Effective Research Thesis and Dissertation Writing* and *The Monkey's Liver Pepper Soup*, and coauthored two books with Molefi Kete Asante, *African Development: Prospects and Pitfalls* and *African Sources of Intellectual Traditions*. He has also contributed chapters to several books and published numerous articles in scholarly journals.

Na'im Akbar is a clinical psychologist in the Department of Psychology at Florida State University in Tallahassee. Considered a pioneer in the development of an African-centered approach to modern psychology, he has authored five books related to the personality development of African Americans and more than 25 articles in scholarly journals.

Joseph A. Baldwin is Professor of Psychology at Florida A&M University. He is a widely published scholar whose work has appeared in *The Western Journal of Black Studies, The Journal of Black Studies,* and the *Negro Educational Review,* and in numerous books and edited volumes.

Yvonne R. Bell is Associate Professor in the Department of Psychology at Florida A&M University. Her research interests are in the areas of African American learning styles and problem-solving behaviors and the development of cultural specific/Afrocentric assessment instruments related to these issues. She is also interested in studying social perceptions among African American children and the role of cultural factors in predicting efficacious and affirmative African American behavior.

Cecil A. Blake is Associate Professor of Speech Communication at Indiana University, Northeast. His research focuses on intercultural communication and world development, rhetorical theory, and analysis. He has coauthored numerous works, including *Handbook of Intercultural Communication* with Molefi Asante and Eileen Newmark, and is author of *Through the Prism of African Nationalism.*

Cathy L. Bouie is Counselor of Nursing at Florida A&M University. Her research has been published in *Journal of Black Studies.*

Janice D. Hamlet is Associate Professor of Speech Communication and Founding Director of Ethnic Studies at Shippensburg University in Pennsylvania. Research interests include African American communication, womanist ideology, rhetorical criticism, and the rhetoric of spirituality. Her scholarly work has appeared in *Journal of Black Studies, Western Journal of Black Studies, Journalism and Mass Communication Quarterly, The Speech Communication Teacher,* and other edited works. She is currently studying the epistemology and methodology of womanist scholarship and practice.

Norman Harris is Professor of Interdisciplinary Studies at Union Institute in Cincinnati, Ohio. He is cofounder of Khepera Institute, an educational and research organization headquartered in Atlanta.

M. Patricia E. Hilliard-Nunn is an independent filmmaker living in Gainesville, Florida. She also owns MAKARE Publishing Company and is Community Activity Coordinator for the Community Outreach Partnership Center at the University of Florida. Her research interests include film audience analysis, media analysis and effects, and African American representation in the media.

Gale Jackson is Assistant Professor at Medgar Evers College of the City University of New York and is pursuing doctoral work in cultural history at the Graduate Center of City University. Her work has appeared in a number of journals and anthologies, including *The American Voice, Kenyon Review, Ikon, Frontiers, Feminist Studies, Callalou,* and *Ploughshares.* She has coedited an anthology titled *Art Against Apartheid: Works for Freedom* and a collaborative book called *We Stand Our Ground.*

Terry Kershaw is Associate Professor and Director of the Institute for Advanced Afrocentric Research in the Department of African American Studies at Temple University. His writings on topics as diverse as male/female relations, race and class, education, methodology, and Afrocentric theory have been published in *Western Journal of Black Studies* and *Journal of Black Studies,* for which he also serves as its coeditor.

Barbara J. Molette is Professor of English at Eastern Connecticut State University, and **Carlton W. Molette** is Professor of Dramatic Arts and Senior Fellow of the Institute for African American Studies at the University of Connecticut. As a result of their research on theater in the African diaspora, the Molettes have presented papers, conducted workshops, and published articles as well as two editions of *Black Theatre: Premise and Presentation.* As playwrights, they have collaborated on several productions, including *Rosalee Pritchett,* staged by the Negro Ensemble Company, the Free Southern Theatre, and several colleges and universities. The Molettes are members of the Dramatists Guild.

Linda James Myers is Associate Professor of Black Studies, Psychology, and Psychiatry at Ohio State University. Her research has focused on the development of an Afrocentric paradigm of psychology functioning. She is author of *Understanding an Afrocentric World View: Introduction to an Optimal Psychology* and numerous articles in scholarly journals.

Peter O. Nwosu is Associate Professor of Communication Studies at California State University, Sacramento and a nationally recognized contributor to multicultural issues, training, and development. His research interests include intercultural, international, and development communications. He is coauthor of *Communication and the Transformation of Society: A Developing Region's Perspective* and has had work published in *Howard Journal of Communication* and *African Media Review: Journal of the African Council on Communication Education.*

Victor O. Okafor is Assistant Professor of African American Studies at Eastern Michigan University, Ypsilanti. His research and writing focus on the theoretical and methodological foundation for Black Studies (Africology), Black politics and public policy, African civilization, multiculturalism, and Afrocentrism.

Robert L. Perry is Professor and Chair of African American Studies at Eastern Michigan University. He laid the foundation for the Department of Ethnic Studies at Bowling Green State University and was Chair of that department from 1970 to 1997. His research interests include juvenile delinquency, issues related to ethnicity and cross-cultural counseling, institutionalizing ethnic studies, and cultural diversity and the Black family.

Jerome H. Schiele is Associate Professor and Chair of the doctoral program in the School of Social Work at Clark-Atlanta University. He has published several scholarly articles and essays centering on intelligence testing, organizational theory, higher education, and academic mobility of faculty of color.

John W. Smith is Assistant Professor of Speech Communication at Ohio University. His research interests are in the areas of political and religious rhetoric.

Alice A. Tait is Professor of Communication at Central Michigan University. Her research interests focus on mass communication theory.

Donald S. Taylor is Assistant Professor of Communication Studies at California State University, Sacramento. His research interests include media uses and effects in both industrialized and nonindustrialized countries. He has published in the area of cultural research and communication and national development.